A CELEBRATION OF 250 YEARS OF

IRELAND'S INLAND WATERWAYS

Ruth Delany

Appletree Press

to my Mother

First published and printed by
The Appletree Press Ltd
7 James Street South
Belfast BT2 8DL
1986

9 8 7 6 5 4 3 2 1

British Library Cataloguing in Publication Data
Delany, Ruth
Ireland's inland waterways.
1. Inland navigation—Ireland—History
I. Title
386'.09415   HE438

ISBN 0-86281-129-5

Cover illustration: *Dublin, from Blaquiere Bridge, Royal Canal* by George Petrie, RHA (1789-1866)

Contents

Author's Notes and Acknowledgements

Most financial transactions in Ireland until January 1826 appear to have been made in Irish currency (the conversion rate is £13 Irish to £12 sterling). All amounts mentioned in the text up to this date are expressed in Irish currency although it is not possible to be completely certain in every case. In the Appendix all the amounts have been converted into £ stg. for purposes of comparison.

Thanks are due to the following for permission to reproduce photographs and illustrations: Department of the Environment for Northern Ireland (Historic Monuments and Buildings Branch), National Library of Ireland, Richard Shackleton, Messrs Arthur Guinness, *Irish Times*, *Irish Press*, Deegan-Photo Ltd, Athlone Printing Works, Institution of Civil Engineers of Ireland, Rosemary Furlong, Denis Macartney.

In addition to thanking Dr Alan McCutcheon as mentioned in the Preface, I would like to thank the staff of the secretary's office CIE at Heuston Station, Dublin, where the records of the Grand Canal Company, the Barrow Navigation Company and the New Royal Canal Company are stored; the staff of the Public Record Office, Dublin, where the records of the Directors General of Inland Navigation and the Board of Works are kept; the staff of the National Library of Ireland and Trinity College, Dublin. I would like to thank Dr Alf Delany, who read the manuscript and made some helpful suggestions, Desmond Barrington for his assistance with photographs and Mary Hanna who tackled the task of drawing maps with enthusiasm. The maps representing areas of the Republic of Ireland are based on the Ordnance Survey by permission of the Government (Permit no. 4481) and those representing areas of Northern Ireland are based upon the Ordnance Survey map with the sanction of the controller of HM Stationery Office, Crown Copyright. Finally, I would like to thank Douglas Marshall of Appletree Press for his helpful advice throughout the preparation of this book.

Abbreviations

CIE	Córas Iompair Éireann
GSR	Great Southern Railway
GSWR	Great Southern & Western Railway
IWAI	Inland Waterways Association of Ireland
MGWR	Midland Great Western Railway
RCAG	Royal Canal Amenity Group

Preface

It is not easy to condense the history of Ireland's inland waterways into a single volume, setting out the basic facts and at the same time retaining the interest of the general reader. I well remember my chagrin on overhearing my late husband, Douglas, confiding in someone that he was 'wading through' my book on the Grand Canal when it was published some years ago. This time I have tried to remind myself constantly that what might seem fascinating detail to a waterway enthusiast may make for dull reading and I have tried to include some of the more entertaining material. For those seeking a more definitive history with all the references cited, *The Canals of the North of Ireland* by W. A. McCutcheon and *The Canals of the South of Ireland,* by V. T. H. and D. R. Delany, though out of print, are still available in most Irish libraries. In addition, there are a number of books which give detailed accounts of individual waterways and these are listed in the bibliography at the end of the book.

Part One deals with the Canal Age from 1715 to the 1830s, during which time the waterways played an important role in the country's developing economy. The story of how the Canal Age evolved is an interesting one: how the works were financed, the engineering blunders which occured and the new breed of Irish civil engineers which emerged. Part Two traces the struggle of the waterways for survival against the railways, each competing for the limited inland trade. It was a struggle which the waterways were doomed to lose from the start. The story might have ended there and it very nearly did, but in recent years many of these old commercial highways have found a new role as recreational and tourist amenities. We came very close to losing for ever this great national heritage but now a new era in its long history is just beginning.

I am grateful to Dr McCutcheon for so readily agreeing that I should include all the Irish waterways in this book so that a complete history could be traced and for allowing me to use material from his book. I hope that this volume will provide the reader with a glimpse into the past which will enable the many who use the waterways today to enjoy them more fully and to appreciate the enormous effort which went into their construction. The book is a tribute to the men who planned and constructed the waterways, to the communities they generated and to those who in more recent times appreciated their potential and fought so hard to preserve them.

Ruth Delany
February 1985

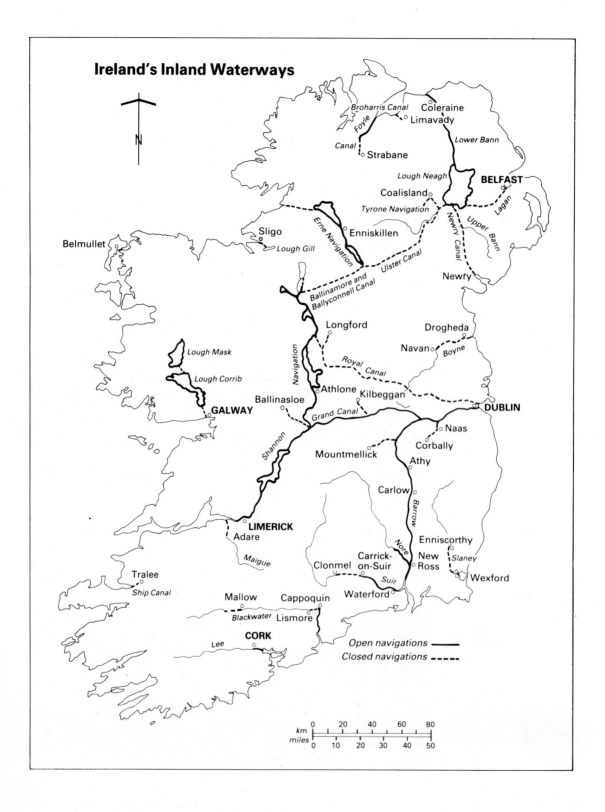

Ireland's Inland Waterways

N

Broharris Canal
Coleraine
Limavady
Foyle
Canal
Strabane
Lower Bann
Lough Neagh
BELFAST
Coalisland
Tyrone Navigation
Lagan
Newry Canal
Upper Bann
Erne Navigation
Sligo
Enniskillen
Belmullet
Lough Gill
Ulster Canal
Newry
Ballinamore and
Ballyconnell Canal
Longford
Drogheda
Navan
Boyne
Lough Mask
Navigation
Royal Canal
Lough Corrib
Athlone
Kilbeggan
GALWAY
Ballinasloe
DUBLIN
Grand Canal
Naas
Mountmellick
Corbally
Shannon
Athy
Carlow
Barrow
LIMERICK
Adare
Nore
Maigue
Enniscorthy
Tralee
Clonmel
Carrick-
on-Suir
New
Ross
Slaney
Ship Canal
Mallow
Cappoquin
Suir
Wexford
Blackwater
Lismore
Waterford
Lee
CORK

Open navigations ——
Closed navigations ----

km 0   20   40   60   80
miles 0 10 20 30 40 50

PART ONE

1
The Canal Age

FROM the earliest dawn of history man has used rivers and lakes as a means of transport and it was inevitable that he would gradually develop engineering techniques to make natural rivers more useful to him. First came the weir, a wall built across the river which held water in the stretch above at a constant level and allowed the surplus water to flow over the top. These early weirs had a threefold purpose: fishing, diverting water into millraces to develop power and improving navigation by raising the level of water over shallows. Some means, however, still had to be found to pass boats through the weirs from one level to the next. Over 2,000 years ago the Chinese invented vertically rising gates through which boats could be hauled upstream or lowered downstream. This was found to be very wasteful of water and so the early Chinese engineers experimented with slipways, which were built into the weirs, but it was very cumbersome hauling boats up and down these slopes and caused damage to the hulls. Eventually, in AD 983, the pound lock was invented, a chamber built into the weir wall with vertically rising upper and lower gates, into which boats could be floated and raised or lowered; the inventor was said to be Chhiao Wei-yo, assistant commissioner on the Grand Canal of China.

The first pound lock in Europe was built on a river in Holland in 1373 but it was left to that greatest of all inventors, Leonardo da Vinci, to invent the swinging or mitre gates which we still use today; apart from mechanising the operation no one has managed to improve on his design since then. At first, short lengths of canal were used to by-pass shallow stretches or places where there were sharp bends in the river, but it was not long before engineers became more ambitious and constructed canals which climbed up to a summit level and dropped down again, making it possible to link watersheds. The remarkable Canal du Midi, built in France between 1666-81 and still in use today, is a fine example of an early still water canal. It established a link between the Atlantic Ocean and the Mediterranean Sea, rising up from Sète on the shores of the Mediterranean to a summit level and dropping down into the River Garonne near Toulouse.

In Ireland, as elsewhere, much use was made of the abundance of slow flowing rivers and large lakes in a countryside which was heavily forested with few roads. Unfortunately, these water highways also gave unwelcome visitors easy access into the interior of the country. The pages of the Irish annalists are full of records of Viking incursions;

Athlone on the River Shannon in the days before the navigation works

there are few more terrible stories than the voyages of terror made by the Dane, Turgesius, in the mid-ninth century up the River Shannon to Lough Ree and up the Bann into Lough Neagh. He plundered and desecrated monastic settlements as he went, declaring himself to be the Abbot of Armagh while his wife, Oda, gave oracles from the violated altar of Clonmacnoise. Maelshechlainn, King of Meath, succeeded in capturing him by a clever ruse. Turgesius coveted the king's daughter and he sent her to him accompanied by fourteen 'maidens' – warriors in disguise – who took the Dane and his followers by surprise. Turgesius was captured and drowned in Lough Owel, ending his reign of terror. In the following century there were further incursions from Scandinavia. In 968 Brian Boru raised a fleet and inflicted defeat on the invaders in Lough Ree but twenty years later he found himself siding with them when his former allies from Connacht deserted him and joined forces with Maelshechlainn II against him. Brian assembled a fleet of 300 ships to do battle with him on Lough Ree but eventually reason prevailed and the two Irish leaders met at the mouth of the River Inny where they agreed to divide the country between them.

There is evidence that weirs were constructed on many Irish rivers, and in the twelfth century an artificial channel was cut through an island at the south end of Lough Corrib which is still used today. It was not, however, until the first half of the seventeenth century that a definite scheme for the development of Irish waterways was put forward when Strafford, the Lord Deputy, suggested linking the major rivers. After the Restoration in 1664, the Duke of Ormonde in his well known instructions included 'making rivers navigable', but it was not until the early eighteenth century that more serious attempts were made to carry out proper surveys and lodge plans before the Irish parliament. Eventually, in 1715, an Act was passed 'To Encourage the Draining and Improving of the Bogs and Unprofitable Low Grounds, and for the easing and despatching the Inland Carriage and Conveyance of Goods from one part to another within this Kingdom'.

Eighteen different schemes were authorised to be carried out under local commissioners or Undertakers but no funds were made available and only two schemes were actually initiated in the years immediately after the passing of the Act. It was, however, subsequently invoked as authorisation for other schemes in the years that followed and it marks the beginning of the Canal Age in Ireland.

The Failure of the Liffey Navigation

It is known that a small amount of work was carried out on the River Maigue near Adare after the passing of the 1715 Act, but it was insignificant. A second and much more ambitious undertaking was also started: to make the River Liffey navigable. In October 1723 Stephen Costello appealed to the Irish parliament for financial help. He explained that he was one of the subscribers of a company set up to carry on this work and that he 'proceeded a Good Way in carrying on the Navigation of the River Liffey, and would have near finished the same had he not been disappointed of Money vigorously to carry it on'. A parliamentary committee recommended that the company should be given £2,000 but, at this stage, the scheme collapsed and the company was dissolved. It was suggested that the South Sea Bubble affair 'had crushed some of the Company' but they could scarcely have taken on a more difficult navigation scheme and references to it in contemporary pamphlets suggest that it was not proving very successful. The work was carried out on stretches of the river between Lucan and Leixlip, 'which was rather to give a specimen of Mr C----l-o's Art, (in order to encourage such Undertakings) than anything else; as may appear by the Narrowness of the Locks, and the Channels, as far as he carried it'. The same writer, John Browne, suggested that such undertakings 'in which the general welfare is concerned, are seldom successful unless, either, there be a fund raised by Act of Parliament for carrying them on, or else, proper encouragement given by tolls, to the particular undertakers of the work'. But another anonymous writer stressed the need for adequate security if public money was to be advanced for navigation schemes, adding:

> I form my Judgement from what has been attempted on the Liffey, I should as soon hope for subscribers from Moscow as from any Gentlemen in this Kingdom, who may, if they please, know (what many feel) the consequence of going rashly to work.

Another writer in the same year, 1729, also referred to the failure of the scheme:

> That Undertaking seemed, for the first two or three years, to be in a very hopeful Way. . . all Men spoke kindly and greatly of it; and hoped still greater things from it, as from an auspicious leading-Card, that was to be the Precedent and Inducement to the like Improvement of our other Rivers throughout the Kingdom. But, how that Favourite Service, so hopeful at

its first setting out, comes now to lye disparaged and neglected; and instead of an Example or Encouragement to be rather a Bar and a stumbling Block to any further Progress in so desirable a Work, is what few Men have been able to comprehend.

The same writer went on to refer to 'Tamperings of Intermedlers and Pretenders to Art at home, as well as of Intruders from abroad, who aided by your own Distractions found Means, first to make themselves necessary as Councellors and Assistants, and by Degrees to work themselves into the whole Management of your Affairs'.

The Irish parliament recognised that the failure of this scheme was acting as a disincentive to private investment in other navigation works and so another Act was passed in 1729 setting up Commissioners of Inland Navigation for each of the four provinces with public funds for carrying on work levied by duties on a wide range of luxury goods: 'Coaches, Berlins, Chariots, Calashes, Chaises and Chairs, and upon Cards and Dice and upon wrought and maufactured Gold and Silver plate'. Canal building had got off to an inauspicious start but it will be seen that this new Act achieved results. In an attempt to satisfy the increasing demand for cheaper coal in Dublin, the Newry Canal was commenced in 1731 to open up access to the Tyrone coalfields with work on an extension from Lough Neagh right into the coalfield area beginning in the following year. Some work was also carried out under the commissioners on the River Boyne and surveys were made of a line for a canal from Dublin to the Shannon. In 1751 parliament extended the appropriation of duties for a further period of twenty-one years and incorporated the provincial commissioners into a single navigation board. In all, by 1755, £89,920 together with £3,200 in grants had been expended on navigation works but, with such limited resources and the reluctance of the private sector to invest, progress was destined to be very slow and, if it had not been for a certain sequence of events, the Irish inland waterway network as we know it today might never have come into being.

The Reign of the Undertakers

The Irish parliament had begun to meet more regularly by the 1740s and to take much more interest in the expenditure of public funds. A constitutional struggle developed between two factions in parliament; one group supported the English administration and the other had a more independent attitude. At that time there was money left in the Irish coffers at the end of each financial year but the Irish parliament had no statutory right to this revenue, which was vested in the Crown. A parliamentary committee revealed that there had been grave misapplication of public funds in the building of barracks. The surveyor general, Arthur Nevill, was held responsible for this but the English administration backed him and this support of a proven perpetrator of irregularities alienated some of the members of parliament. Nevill was eventually dismissed but the damage was already done and those who were against the administration found themselves with a majority in the House. Resenting the Crown's right to the hereditary revenue, this group, who became known as the 'Undertakers', decided that in future there would be no surplus revenue for the King. Commencing in 1755 they voted large sums each session for public works and for the encouragement of industry. Navigation works were an obvious choice at that time and the Commissioners of Inland Navigation, many of whom were members of parliament themselves, were able to obtain large grants for schemes.

Inevitably there were abuses as members sought schemes for their own aggrandisement. The greatest jobbery occurred in the grants for industry but navigation schemes came in for considerable criticism in the years that followed. Sir George Macartney, who had been chief secretary in Ireland at the time, wrote in 1773:

> And now, after near twenty years' distribution of the national treasure in this manner, what have been the fruits of it? Intercourse, without commerce; means of conveyance, where there is nothing to convey; coalworks, where turf is still the fuel even of the colliers; harbours, which present shipwreck, instead of safety; bridges impassable and navigations unnavigable.

Richard Griffith, writing in 1795, a little further removed from the time, referred to the 'chance-medly manner in which the whole business was conducted'. He computed that £592,200 0s 8½d had been spent by the commissioners between 1730 and 1785 on no less than twenty-three different navigation schemes:

> Every member had his favourite work, the fund was divided and subdivided into various channels, and at least one third of the whole expended in salaries to officers, whose interest it was to make their place perpetual by retarding the completion of the works, and the remainder in discount for money advanced, and in jobs to contractors whose accounts were never adjusted. . . . In England canals were the effect of internal wealth, in Ireland an efficient cause of producing or at least as the best means of facilitating these happy effects.

In fact, as the story of each of the waterways unfolds, it will become clear that the greatest waste of money was caused not so much by jobbery but by faulty surveys and the inexperience of the early engineers. That great historian, William Lecky, was nearer the truth in his assessment of the situation:

> There was no doubt much corruption, but it is not clear that there was more than in England. . . . It is, at all events, certain that the great period of political corruption in Ireland was not the period of the Undertakers but that which immediately followed their overthrow. . . much the greater part seems to have been expended on inland navigation and the grants do not appear on the face of them either excessive or misapplied.

The Newry Canal had been completed successfully and the potential of inland navigation became obvious to all. The commissioners had embarked on implementing the grand concept which had been in men's minds for some time: connecting up Ireland's major rivers. In the words

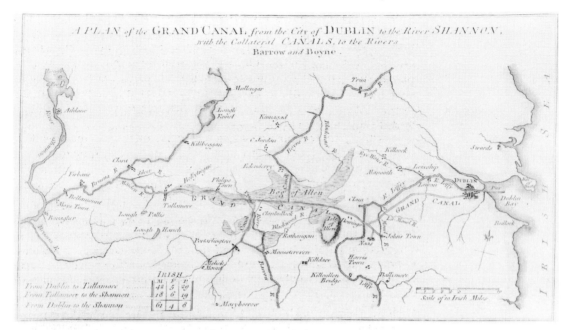

An early survey of central Ireland illustrating the grand concept of linking up the principal rivers

of Henry Brooke, writing in 1759, the waterways would be like a giant spider's web enabling Ireland 'to spin her own web of happiness out of her own bowels'. Based on the excavation work on the Grand Canal which had begun at that time, he estimated that it required 3,640,000 cubic yards of excavation to complete that canal to the Shannon and, working on the basis that one man cuts two cubic yards per day, he suggested that twelve such canals should be constructed providing a national navigation system:

> and it follows, as surely, that 80,000 of our Idle hands, if employed therein, would in much less than one year, accomplish the Business, and might amuse themselves on the water the Remainder of the Term.

This sort of comment is an indication of the canal mania of the time. One thing is clear, the Undertakers set in motion a programme of canal building in Ireland which was to lay the foundation of the waterway network as we know it today, and there is little doubt that if it had not been for this initial phase many of the works would never have been undertaken.

The Fall of the Undertakers

The financial bonanza was shortlived. The English administration used the accusations of jobbery to discredit the spending spree and by 1767 the Castle administrators had brought about the fall of the Undertakers and reimposed control over public expenditure. By this time Ireland had an annual deficit instead of surplus revenue and the question was what to do with all the incomplete navigations. In England there had been little government intervention in canal building; canals had been built to service industry which was already there. In Ireland public confidence did slowly increase in this new means of transport which was supposed to lead the country into the new Industrial Age. The government encouraged private companies to take over the partly completed navigations and substantial sums were subscribed which were vast by the standards of private enterprise in Ireland at that time. Arthur Young, the English writer, visiting Ireland in the 1770s warned: 'Have something to carry before you seek the means of carriage'. His warning was to prove very accurate. The Irish waterways failed to generate industry; the anticipated Industrial Revolution did not cross the Irish Sea.

In 1787, following an inquiry into their financial affairs, the Commissioners of Inland Navigation were dissolved and the navigations which were still in their charge were transferred to local bodies. Forced to rely on the meagre income from tolls on the incomplete navigations, these bodies did little in the closing years of the century. In 1789 a debenture scheme was introduced to give financial help to private companies. Loans at four per cent of up to one third of the cost of construction work were made available but proper accounts had to be submitted to the Commissioners of Imprest Accounts showing that the money had been expended before each instalment of the loan was issued.

In 1800 the Irish parliament carried out an inquiry into inland navigation and it became obvious that a further injection of public funds was needed. In its dying moments, before its Union with Westminster, the Irish parliament appointed five Directors General of Inland Navigation with a fund of up to £500,000 at their disposal. For the next thirty years it was this body which controlled waterway development in Ireland.

The Directors General of Inland Navigation

William Parnell, writing in 1804 in his *Inquiry into the Causes of Popular Discontents in Ireland* remarked: 'The surrender of political rights to a foreign power for the sake of improving domestic government, calls to mind the Pelew islanders, who jump into the sea to shelter themselves from a shower of rain'. There is no doubt that Ireland's domestic affairs were neglected as a result of the Union. The Westminster parliament adopted a policy of leaving well alone as long as the administrators in Dublin Castle preserved tranquillity in Ireland and built up the defences of the country. One Englishman, John Gough, who visited Ireland in 1813-4 remarked: 'Ireland is a country that Englishmen in general know less about, than they do about Russia, Siberia and the country of the Hottentots'. If was considered that the waterways had been well taken care of, a large fund had been allocated to them and it was up to the Directors General to get on with it as they thought fit.

In their wisdom, the Directors General saw it as part of their role to try to standardise tolls at as low a rate as possible and they adopted

a policy of forcing companies to reduce tolls in return for financial
assistance. This proved very shortsighted because it forced the companies to operate uneconomically which in turn led to a deterioriation
in the maintenance of the waterways. The Canal Age had introduced
a much cheaper form of transport into the country. In the 1790s the
average cost per mile of carriage of goods by road was 1s. The early
canal company charters allowed them to charge up to 3d per ton per
mile and 2d per ton per lock. The lockage charge was found to be too
cumbersome to operate and was soon dropped but the mileage charge
was not increased. The Directors General sought to impose even lower
tolls: 2d on general goods and 1d on corn, grain, meal, malt, flour,
potatoes, lime, sand, fuel, manure, iron and military equipment.

Negotiations between the Directors General and canal companies
always seemed to be very protracted, which led to much frustration;
matters were conducted through lengthy correspondence and no effort
was made to sit down together to discuss them. Over the years, more
than one quarter of the funds was swallowed up in the running of the
establishment. The chairman was paid a salary of £738 9s 4d and each
of the other four Directors General £461 11s 9d. The first chairman,
the Hon. Sackville Hamilton, fancied himself as an inventor and nearly
£1,000 was wasted on his 'shoal scrubber' for preventing the accumu-
lation of sand banks in Dublin Bay:

> from the operation of which the sands of the Bar may be removed by the
> Winds and Currents. . . a Boat or Vessel of so buoyant a Form as to be
> easily moved by the Undulations of the Sea, with strong iron framework
> supporting loose poles with a Scrubber on each of a spherical form shod
> and pointed with iron.

Most of the navigation establishments were very small but a larger
concern like the Grand Canal Company had as many as 160 on its
payroll in 1810. Tolls were collected at the loading places by toll
collectors or agents but sometimes by the lockkeepers. Each boat was
'weighed' when it went into service: it was gradually loaded in controlled conditions and its 'depth sheet' was filled in, indicating the
reading on the depth gauge on the bow of the boat as each additional
ton was added. The boatmaster had to carry his depth sheet at all
times together with a manifest of the weight and destination of his
cargo. Legislation, which was not changed until 1845, precluded canal
companies from acting as carriers on their own canals but they were
allowed to operate passenger services.

In the first decade of the nineteenth century the war with Napoleon
gave a temporary boost to the Irish economy and the canal companies
shared this boom. Then the country gradually sank into a period of
depression; unrest and unemployment grew and while politicians,
administrators and economists argued about what should be done,
the distress of a large section of the population increased. Many questioned whether it was good policy to fund public works just to give
employment; the *laissez-faire* doctrine operating so successfully in England dominated thinking. Edward Wakefield, writing in 1812, typifies
this:

If this be a sufficient reason for cutting canals, when is the labour to cease? If the object be to prevent idleness and all its consequent evils, the same might be effected by filling them up again, or conveying the produce of Ireland from one place to another in wheelbarrows; the fact is that cutting canals is not a regular, permanent and profitable employment. It is characteristic of the Irish to cut a canal in the expectation of trade rather than to wait till trade demands it.

For the many unemployed and their families conditions worsened, aggravated by bad harvests in 1816 and 1817 with the consequent spread of fever. The people's plight gradually became known from descriptions of travellers and reports of parliamentary inquiries. The granting of debentures to assist navigation works had ceased in 1800 with the establishment of the Directors General. Now, new loan schemes were introduced to encourage all types of public works but at first the repayment terms were so stringent that fews companies could avail of them. These terms were relaxed in the early 1820s as conditions in the country worsened, but no attempt was made to set up adequate administrative machinery to co-ordinate and control the funds. The navigation board had by this time become a very ineffectual body and it failed to avail of the opportunity to encourage navigation works.

Eventually, in 1831, legislation was passed setting up Commissioners for Public Works to take over the functions of a number of boards including the navigation board. The new commissioners were to embark on navigation and drainage works to provide employment but, ironically, by the time some of the works were in hand, emigration and famine had so reduced the workforce that it became difficult to find labourers. These new navigation works coincided with the start of the Railway Age in Ireland which was to have such a disastrous effect on the waterways.

It will be seen in the chapters that follow that most of the waterways facing into the 1830s had reached a relatively improved position. Given the low density of industrial activity and the concentration of that activity on the coastal towns, it was inevitable that traffic on the waterways would remain low. They were doomed to low profitability, and matters were made worse by the high capital costs of their construction and mismanagement. However, the traffic carried was far from insignificant in relative terms and the waterways did make a large contribution to the expansion of inland trade by considerably reducing transport costs. By the early 1830s some 500,000 tons per year were being carried by water, which represents a high proportion of the total inland trade of the country at that time but, to set this figure in perspective, a similar tonnage was being carried on the Oxford Canal alone in England at that time. The success or otherwise of navigations was determined by the economic environment in which they operated.

The towns and communities which lay along the path of the waterways enjoyed a new prosperity in the first half of the nineteenth century; some of them, like Tullamore, became important market and distribution centres. Then the railway companies arrived to compete for the limited trade and succeeded only in preventing the waterways from prospering without securing financial stability for themselves; towns by-passed by the railways and exclusively dependent on inland navigation fared badly. But history was to show that the aspirations of the new railway entrepreneurs were no less inflated than those of the canal builders before them.

2
Northern Waterways

The Newry Navigation

IN the early eighteenth century Dublin expanded rapidly and became the fashionable centre for the gentry and aristocracy. The demand for coal increased but, because land carriage was so expensive, it was cheaper to import it from across the water than to use local resources. Coal seams had been discovered in Co. Tyrone in the 1690s and it was not long before people began to consider ways of conveying the coal from there to Dublin. A glance at a relief map of Ireland will show that a natural corridor existed between the Upper Bann and the Newry river, a distance of about twenty miles, with the land which separated the two watersheds never exceeding 80ft (24.4m). The colliery area was located about five miles from the west shore of Lough Neagh and coasters could transport the coal from Newry to Dublin so all that was needed was the canal link. It seemed to be a practical and attractive proposition.

Many years earlier during the Cromwellian campaign the land had been surveyed for a 'navigable trench' to link the two watersheds. Again, in 1703, it had been surveyed by Francis Nevil, Collector of Her Majesty's Revenue, at the request of some members of the Irish parliament, when Nevil estimated that a canal could be made for £20,000 to accommodate twenty ton boats. He was paid a fee of £200 for his pains. Six years later Thomas Knox, one of the Tyrone colliery proprietors, petitioned parliament for aid to build a canal but, despite an encouraging response, nothing happened.

In 1717 the Irish parliament took the unusual step of offering a reward of £1,000 to the first person to produce 500 tons of native coal in Dublin. The proprietors of Ballycastle Colliery in Co. Antrim claimed this reward in 1721, shipping the coal by sea to Dublin, and went on to receive further grants to develop the harbour there. A number of pamphlets were written recommending the canal link with Newry, probably instigated by the proprietors of the Tyrone collieries, and the whole issue seems to have become a subject of general discussion. One anonymous writer in 1729 commented, 'the Supplying of our Selves with our own Coals, is become the subject of almost all Conversations'.

The failure of the Liffey scheme discouraged private investors but, with the establishment of the provincial Commissioners of Inland Navigation and their appropriated funds in 1729, there was a strong case for the work to be put in hand. Thomas Burgh, the Surveyor

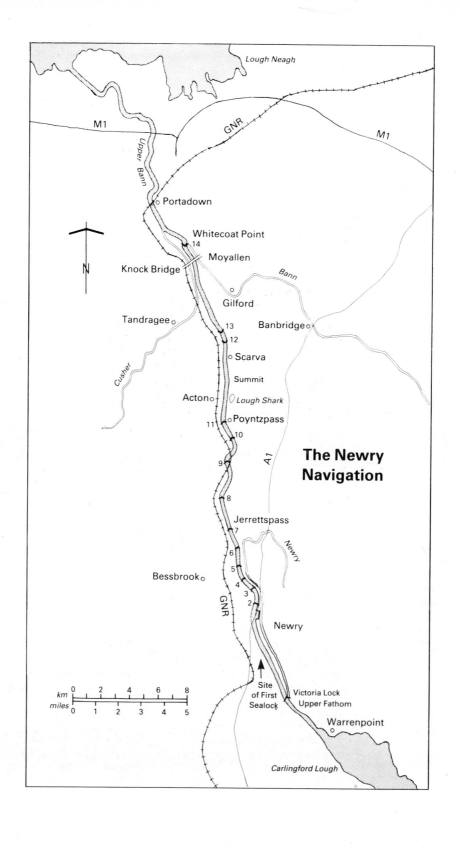

Lough Neagh

M1

GNR

M1

Upper Bann

Portadown

Whitecoat Point

14

Moyallen

Bann

Knock Bridge

Gilford

Tandragee

Banbridge

13

12

Scarva

Cusher

Summit

Acton

Lough Shark

The Newry Navigation

11

Poyntzpass

10

9

A1

8

Jerrettspass

7

Newry

6

5

Bessbrook

4

3

2

GNR

Newry

Site of First Sealock

Victoria Lock
Upper Fathom

Warrenpoint

km
miles

0   2   4   6   8
0   1   2   3   4   5

Carlingford Lough

General, who was responsible for civil works, had a financial interest in the rival Ballycastle Colliery, but he died in 1730, and Edward Lovett Pearce, who succeeded him, began work on the Newry Canal in the following year.

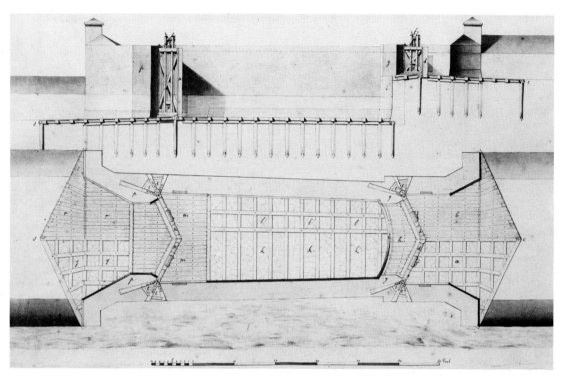

A plan of a lock by Richard Castle in his Essay on Artificial Navigation *addressed to the Commissioners of Inland Navigation in the 1730s*

Richard Castle's signature which demonstrates that he used this form of his name at this time

Pearce was busily engaged in the building of the new Parliament House at this time and it was his young assistant, Richard Castle, who actually took charge of the work. He had arrived in Ireland a few years earlier and was later to establish his own name as an architect of note. It is interesting that while he later became better known as Richard Cassels, he used the anglicised spelling of his name at this time. When Pearce died prematurely in 1733, Cassels made a determined effort to be retained as engineer to the Newry works in preference to the new Surveyor General, Arthur Dobbs. He addressed an *Essay on Artificial Navigation* to the commissioners, in which he showed his detailed knowledge of canal engineering which he said he had acquired 'in Holland and other Places through which I have travelled'. He pointed out how important it was to have competent directors of such works:

The carelessness of Workmen is not less worth notice, for let them be ever so well qualified they will slobber any work over in a negligent manner provided it be the easiest manner for themselves, and more particularly if they find the Director knows nothing, but to make a noise now and then, for the truth of which I appeal to any Gentleman who had his hands in building.

The commissioners must have been impressed because he continued to direct the works until he was 'discharged' in December 1736 – probably because by this time he was neglecting the works for his increasing architectural pursuits.

Thomas Steers, a Liverpool engineer of 'established character', was acting as consultant engineer to the troublesome Ballycastle Harbour works at this time and he had been asked for his opinion about the Newry works earlier in that year even before Cassels was dismissed. He now agreed to accept a contract to complete the canal, but the work took longer than he anticipated and another engineer, called Gilbert, was also involved. The work was finished by 1741 but the actual opening was delayed by legal disputes until the following year. An anonymous pamphlet published in 1773 called *A True Account of the Canal between Lough Neagh and Newry* was very critical of Steers's work. It said that he had built five of the locks and 'his ill Conduct bears a near Relation to the present State of the Work'. It defended Gilbert who had built ten of the locks but added: 'There is however but too much reason to suspect, that the great Salarys allowed to the first Undertakers, who being little acquainted with the Business, committed it to Underlings as ignorant as themselves, were the Chief Cause of its delay. The chief Managers were willing to protract an Employment that was so Beneficial'.

It was a considerable engineering achievement, although imperfections were soon to be realised. It was the first canal undertaking to be completed in these islands. Extending eighteen and a half miles, it climbed up from a tidal lock at Newry through ten locks to a summit level near Poyntzpass, 78ft (23.8m) above sea level, before dropping down through three locks to join the Upper Bann about one mile south of Portadown, from where the river was navigable into Lough Neagh. The first cargo of Tyrone coal arrived in Dublin on 28 marach 1742 aboard the *Cope* which 'had a flag at her topmast head and fired guns as she came up the Channel'. The coal still had to be brought overland to the shores of Lough Neagh because the construction of the Tyrone Navigation which had begun in 1732 was not to reach completion for many years.

A report by the manager, Acheson Johnston, to the Irish parliament in 1750 indicated that delays were being experienced because of defects in some of the locks and because of a shortage of water and the narrowness of parts of the summit level. The Newry merchants, however, looked upon the development of the port as a higher priority than the improvements of the inland canal. They obtained a government grant to build a ship canal so that boats could come right up to the town. They fell out with the first contractor, John Golbourne of Chester, and the work was taken over by Thomas Omer, an engineer who had been invited to Ireland by the Commissioners of Inland Navigation.

It will be seen as the story infolds that the Canal Age was to bring forward a new generation of Irish civil engineers. Up to this time all the Irish engineers involved in public works had learned their trade in military service and they had been assisted from time to time by engineers from England or Europe who were invited to Ireland to act as consultants. There was no engineering training as such and it was a matter of establishing a reputation. For example, Acheson Johnston appears to have been some sort of a cleric because he is referred to sometimes as 'Pastor Johnston'. It will be seen that in addition to being manager of the Newry Canal he was engineer in charge of the Tyrone Navigation works – with somewhat disastrous results.

Thomas Omer and his compatriot, William Ockenden, who came to Ireland in 1755 and 1756 respectively at the invitation of the commissioners, are thought to have originally come from Holland, but there is evidence that Omer had worked in England on river navigation works. Between them they were to supervise all the major new schemes undertaken at this time. It will be seen that their work was subsequently found to be very suspect, but initially they were looked up to as the experts in their field. One writer of the time, Henry Brooke, extolled their virtues in 1759:

> Should these Men persevere, for a few Years more, with the same Spirit and Success, they will be Instruments in the Hands of our Parliament and Commissioners for doing the greatest of all Human works, that of making a great Little Nation, they will thereby intitle themselves to a National Acknowledgement, and the names of Omer and Ockenden will be honourable to our Posterity.

Brooke's faith in these engineers was to prove misplaced and those who came after them and had to cope with their blunders had little cause to honour their names.

Omer decided to lay out a completely new line for the Newry ship canal to larger dimensions accommodating vessels of up to 120 tons. Nearly two miles long, with a large lock at the seaward end, it was completed by 1769 and greatly boosted the trade of the port. This in turn added to the trade on the inland canal, despite its shortcomings, and a considerable trade developed. The trade in coal, for which the canal had been constructed, was not very great; instead, it was bulk agricultural cargoes like grain which developed, together with imports of general merchandise. The canal assisted in the growth of the linen industry in Tyrone and Down and encouraged the establishment of centres of marketing and commerce in produce such as butter for export through Newry port. By the end of the century tolls amounting to over £7,000 per annum were being collected on the inland canal but little was being done to maintain or improve the navigation by the local body which had taken over its administration on the dissolution of the commissioners and it was allowed to deteriorate into a ruinous condition.

The Directors General Take Over

The Directors General assumed control of the canal in 1800 and dispatched one of their engineers, Henry Walker, to take charge and to put the canal into good working order. At this stage the serious state of the canal does not seem to have been appreciated by the board. Work began but Walker was found to be returning false vouchers. He was prosecuted and convicted but after spending three years in prison he agreed to voluntary transportation to America. The senior engineer, John Brownrigg, in the meantime prepared a detailed report in which the ruinous condition of the canal became clear. Walker and Brownrigg are examples of the new generation of Irish engineers. Walker was apprenticed to Brownrigg and had worked with him on the Boyne navigation works in the 1790s where they both gained valuable experience. Brownrigg was to have a long, if somewhat controversial, career in Irish canal building.

Newry Canal: a lighter under sail near Moneypenny's lock, the last lock before the canal joins the Upper Bann. The sails were essential for the Lough Neagh crossing

Brownrigg reported that many of the Newry Canal locks were 'little better than ruined makeshifts pieced and patched from time to time these sixty years'. They had been built to Cassel's design of brick with deal plank floors and had not withstood the test of time. Despite Brownrigg's gloomy forecast that restoring the canal would prove 'little

less expensive than making a new one of the same length', the board felt that there was no option but to embark on an extensive restoration programme.

Nine local 'conductors' were appointed to administer the navigation and oversee the work which was to drag on for the next ten years. A number of the locks and bridges were completely rebuilt, the summit level was widened and deepened, the water supply was improved and the tidal lock on the ship canal was restored. Attempts were made to keep the trade moving while repairs were in progress but, inevitably, the canal had to be closed for long periods; trade was lost to road transport which was going to prove very difficult to win back. There were constant problems with two of the contractors, John Chesby and Edward Cooke. The labourers refused to work because they said that they were not being paid regularly 'and being strangers coming from thirty or forty miles to the work they found they could not pay or satisfy the people they were entertained or supported by'. These were the boom years for the Irish economy because of the war with France, with full employment and high prices, and it was reported that 'the dearness of provisions puts it out of the power of the labouring people at Newry to work for more than one week without payment of their hire'. The men were paid a daily rate and not by task: the wage was about 2s per day but a few years later when the war boom was over, wages fell to about 1s 6d.

Even after the work had been completed in 1811, trade did not improve, although the canal did show a modest profit. In the ten-year period from 1818 to 1827 the income from tolls amounted to an average of £2,546 per annum. The establishment cost about £600 per year to run and maintenance accounted for about £1,000, leaving a net profit of about £800. The Directors General had taken over the concern showing a credit balance of £8,520 in 1800 and by 1829 this had been increased to over £28,000 but this did not take into account the £57,000 spent on restoring the canal so it could be argued that the concern was still heavily in debt to the public. Once the work had been completed the conductors were dispensed with, which reduced the cost of the establishment. This left a secretary, treasurer, check clerk, harbour master, storekeeper, two inspectors of works and the lockkeepers on the payroll.

A passenger service was introduced in 1813 by a private operator, William Dawson. The journey from Knock Bridge, near Portadown, to Newry took four hours and the round trip cost 3s 4d first class and 2s in the common cabin. Dawson made frequent unavailing appeals for a lowering of his tolls, which suggests that the service was not a great economic success, but he continued to operate for many years, eventually connecting with the new railway service at Portadown.

It will be seen in the next section that even after the Tyrone Navigation was completed to Coalisland, the coal trade did not materialise to any greater extent. Another factor which affected trade on the Newry Canal was the decline in the port of Newry while Belfast greatly

Scarva Quay in the early 1900s

increased in importance and the trade generated by the increasing industrial activity in the Lagan valley found its way up and down the Lagan navigation to that port. One of the reasons for the decline in the port of Newry was the inadequate size of the ship canal; the development of steam ships had greatly increased the size and draft of vessels. In addition, large accumulations of mud below the sea lock limited the draft of boats even further. A number of experts were consulted: the Irish engineers, John Brownrigg and John Killaly, Alexander Nimmo from Scotland and Sir John Rennie from England. They all agreed that the ship canal should be enlarged and extended to deeper water with a new sea lock. In 1829, in response to appeals from the Newry merchants, the government agreed to transfer the entire Newry Navigation concern, inland and ship canals, to a private company under the chairmanship of the Marquis of Downshire. This made the Directors General very angry; they were not even consulted and they made it plain that they considered it quite wrong that works which had been constructed entirely at public expense should be handed over to a private company. Part of the deal, however, was that the new company would spend £80,000 over a period of twenty years in improving the ship canal. The company kept its word, and extensive works were carried out which were completed by 1850: the ship canal was enlarged and extended one-and-a-half miles with a new sea lock almost twice the size of the old one, the river channel to the sea was dredged and a large basin, the Albert Basin, was constructed in Newry to accommodate the larger ships. The transfer of control to a private local company proved an advantage to the inland canal as well: in the 1830s the tonnage carried was doubled to over 100,000 tons per annum, raising toll receipts to over £3,500. In common with most Irish waterways this pattern of improvement was maintained through the 1840s, but the railways were soon to establish a stranglehold in the north-east corner of the country.

The Tyrone Navigation

On the face of it, it should have been a much easier task to make a navigation from Lough Neagh to the area of the Tyrone coalfields at Drumglass – a distance of about six miles as the crow flies – but, in fact, it was a very difficult engineering undertaking because a rise of about 250ft (76.2m) had to be overcome. The obvious route was to make use of the natural navigation provided by the River Blackwater from Lough Neagh for a distance of about three miles to its junction with the River Torrent. From here a canal would have to be made following the valley of the Torrent to Coalisland, a distance of about four and a half miles. Although this would bring the navigation to within about two and a half miles of Drumglass, there would still be a rise of 200ft (60.9m) to be overcome, which was to test the ingenuity of the engineers. In 1732, with work on the Newry Canal already in hand, the commissioners began work on the first stage of the Tyrone Navigation, the Coalisland Canal.

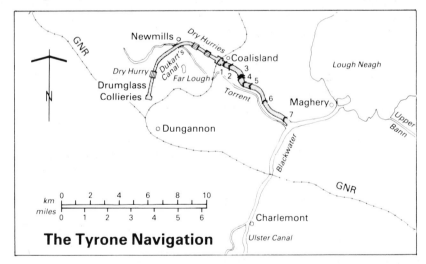

The Tyrone Navigation —the Coalisland Canal and Dukart's tub-boat extension to the collieries

The direction of the works was given to 'Pastor' Acheson Johnston, who as we have seen was subsequently manager of the completed Newry Canal. He displayed a complete lack of engineering skill: he sited three of the seven locks in poor locations in swampy ground and two of the others in loose sandy soil. In both cases he should have used piling and paved the chamber floors. The first one-and-a-half

miles of the canal were so close to the Torrent that it flooded into the canal in winter and drained the water out of it in the dry season. At Coalisland the canal terminated in a large basin into which the main water supply fed from the Torrent which, when it was in flood, brought down large quantities of sand and gravel causing the basin and the first two levels to silt up. It is not quite clear when, if any, boats managed to pass through the canal and, certainly, Dublin failed to gain any benefit from cheaper coal supplies. An anonymous open letter addressed to the commissioners in 1752 complaining about the state of both the Newry and Coalisland canals said:

> It is above twenty years, since this wonder-working Canal was first set about, and, except a few Puffs in Faulkners News Papers, What relief has the City of Dublin had, by the mighty Produce of the Tyrone Collieries?

The writer pointed out that the canal was fully three miles from the Drumglass collieries and the canal 'in Truth, extremely defective, and incompletely finished'. The commissioners replied in their own defence that 'excessive rains had prevented the completion of the canal that summer'; they were aware of the defects and imperfections and 'will thro' their usual Regard to the national Interest, and the Propensity of our own home Collieries, soon remedy every Defect complained of'.

Three years earlier, in 1749, the colliery proprietors, led by the archbishops of Armagh and Tuam, had come together to form a company to improve transport between Drumglass and Coalisland. In 1753 this company was granted £4,000 by parliament to construct a roadway and two years later the same company entered into a twenty-one year contract with the commissioners 'to repair and maintain' the canal. Nothing much seems to have been done, because a parliamentary committee heard evidence in 1758 that the company had failed in its contract and the works were 'in a very bad state'. In 1760 Thomas

Coalisland Canal: the harbour at Coalisland about 1910. Note the silting caused by the River Torrent supply which fed the canal

Omer reported that several of the locks would have to be pulled down and rebuilt and that most of the gates needed replacing. Despite this gloomy report, the Irish parliament now embarked on a series of ambitious schemes to extend the navigation to Drumglass instead of putting right the defects of the Coalisland Canal.

At this time Omer was working on the Newry ship canal and the idea was conceived that a ship canal should be extended all the way from Newry to the coalfields in Tyrone capable of accommodating boats of up to 100 tons. This would have meant that the Newry and Coalisland canals would have to be rebuilt to larger dimensions and an extension constructed from Coalisland to Drumglass. In line with this ridiculous idea of a ship canal right into the heart of Tyrone, Omer was instructed to commence work on the Drumglass extension to these enlarged dimenions. He decided to canalise the River Torrent, and work began on a large ship lock, 125ft (38m) by 22ft (6.7m) near Coalisland under a young assistant engineer, Christopher Myers. After he had partly completed the lock, Myers realised the impracticability of the scheme and he advised a parliamentary committee that it would be much more sensible just to extend the Coalisland Canal and forget about constructing ship canals. Instead of accepting this sensible proposal, parliament favoured a scheme put forward by an engineer of Franco-Italian descent, Davis Dukart.

Dukart's Canal

Dukart's plan was to build a 'tub-boat' canal of much smaller dimensions than even the Coalisland Canal, part of which would be in a tunnel right into the heart of the collieries. Parliament made the change from 100-ton ships to tub-boats and approved his scheme. After commencing work on the tunnel Dukart decided to abandon it and use a new technique to carry the canal up to the level of the coalworks.

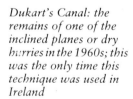

Dukart's Canal: the remains of one of the inclined planes or dry hurries in the 1960s; this was the only time this technique was used in Ireland

Instead of using a staircase of locks, he proposed building three inclined planes or 'dry hurries'. The tub-boats would be floated on to cradles, pulled from the water and drawn up these slopes on rollers, much in the way the ancient Chinese had manhandled boats up slopes in the early weirs. This was the first attempt to construct inclined planes in these islands and was to prove a failure, but the technique was later to be used successfully in England. It proved very difficult to haul the boats up the ramps and William Jessop, an English engineer, was asked for his advice. He suggested doubling up the width of the ramps and operating a counterbalancing system, the weight of the descending laden boat being used to haul up the empty boats. This was more successful, but there were problems because the rollers frequently jammed and so tracks were laid instead with wheels on the cradles. By 1771 it was reported that tub boats were arriving in Coalisland, but so much money had been diverted to Dukart's canal that the Coalisland Canal itself was neglected and impassable. An anonymous pamphlet written in 1780 referred to Dukart's lifts as 'a monument of eccentric ability without foresight' and his canal was known locally as 'Dukart's Whim'. It must have continued to give problems because it does not seem to have been used for long and suggestions that it should be replaced by a tunnel received a cool response from the Irish parliament. The Coalisland Canal appears to have remained in a very imperfect state. William Chapman said of it in 1787, 'it is an old work, requiring frequent and expensive Repairs, and that there is no Toll now paid by Boats on that Navigation'. In that year it was transferred to local commissioners and when the Directors General took it over in 1800 it was reported to be in a ruinous condition, although there was some traffic on it. No further attempt was ever made to extend the navigation from Coalisland to Drumglass and so the coal had to be transported by road. In addition to coal, flaxseed, grain, timber, rock salt, fish, hardware and general provisions were carried by water to and from Coalisland across Lough Neagh and via the Lagan and Newry navigations.

The Directors General Take Over

The Directors General immediately started major repairs on the Coalisland Canal and the engineer given charge of the works was Daniel Monks who had earlier worked as an assistant engineer on the Boyne. The entire canal was dredged and deepened, the third lock – a double chambered lock through which it was reported to take half an hour to pass boats, so badly did it leak – was completely rebuilt, the other locks were repaired and the wooden floors replaced with paving. Some of the lockgates had to be replaced and the banks staunched where the canal and river were too close together. A short canal cut was made at Maghery, where the Blackwater entered Lough Neagh, and a great deal of work was done at the basin at Coalisland; it was dredged, boundary walls were erected and quays and warehouses constructed. Traffic frequently had to be held up and the works dragged on – much to the annoyance of the Coalisland merchants. They eventually held a protest meeting in 1809 to complain about the 'many unnecessary interruptions and to call for an investigation of the delays and disbursements'. It must all have been too much for Daniel Monks because he died in the following year and his father, William Monks, was appointed to administer the canal. By this time the canal had been permanently reopened and trade had begun to pick up.

Coalisland Canal: the 5th lock in 1945. It bears the date 1749 and Acheson Johnston's name

In 1820 the Directors General found themselves questioning their own earlier policy decision to keep toll rates as low as possible on all the waterways. The wages for the Tyrone concern came to just under £200 per year but the income from tolls was only just over £100 so that there was a loss even before annual maintenance was considered. Trade did improve in the 1820s and in some years the income was sufficient to meet the expenditure and leave a small profit. By 1829 a balance of £71 14s 0½d stood in the Tyrone account, a poor return set against the estimated £31,417 spent on the construction of the Coalisland Canal and the additional £21,716 which had to be spent on its restoration, not forgetting the sum of nearly £20,000 wasted on Dukart's Drumglass extension.

The chief disappointment was the failure of the coal trade to develop. It now took just three days for a seventy-ton lighter to make the journey of sixty-one miles from Coalisland to Belfast and two days to cover the forty miles to Newry, but coal made up only a small proportion of the cargo to Newry and no coal was sent to Belfast; the coal trade on the Lagan Navigation was all in the opposite direction, with imported coal from Belfast. With free trade between England and Ireland after the Union, a ton of English coal could be marketed in Dublin for 30s. The pithead price of Tyrone coal was 16s and it cost another 10s to transport it to Dublin. Although slightly cheaper, it was considered to be of inferior quality and there was little demand for it. However, in the Coalisland area, with local supplies of coal available and improved water communications, industries developed, the raw materials came in and the finished goods were exported. By 1837 Coalisland was described in Lewis's *Topographical Dictionary* as 'a place of considerable trade, with thirty-five large lighters or barges, which frequently make coasting voyages to Dublin, and sometimes across the channel to Scotland. . . there are exports of coal, spades, shovels, firebricks, fireclay,crucibles, earthenware, linen cloth, wheat, oats and flour etc., while the imports are timber, deals, iron, salt, slates and glass.' In fact, there is not much evidence to support the suggestion that the lighters were used at sea, although they did have to be good sea boats to make the Lough Neagh crossing under sail. When the new Commissioners of Public Works took over the canal in 1831, there was a credit balance of £5 1s 8d to its name but it was, at least, moving into a period of greater prosperity.

The Lagan Navigation

In the same way that canal entrepreneurs in Dublin had looked to the Liffey in the early years of the eighteenth century, the merchants and landowners of east Ulster had turned their attention to the Lagan as an obvious trade route. The river carved a way through the hills to within about six miles of Lough Neagh and when coal was discovered in Co. Tyrone in the 1690s the idea of creating a navigable link with Belfast became very attractive. The construction of the Newry canal in the 1730s added a new urgency to the situation if Belfast was to be encouraged to develop as a competing port. Although a survey of the Lagan was made by the Surveyor General, Arthur Dobbs, in 1741, it was not until 1753 that a petition finally made its way before the Irish parliament looking for support for the scheme. The plan was based on a new survey undertaken by Acheson Johnston, whose engineering abilities, as already shown, were somewhat suspect. He estimated that the Lagan could be made navigable from Belfast to Spencer's bridge, about seven miles from Lough Neagh, for £20,000 and from there a pass through the hills would provide a good route for a canal to the lake.

Parliament supported the scheme but the Commissioners of Inland Navigation were not in a position to fund it from their limited appropriated duties. An Act was passed, therefore, in 1753 which authorised a special tax of 1d per gallon on ale and 4d a gallon on spirits to be levied in the districts which would be served by the proposed naviga-

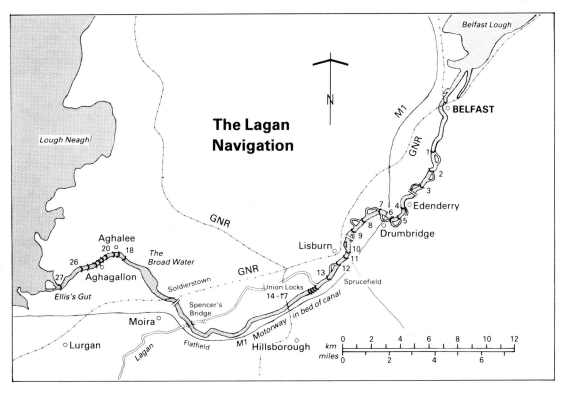

tion. This produced an annual sum of about £1,000, not very much to finance such a scheme, but the floodgates for public works were about to be opened in the next session of parliament, supplementing the funds available. Fortified by a grant of £6,000 the commissioners began work in 1756, dispatching their new engineer, Thomas Omer, to supervise the scheme.

The writer Henry Brooke recorded that six miles of navigation had been completed by 1759 and he praised the quality of the stonework. Parliament continued to lend support to the work and the navigation was opened to traffic from Belfast to Lisburn in September 1763 amid scenes of great enthusiasm described in the *Belfast Newsletter*. The first boat to make the passage was the *Lord Hertford*, owned by Thomas Greg of Belfast, carrying a load of coal and timber for Lisburn – was it an omen that the first load of coal on the canal was imported from across the water and was travelling in the opposite direction to that intended?

> Mr and Mrs Greg had upon this occasion invited a numerous company of ladies and gentlemen to make the voyage and to dine on board. The day was indeed a happy one, the weather was fair, the prospects diversified with bleach greens breaking upon every reach of the river, together with the woodlawn and meadow and the happiness and jollity of the reapers in nearly every field cutting down their harvest, all diffused with joy and pleasure. The party was met at Drumbridge by the principal gentlemen of the town of Lisburn who came on board and the whole company were

entertained by Mr Greg and his family in the most elegant and polite manner with a cold collation and wines of all sorts. A band of music played the whole way to over one thousand persons who accompanied the lighter on the banks of the waterway as far as Lisburn where the inhabitants expressed their unfeigned satisfaction at the completion of this great and truly useful work up to their town and at the very near prospect of its being rendered much more advantageous by having the passage by water opened to Lough Neagh.

For the next four years work continued, but the river was becoming increasingly unsuitable for navigation works and the navigation was extended only a short distance upstream to the thirteenth lock at Sprucefield. Parliamentary grants ceased in 1767, by which time a total of over £40,000 had been spent on the works. The appropriated duties continued, but £1,000 per year was not enough to keep the works in progress and by 1768 all work had ceased. Omer had disappeared from the scene by this time; it is not clear whether he died or just left the country. All was far from well with the part of the navigation that had been completed. Severe floods in winter and a shortage of water in summer were aggravated by the fact that the linen barons considered that they had a prior right to the water.

Lagan Navigation: Robert Whitworth's survey in 1768 showing his suggested route for completing the navigation to Lough Neagh and replacing the existing river navigation with a new canal

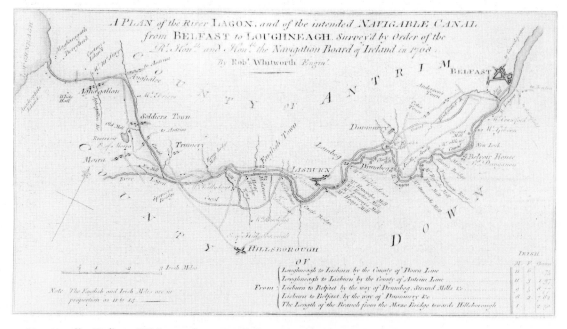

Eventually, Robert Whitworth, an English engineer who had worked under the famous English canal engineer, James Brindley, was consulted. He was not very encouraging. He said that there was very little that could be done to solve the problems, the fact of the matter was that the river was really unsuitable for navigation works and it would have been easier to have constructed a canal all the way from Belfast to Lough Neagh. It became obvious that the commissioners had neither the funds nor the will to undertake such drastic measures and parliament decided to establish local commissioners with powers to borrow up to £10,000 to supplement the income from the duties. This did not prove very satisfactory and in 1779, following the lead shown by the Grand Canal Company, a private company was incorporated in which the Marquis of Donegall held the controlling interest, and the works were handed over to the new company.

Lagan Navigation: Union locks near Lisburn which were removed to make way for the M1

The Marquis enlisted the help of yet another English engineer, Richard Owen. Financing the work almost entirely out of his own pocket, he instructed Owen to complete the navigation to Lough Neagh, ignoring Whitworth's gloomy view of the existing works from Belfast to Lisburn. From Sprucefield, Owen carried the navigation up through four locks, the Union locks, in the space of 100 yards (91m) to a summit level eleven miles long. He constructed the canal to the south of the River Lagan, converging with the river and ultimately crossing it near Spencer's Bridge. From here he used the natural gap in the hills to drop down 70ft (21m) through ten locks to Lough Neagh at Ellis's Gut. In December 1793 Owen, who had a house near Moira, conveyed the Marquis from there to the lake by lighter where they were greeted by the firing of a canon and the cheers of the crowds. Owen seems to have developed a liking for Ireland because on 13 January 1830 he was buried in the little churchyard at nearby Soldierstown looking out over the stretch of canal known as the Broad Water.

The Struggle for Trade

Thus, with the Tyrone Navigation already opened to traffic, the Lagan company had now completed the final link in the northern network connecting Newry, Coalisland and Belfast. Whitworth's warnings, however, proved only too accurate and there were frequent delays on the river navigation: floods damaged the banks and caused silting and there was a constant shortage of water in summer. The company had spent £62,000 on the works, most of it subscribed by the Marquis, but he showed little inclination to finance further work. In 1810 control of the company passed from the Donegall family to a group of prominent Belfast businessmen and merchants who set about investigating what should be done to improve the navigation. Various plans were considered to separate the navigation from the river but a crucial difficulty arose over a water supply. It involved turning water from the Lagan into the summit level to create a sufficient supply for the new canal section and the vested interests of the Lagan linen manufacturers was strong enough to prevent this being done. An Act was passed in 1814 authorising the company to construct the new navigation, with a reservoir to supply it, but negotiations with the Directors General to obtain half the cost of these works came to nothing and in the end the whole idea was abandoned and work was confined to trying to improve the existing navigation. These improvements did lead to a marked reduction in the time needed to pass boats through, and traffic increased considerably. A loaded boat could make the passage from Belfast to Lough Neagh in about twenty-eight hours, a distinct improvement from the early days when it could take anything from one to three weeks, and it was humorously said that a vessel could make a round trip to the West Indies in the time taken to pass through the Lagan Navigation.

Despite its inability to carry out any large scale improvements, the company did manage to maintain a high standard of maintenance of the banks and locks and to keep the river channel well dredged so that traffic continued to increase. Trade between Belfast and Lisburn was an important element but because of road competition on this short haul, tolls had to be carefully regulated. The company introduced a 25 per cent reduction in tolls and even allowed the carriage of potatoes, hay and straw free of toll downstream to fill the empty returning lighters. In 1819 it is recorded that 479 laden lighters made the outward trip from Belfast; nearly half of these did not travel beyond Lisburn and less than one quarter of them returned with loads to Belfast. The

The aqueduct over the Lagan near Moira, built by Richard Owen between 1782 and 1785

chief cargoes carried from Belfast were imported coal for the industries of the Lagan valley and lime; grain was carried on the return journey.

The company made efforts to obtain a loan from the Exchequer Loan Commissioners to finance canal sections at two of the most difficult places in the navigation, at Lisburn and at the seaward end, but the company had not been able to realise any net profits because of the high annual maintenance costs and the commissioners considered that there was insufficient security for the repayment of the loan. It is a measure of the muddled thinking of the time that loans were issued for completely new navigation works on the security of the 'anticipated' revenue from tolls which usually proved to be very over optimistic, whereas loans to existing companies were often refused.

Water transport continued to compete successfully with road transport in the north-east of Ireland in the 1820s and 1830s. The average annual tonnage carried on the Lagan Navigation in the 1830s was 40,000 tons, yielding gross toll receipts of about £1,500. Some loss in revenue had to be conceded by the reduction in tolls. The freight rate was about 6-7s per ton for the through trip including tolls which amounted to about 9½d per ton. In 1821 James McCleery brought the paddle steamer, *Marchioness of Donegall,* to Lough Neagh, the first steamer to arrive on Irish inland waters. Built in Belfast by Ritchie and MacLaine, her engine, supplied by David Napier of Glasgow, developed thirty horse power, giving a speed of six knots. She was used to tow lighters between Ellis's Gut and the Tyrone Navigation at Maghery, but was very expensive to run and was eventually laid up in the mid 1840s. The company was still precluded by law from operating its own lighter service but McCleery, the secretary of the company, operated a private goods service with a fleet of seven lighters. There were also a number of smaller operators and some of the large industrial firms had their own fleets. The completion of the Ulster Canal from Lough Neagh to Upper Lough Erne, which was constructed in the 1830s, was eagerly awaited. It was hoped that it would lead to an expansion of traffic and help to fight road competition, but a new and much greater threat was already beginning to emerge with the start of railway contruction in this area in 1837.

Strabane and Broharris Canals

In 1791 an Act was passed authorising the construction of a four-mile canal from the tidal waters of the Foyle, about ten miles upstream of Derry, to Strabane. It had two large locks which could accommodate boats up to 100ft (30.4m) long and it was opened to traffic on 21 March 1796. The cost of the works was about £12,000, one third of which was obtained as a loan through the debenture scheme for public works, but the rest of the money was put up by the Marquis of Abercorn who had conceived the idea. He had obtained technical advice from the English engineer, Richard Owen, who was working at the time on the final stages of the Lagan Navigation, and the marquis looked upon the canal as an important factor in increasing the wealth of Strabane and the surrounding area which lay within the boundaries of his estates, opening up the area to the sea-going trade. (See map, p. 165.)

The *Londonderry Journal* praised the 'noble and liberal patron' and the *Strabane Journal* described the scene as the canal was opened:

> Early in the morning all the boats on the river assembled at the mouth of the canal in order to try their dexterity on the still-water navigation and to see which would have the honour of first arriving at Strabane. . . . In the evening a number of respectable inhabitants met and dined at the Abercorn's Arms and drank many loyal toasts suitable to this day; the populace was regaled with ale and bonfires and illuminations and other demonstrations of joy closed the night.

It was suggested that Lough Foyle should be linked by canal with Lough Swilly but nothing came of this plan. The Duke's canal did bring considerable prosperity to Strabane in the first quarter of the nineteenth century and the town became a flourishing market for all sorts of agricultural produce. Lewis's *Topographical Dictionary* describes the busy scene on the canal: 'on its banks are large ranges of warehouses and stores for grain with wharfs and commodious quays, well adapted to the carrying on of an extensive trade'. In 1836 just over 10,000 tons were handled on the canal; with the advent of steamers, a towing steamer brought the boats up the tidal river and horses towed the boats up the canal.

In the 1820s a cut was made about two miles long on the south shore of Lough Foyle near Ballykelly towards Limavady. It served both as a drainage channel and a navigation with goods being brought from the port of Derry. It was also used to bring in shellfish and kelp from the sand banks along the shore. An appeal from the inhabitants of Limavady for a canal the whole way to the town from Lough Foyle was turned down and the cut, known locally as the Broharris Canal, was the nearest they came to achieving a navigable link with the lough.

Meanwhile, the Duke had leased his interest in the Strabane Canal in 1820 and all had gone well until 1847, when the railway from Derry to Strabane was opened. This line was extended and Strabane was linked with Omagh, Belfast and Enniskillen by the early 1860s. The company which had obtained the lease of the canal went into liquidation in 1860 and a new company, the Strabane Steam Navigation Company, took over the lease with an option to renew. This company suffered a similar fate and yet another company, the Strabane Steamboat Company, was established in 1890. It paid a fixed annual rent to the Duke of £300. By this time the condition of the canal had deteriorated and the bye-traders using it complained to the Board of Trade that the tolls were unreasonable because of the poor state of the waterway. This led to a legal wrangle as to whether the Board of Trade had any jurisdiction over a private company and in the end an inquiry was set up to investigate the matter. The inquiry concluded that it was a public company, and imposed a tonnage rate of 6*d*, a great deal less than the company's proposal of 2*s*, and found that the accusations about the shallowness of the channel and the poor condition of the locks were justified but 'it cannot be fairly said that the canal is in an unnavigable state'. The company, angered by the whole affair, made no attempt to improve the canal for the traders.

By 1910 there was less than 2ft (0.61m) in places in the canal because of seepage through the banks and leaking lockgates, and the lighters were forced to reduce their loads. Shoals and sandbanks in the river were also reducing the depth of the boats and new bridges restricted the width and headroom so that most cargoes had to be transhipped at Derry and sea-going craft could not get through to Strabane. However, bulk cargoes of grain and timber for the mills along the canal still arrived by water as did goods for the brewery and tannery; the existence of water transport helped to keep down railway rates. In 1912 yet another company, the Strabane and Foyle Navigation Company, took over and this time the Duke sold his interests outright though he remained a tenant for life. The new company did make efforts to improve the depth in the canal and acquired a steam tug, the *Shamrock*, to tow strings of lighters along the canal. But it was to no avail; by the early 1930s there was no traffic and parts of the canal were officially abandoned in 1962, the rest remaining disused. The basin at Strabane was filled in and the contribution of the canal to the early prosperity of the town is now largely forgotten.

3
River Navigations

The Boyne Navigation

I
N the early years of the eighteenth century, when navigation schemes were all the rage, the Boyne had figured large in the overall grand concept of linking up Ireland's major rivers. It was an important fishing river with a number of weirs navigated by shallow draft boats making use of the compulsory 'King's Gap' in the weirs. It has been seen that the Commissioners of Inland Navigation decided to channel their funds in the first instance into the Newry and Tyrone navigations, but in the 1740s, with the Newry Canal completed, they asked Thomas Steers to carry out a survey of the Boyne, a task of additional interest to him because, as a young man, he had forded the river with William in 1690 to engage King James's forces at the Battle of the Boyne.

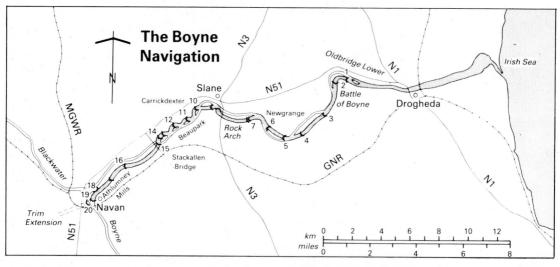

Work began in 1748 under the direction of the now elderly Steers and his deputy, John Lowe, and by the time Steers died in 1750 the tidal lock at Oldbridge had been completed. Underground springs at the site made this a difficult task and, in fact, this lock subsequently had to be rebuilt in the 1830s. Following the death of Steers, work continued slowly until 1756 when, in common with other navigation schemes, it received a boost from the public works bonanza. Over the next twenty-seven years, £40,621 was issued for the works but apart from occasional progress reports to the Irish parliament the whole system of accounting appears to have been very lax. In the 1780s, when the navigation board came under scrutiny, the accounts were found to be 'defective in materials and involved in much perplexity'. Lord Bective, who acted as chairman of the local body overseeing the work, was asked to account for the money by producing proper vouchers but he replied:

> Gustavus Lambert Esq of Beaupark on the Banks of the Boyne, conducted that Navigation for some years and received the Money granted for that Purpose from the Treasury. As he was a Man of Business, he does presume he regularly accounted for the Money he received, as he lived several years after the Conduct of that Navigation was put into other Hands; and that his [Lord Bective's] Name was only made Use of in the Grant, for he lived at too great a Distance to be concerned.

David Jebb, the engineer in charge in the 1760s, had a personal interest in the work. In 1766 he had completed a large mill at Slane. It had been reported three years earlier in the *Gentlemen's Magazine* that the navigation was open to Rosnaree, about one and a half miles downstream, and that a forty-ton vessel had arrived there with a load of Tyrone coal, so it is probable that it was extended to Slane in time for the opening of his mill. He provoked a storm of protest from the salmon fishermen upstream by adding 2ft (0.61m) to the weir at Slane to give a better head of water in his millrace.

It had taken just under twenty years to complete the nine miles of navigation from the tidal lock at Oldbridge to Slane. Less than one third was in the river; there were four stretches of canal with a total of seven locks, the last of these at Rosnaree, a double chambered lock. One of the stretches of canal was on the north bank of the river and the others on the south bank, and there were no bridges at either end of this canal to get the towing horse across the river. Platforms, or 'horse-jumps' as they were called, were constructed from which the horse stepped on to the boat he had been towing which was then poled across the river, a difficult and hazardous operation when the river was in flood.

Some work had also been carried out upstream of Slane in the 1750s by Thomas Omer but, as with so much of his work, it displayed a lack of understanding of the problems of river navigations. He used short lateral canals with narrow walls separating them from the river. These were very vulnerable to damage from winter floods, and the locks soon became ruinous, so that this part of the navigation had never been opened to traffic.

The Navan merchants were aggrieved that so little progress was being made on the navigation upstream of Slane. In 1782, when they heard that plans were afoot to make a new lateral canal on the south bank of the lower Boyne to overcome the difficulty of the navigation changing sides, they were incensed and demanded an inquiry into the state of the works between Slane and Navan. Arising from this inquiry, Jebb was instructed to proceed with the upstream works but, apart from building a guard lock, or single set of gates, at the upstream end of the Slane canal to prevent flood water damaging the canal, he did not proceed any further. In 1787, when the Commissioners of Inland Navigation were dissolved, local commissioners were appointed to take over the navigation and Jebb was retained as engineer. About 6,000 tons a years were now being carried on the navigation between Drogheda and Slane, mostly coal and wheat upstream and flour downstream. This produced a gross income of about £400, which was not even enough to meet the costs of the establishment and maintenance, so there was little chance that the navigation would be extended.

In 1790 parliament agreed to the incorporation of the Boyne Navigation Company, but in response to a petition from the millers on the upper part of the river safeguards were written into the Act to ensure that the navigation would be extended. It was laid down that the completed part of the navigation from Drogheda to Carrickdexter, just upstream of Slane, would not be fully vested in the new company until the navigation was completed to Navan. It was further decreed that if the navigation was not extended to Trim within five years of being completed to Navan, then the Lower Boyne would once again revert to public ownership. The new company applied for debentures and was granted loans of up to one third of the estimated cost of completing the navigation to Navan, which was £37,500.

The company was faced with a difficult task. General Charles Vallency, one of the old-style military engineers, had inspected Omer's works above Slane about twenty years earlier and had reported that they were 'executed with such bad materials and with so little judgement that most of them are in ruins without having been used'. The company entrusted the work to Richard Evans. Evans had learnt his engineering skills with the Grand Canal Company working under an elderly military engineer, Charles Tarrant. Evans had gradually assumed control of the works and was responsible for completing many miles of this canal. His fame spread and his services were sought by other companies. The board of the Grand Canal Company accused him of neglecting their works and when he appeared unrepentant he was dismissed and he took up employment with the rival Royal Canal Company, which adopted a more liberal attitude to his consultancy work. Evans appointed as his assistant engineer on the Boyne works Daniel Monks, who, as we have already seen, ended his days on the Tyrone Navigation. His other assistant engineer on the Boyne was John Brownrigg, who had the young apprentice Henry Walker working for him; the one was starting out on a long career as a canal engineer, the other destined to leave the country in disgrace. Brownrigg was later to cross swords with Richard Evans in connection with work on the Royal Canal, but it is interesting to find so many of them working together on these early Boyne works which were a good testing ground.

Evans decided to use Omer's partly completed scheme from Slane to Stackallen, which was a series of short canals by-passing shallows. He changed the location of one of the canals and made a new lock at

Stackallen to replace Omer's guard lock as it was impossible to open the gates for five months of the year because of the strength of the current. The high rock formation near Beaupark made it impossible to continue the navigation on the south side of the river, and Omer had begun to build a bridge for bringing the towing horses across. Evans decided that the piers of the bridge were obstructing the flow of water and he removed them. This meant that at this point the same system had to be used as was the practice downstream whereby the horses had to be brought across the river on board the boats which were poled across, a dangerous and cumbersome operation. Possibly because of the many difficulties he encountered, Evans decided to avoid using the river in the last four and a half miles of navigation from Stackallen to Navan, and used a single length of canal instead.

The work was divided between a number of contractors and was carried on simultaneously all along the line; eight contractors excavated the canal sections and others built the locks and bridges. Some of the prices paid for the work are interesting: John Monks received £260 for ten pairs of lockgates; Thomas Martin was paid £241 15s 9d for building a new lock at Stackallen; £214 0s 10d was issued for whiskey 'occasioned by the necessity of employing for some time, during the day and the night, more than one hundred persons in keeping the locks free from water during the heavy rains.' On 1 April 1800 the navigation to Navan was opened to traffic and, in accordance with the terms of the 1790 Act, the Lower Boyne became vested in the company. There were seventeen locks between Navan and the tidal lock at Oldbridge Lower, with three additional locks at Navan. One of these gave access to the river and town quays below the weir, the other locked out into the river above the weir for the continuation of the navigation to Trim and the third was a partly completed lock at the entrance to the Trim extension.

While the works were in the final stages of completion, the company had gone back to the Irish parliament looking for a further advance of debentures to continue the works from Navan to Trim. The directors said that 'by reason of many unforeseen difficulties and fatalities incident to such undertakings' they had already expended more than the entire original estimate and had nothing left to complete the works to Trim. They explained that they were advised that the river would not be suitable for this extension and that it would be necessary to adopt the more expensive option of making a lateral canal. Their petition did not come before the House on a very good day. The following uncompromising resolution had just been passed:

> Resolved that no Money be granted this session of parliament for any Pier, Harbour, Quay, Canal, Navigation, Colliery, Road, Bridge, Mill Millwork, nor for building nor rebuilding any particular Church or Cathedral, or for any Charity or Public Institution, except Hospitals and Schools, which has not usually or regularly received Parliamentary support.

It must have seemed that salvation was at hand when the Directors

General were appointed in 1800 with their £500,000 fund. The Boyne Navigation Company was one of the first to apply for aid. Not content with seeking help to make the navigation from Navan to Trim, the company put forward an ambitious scheme, devised by Daniel Monks, to extend the Boyne Navigation to Athboy, to canalise the Blackwater from Navan to Kells and to construct a canal from Trim to link with the Grand Canal at Edenderry. This plan seemed to ignore completely the Royal Canal, and would have involved crossing its intended line. The company had made an error of judgment in seeking finance for such a grandiose scheme and not only did the Directors General turn it down, but they came to the conclusion that there was not even a case for lending support to the more modest extension to Trim. With no further public assistance forthcoming, the company seems to have abandoned all thoughts of continuing the work knowing there was no possibility of financing it from current profits.

The gross takings of the company in 1800 were only £279 19s 1d. The navigation should have been faring better. In the early 1780s the port of Drogheda had been greatly improved by works carried out by John Golbourne, the English engineer who had been connected for a short time with the Newry Ship Canal. In the Boyne estuary he adopted

Boyne Navigation: the approach to Carrickdexter lock, the dividing line between the Upper and Lower Boyne navigations, in about 1890

a technique which he had used successfully on the Clyde; he confined the channel by constructing a series of low walls of gravel and clay at right angles to it. Although the work was never properly completed, it greatly improved the depth on the approaches and encouraged trade to the port. In addition to the mills which had already existed in Navan, new mills had sprung up along the navigation. A large mill complex was established at Athlumney, a short distance downstream of Navan. Here there was a thriving flour mill with a flax mill, built astride the canal, with facilities for loading and unloading directly into the mill from the boats. A cotton mill was built at Stackallen further downstream in 1802 and Jebb's Slane mill was still enjoying the period of prosperity before the repeal of the Corn Laws. These should, therefore, have been good years for the company but, apart from trade with the mills, there was little other traffic. Road transport from Navan to Dublin was more direct than the canal and sea journey, and the Royal Canal, with its reduced tolls imposed by the Directors General, was beginning to attract trade from the same hinterland. By the 1830s there were only about 10,000 tons a year moving on the navigation, and the income from tolls was insufficient to meet the cost of the establishment. In the early years of the century lockage charges had been replaced by a fixed rate of $1\frac{1}{4}d$ per ton per mile, collected at the loading point. The lockkeepers were paid £7 per year, with a free house and garden, and a 'collector' at Drogheda received £50 per year and was assisted by an overseer who was paid according to the tonnage he supervised. There were never more than about twelve boats plying, carrying loads of from forty to sixty tons.

Everybody had quietly forgotten about the clause in the 1790 Act which had stipulated that if the navigation was not completed to Trim within five years of reaching Navan then the Lower Boyne would revert to public ownership. Things might have remained that way but, in 1834, one of the traders, seeing a copy of the 1790 Act, refused to pay tolls on the lower river because he maintained that the company had no statutory right to own it. Whether this incident was responsible for drawing attention to the situation or not, the company was asked to surrender the Lower Boyne on 1 August 1835 and was left with the navigation from Carrickdexter, above Slane, to Navan. The lower Boyne was placed under the control of the new Office of Public Works, thus creating a very unsatisfactory arrangement of dual control. Whatever chance the Boyne Navigation Company might have had of making the company more productive, it was certainly impossible now with such a short length of navigation under its control. In fact, its troubles were only just beginning, because soon a railway running along its route was to add to its difficulties.

The Shannon Navigation

The Shannon Navigation today is 160 miles long from Acres Lake in Co. Leitrim to Limerick, occupying some eighty square miles and passing through fifteen lakes. In all this length there is a fall of only

160ft (48.7m), and 100ft (30.4m) of this are in the last few miles between Killaloe and Limerick. For most of its length, therefore, it meanders its way south, wide and slow-flowing, a natural navigation.

It is little wonder that it played an important part in history from early times; offering attractive sites for monastic settlements, as a trade route for shallow draft boats, as a means of gaining access to the interior of the country for unwelcome invaders and as a line of defence with its major fording places – particularly Athlone – it figures large in stirring stories of bravery. Giraldus Cambrensis who visited Ireland in 1185 with Prince John said:

> The Sinnenus [Shannon] rightly holds the chief place among all the rivers of Ireland whether old or new both on account of the magnificence of its size, its long meanderings and its abundance of fish.

Shannon Navigation: the Martello Tower at Banagher, part of the defences against a Napoleonic attack from the west erected in 1812

As recently as Napoleonic times the Shannon was once again used as a line of defence against a possible French invasion from the west. Massive fortifications were erected by the military authorities at Meelick, Banagher, Shannonbridge and Athlone, which would have served little purpose if the French had arrived in force; Napoleon's Irish friends had briefed him about their location and strength and his army would have come prepared to ford the river elsewhere. The fortifications still stand today as solid as the day they were built, a curiosity and a fine example of the military architecture of this period.

It was only natural that the Shannon should figure prominently in proposals for navigation schemes in the early years of the eighteenth century. In 1697 the 'Grand Jury, Justices of the Peace, Gentlemen

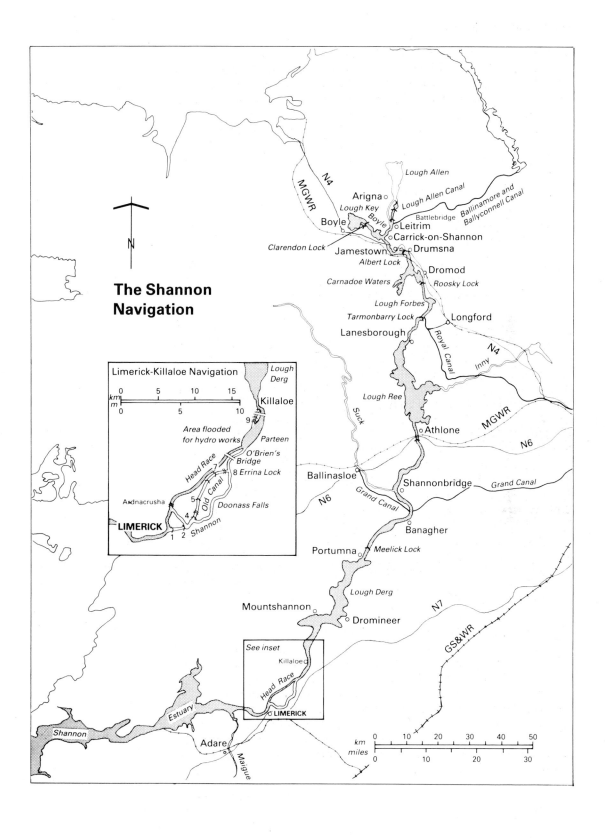

The Shannon Navigation

N

MGWR
N4

Lough Allen

Arigna
Lough Allen Canal

Lough Key
Battlebridge
Ballinamore and
Ballyconnell Canal

Boyle
Boyle
Leitrim

Carrick-on-Shannon

Clarendon Lock
Jamestown
Drumsna

Albert Lock
Dromod

Carnadoe Waters
Roosky Lock

Lough Forbes

Tarmonbarry Lock
Longford

Lanesborough

Royal Canal
N4

Inny

Suck
Lough Ree

MGWR

N6

Athlone

Ballinasloe
Shannonbridge
Grand Canal

N6
Grand Canal

Banagher

Portumna
Meelick Lock

Lough Derg

Mountshannon
N7

Dromineer

GS&WR

See inset
Killaloe

Head Race

LIMERICK

Estuary

Shannon

Adare

Maigue

km
miles

0 10 20 30 40 50

0 10 20 30

Inset: Limerick-Killaloe Navigation

Limerick-Killaloe Navigation

km 0   5   10   15
m   0   5   10

Lough Derg

Killaloe

9

Area flooded
for hydro works
Parteen

O'Brien's
Bridge
Head Race
8 Errina Lock

7

Ardnacrusha
5
Old Canal
Doonass Falls

4

1 2 Shannon

LIMERICK

and Freeholders of the County of Galway' suggested that the cost of making the Shannon fully navigable would not exceed £14,000. A select committee of the Irish parliament was appointed to prepare a bill but it was not until 1709 that more positive action was taken when Mortimer Heylen and Stephen Costello (of Liffey Navigation fame) petitioned the House saying that they had been 'at great pains and charges for a public good to sound and fathom the River Shannon from Limerick to Carrick' and they were given leave to bring in the heads of a bill.

Eventually, in 1715, parliament did decide to authorise many schemes including the Shannon, but there was still no effort made to do any work on it. Navigation schemes for the Shannon continued to occupy public attention. In 1746 an anonymous pamphleteer quoted the fact that the 'curious and very learned Dr Bolton, late Archbishop of Cashel, frequently declared that he would undertake to have all the difficulties removed so that vessels of thirty tons might pass and repass easily at all times of the year, for the sum of £3,000', and suggested that the existing shallows could easily be overcome. 'The ingenious Mr Gilbert', who was associated with the Newry Canal works with Thomas Steers, estimated that the river from Killaloe to Limerick could be made navigable for £21,000. In a pamphlet about schemes for inland navigation written by Matthew Peters in 1755 he said that in the latter part of the summer season of 1753 he was ordered from the Shannon, 'being then employed by the Rt Hon. the Navigation Board as Pay Clerk and Assistant to that Work, which was then under the Direction of the late Mr Scanlan'. This suggests that the Commissioners of Inland Navigation had begun survey work on the river even before the celebrated 1755-7 session of parliament gave impetus to the work.

In 1755 the commissioners ordered their newly-arrived engineer, Thomas Omer, to commence work on the Shannon, and an application was made to parliament for a grant. Omer tackled the middle Shannon first. There were four places where the natural navigation was obstructed between Lough Derg and Lough Ree: Meelick, Banagher, Shannonbridge and Athlone. The Meelick shallows were extensive and he had to construct a lateral canal with a lock which had a 7ft 3in. (2.2m) fall. At Banagher he had to overcome a 3ft (0.9m) fall and so he built a short length of canal and put in a single set of gates, or flash lock, through which boats had to be hauled against the stream. There was only a 9 in. (0.2m) fall at Shannonbridge so again he made a short canal with a flash lock which was only separated from the river by a wall. *Faulkner's Journal* on 23 July 1757 reported that 'Mr Omer arrived in Athlone on Thursday and appointed a spot for erecting a lock on, where contrary to expectations there was a fine foundation. There are thirteen gangs at work of twenty-five men each, which makes in the whole 325 men on the canal'. The Athlone Canal was one and a half miles long and the lock, 120ft (36.5m) long by 19ft (0.9m) wide, had a fall of 4ft 6in. (1.3m). In addition, Omer put a guard lock with a single pair of gates at the upper end of the canal which could be closed in time of flood to protect the works. By 1759 it was reported that he had completed five locks, so he must have finished the work in Lanesborough, north of Lough Ree, by that time. Here again there was a small fall of only 1ft (0.4m) and so he built a short canal and flash lock which, like Shannonbridge, was only separated from the river by a wall. At each of these five places he built a lockhouse. The first house at Meelick was single storey but the others were built to his own special design, which he used on the Grand Canal and the Lagan, a small square two-storey house with semi-circular arched recesses in the sides and front and with a spiral staircase in one corner giving access to the upper floor. The house at Lanesborough was built astride the canal and it and the house at Athlone have not survived but the other houses are still there today, two of them still occupied.

Shannon Navigation: the attractive lockhouse at Shannonbridge designed by Thomas Omer in the 1750s, similar to the houses he designed for the Grand Canal and Lagan Navigation

North of Lanesborough from Tarmonbarry to Lough Forbes the river was shallow in many places and so Omer used the nearby River Camlin by locking up into it. At Roosky a lateral canal and lock were needed and at Jamestown he was able to by-pass the shallows by cutting a canal across the natural loop in the river. Omer's employment with the commissioners ended in 1768 and it was stated before a parliamentary committee that the navigation was completed to Roosky in November 1769. The Jamestown Canal was probably finished in the early 1770s, but it was not recorded who took over the works.

The Limerick-Killaloe Navigation

In the meantime, while efforts to make the Shannon navigable from

Killaloe to Carrick could be said to have progressed reasonably well, it was a very different story south of Killaloe, where enormous difficulties were encountered in the few short miles to Limerick in which the river fell 100ft (30.4m). William Ockenden, the other new arrival in Ireland, was placed in charge of these works by the commissioners. According to Maurice Lenihan, the Limerick historian, work began on 13 June 1757. Ockenden was also in charge of work on the Nore and the Munster Blackwater at the same time with, as we shall see, equally disastrous results. Ockenden commenced work at the Limerick end of the navigation where the Shannon made a great loop approaching the town. He by-passed the loop by constructing a canal with two locks. By 1759 he reported to a parliamentary committee that he had spent the initial grant of £8,000 and that this first stage of the navigation was nearing completion. Two years later his deputy, Edward Uzuld, who was later to become a partner in a large mill here, reported that they had spent another £4,000 and the same length of canal was still 'nearing completion'. Ockenden died in June of that year and work seems to have ceased because in 1763 it was reported that a further grant had not been claimed and there was a dispute about how to tackle the work.

In 1767 parliament gratefully agreed to the incorporation of the Limerick Navigation Company and handed over the concern to it. Under the terms of the Act the new company was to receive a grant of £6,000 to add to their subscriptions of £10,000. Sixteen years later, in 1783, a committee was appointed by parliament to investigate progress on the navigation, and it heard evidence that work was now in progress on another lateral canal about five miles long with six locks and that yet another lateral canal would be needed near Killaloe. It was stated that much time had been wasted because the original line had not been properly laid out and that the company 'laboured under many difficulties from the ignorance and knavery of the persons concerned under the first and subsequent public Acts'. The committee concluded that the navigation would be of great value to Limerick and the surrounding country, particularly in the provision of fuel, as 'many poor families had almost perished for the want of it last winter'. Although the committee recommended that the company should be given aid, the petition for £10,000 appears to have fallen on deaf ears. Two years later the company was back again looking for help and said it would take six more years to complete the navigation to Killaloe.

When the debenture scheme was introduced, the Limerick company quickly applied for a loan. The works were stated to be 'in great forwardness' but it was estimated that over £24,000 would be needed to complete them and debentures up to one third of this amount were guaranteed. At this stage the company decided that it had better seek the advice of an expert, and William Chapman was consulted. Chapman had come to Ireland as an agent for Boulton and Watt steam engines to supervise the erection of an engine at the Tyrone collieries and had decided to stay in Ireland and make a career in canal engineering. He established his name as engineer to the Kildare Canal Company, building the Naas Canal, and then became a consultant engineer to the Grand Canal Company. He subsequently returned to England, where he became one of the leading engineers of his day. His report, prepared for the Limerick company, gives a good indication of how little progress had really been made by 1791.

Chapman said that all the locks had been built to different sizes and designs and some of them would have to be rebuilt. There was a triple chambered lock at Errina, at the upper end of the long lateral canal below O'Brien's Bridge, and the chambers of this lock were 20ft (6m) shorter than all the other locks. He recommended doing away with the middle chamber and extending the upper and lower ones to make it into a double lock which would conform with the others. Chapman was invited to join the company and remained for three years carrying out the work at Errina and rebuilding a number of the other locks. He laid out the line for the final stretch of canal at Killaloe, but unfortunately left the company before it was completed and the works dragged on until 1799 when at long last boats began to ply. It was reported that over 1,000 tons of corn came down the navigation to Limerick in that year, together with cargoes of slates and turf. The fuel was particularly welcome because English coal was very expensive, selling at £2 10s per ton. In that year, £102 10s was received in tolls, which was almost enough to meet the cost of the small establishment of secretary, treasurer, overseer and nine lockkeepers. The navigation, however, was still far from satisfactory. There were no towpaths on the river sections, and shoals were a hazard when the river was low in the summer, while floods made it impassable in places in the winter. There were ten boats operating but the maximum load they could carry in safety was fifteen to twenty tons. It was obvious that more work was needed and it would be some time before the company could declare a dividend, but at least the navigation was now open and the company was only about £1,000 in the red.

The Middle and Upper Shannon

With expenditure on public works severely curtailed from the 1770s, the commissioners made no effort to carry out any further works on the Shannon upstream of Killaloe, nor even to maintain the works that had been completed. Richard Evans was asked to investigate the state of the works upstream of Killaloe by the parliamentary committee set up in 1783. He found the lock at Meelick in very bad condition. At Banagher it took a great number of men to haul boats through the flash lock and he recommended that a chambered lock was essential here. The small fall at Shannonbridge did not present any difficulty, but Athlone lock was 'much out of repair', the cills and floor bulging, making it nearly impossible to pass boats through. He was told that the guard lockgates had never worked and when the river was in flood the water rushed down the canal, damaging the banks which had fallen in. North of Athlone the works were still in reasonable repair, having been completed more recently. The same committee heard evidence from Colonel Charles Tarrant that the work of extending the navigation into Lough Allen would cost £12,000. The committee resolved that the entire navigation should be put into repair and extended into Lough Allen by the commissioners, with contributions from the Grand Juries of the adjacent counties. Tarrant did begin work on a lateral canal to Lough Allen on the west bank but this work seems to have ceased shortly afterwards and no improvements were carried out further south.

Both the Limerick Navigation Company and the Grand Canal Company now became concerned about the state of the works. There was little point in making the connection with the Shannon if it was becoming impassable. The Limerick company had asked William Chapman to look at the rest of the Shannon in 1791, and he confirmed Evans's report. He said that Meelick was in a particularly bad state of repair, 'the present gates are in such a wretched state through want of swing beams, sluices etc. . . , that even with the help of loose boards to stop the openings, and other contrivances, it requires near three hours and a considerable force of men to pass a boat through the lock'. By this time the Commissioners of Inland Navigation had been dissolved and the Shannon was being administered by twenty-seven local commissioners. They do not appear to have done anything at all, and did not even pay the lockkeepers because later, in 1804, the lockkeepers at Meelick and Banagher said that they had received no wages for fourteen years.

In 1794 the Grand Canal Company asked its English consultant engineer, William Jessop, to inspect the Shannon. He pointed out the need for towpaths on the river stretches and said that the banks would need to be built up two feet and a channel made up one side of the river. He also suggested a seven-mile canal to by-pass the large lakes of Bofin and Boderg; because there were no towpaths, boats had to be either sailed or poled on these lakes and there were frequent delays caused by weather in addition to the problems of the badly maintained locks. Arising from this report, the Grand Canal Company directors proposed to the Irish parliament that they would take over the middle Shannon from Lough Derg to Lough Ree, put it in order and maintain it if a grant was issued to them based on Jessop's estimate.

The Shannon under the Directors General

The Limerick Navigation Company and the Grand Canal Company were not slow to apply to the new Directors General for financial assistance. The Grand Canal directors now viewed the matter with urgency because their canal to the Shannon was almost finished, and they succeeded in obtaining approval from the Directors General in September 1801 for the company 'to lay out a few hundred pounds on some of the locks' while negotiations continued. The Directors General sent their own engineer, John Brownrigg, to view all the Shannon works in 1801 and his detailed reports provide a clear picture of the state of the navigation at this time.

He began his inspection at Limerick and he reported that the floating dock there, started in 1757, had never been fitted with gates; there were no harbour facilities and 'nothing can equal the inconvenience of the termination of the navigation in this city'; the boats were tracked by men, not by horses, 'then some take to oars, some oars and square sail, men jump into the boats and out again to pass the places that they can track'; some of the old locks were strange shapes and had been pulled down and altered very often; the new locks built more recently under contract had lacked supervision, the stone work looked good to the eye but the stones were placed on edge instead of being laid horizontally with unconnected rubble behind, 'well known on the Grand Canal by the name of "Starters"'; one stretch of the canal was almost impassable because the contractor had never finished his work; and so it went on. In one place he witnessed a boat with about eight tons of slate for Limerick which had to be lightened by using cotts: 'she had to do this three times in her journey, can anything exceed such labour, or be more disheartening, dangerous and expensive'. He described the various types of boats used on the navigation: sand boats which carried from six to eight tons; lighters of twelve to sixteen tons crewed by four men with two oars and no rudder but steered by an oar in the stern; half keeled boats with a falling mast, square sail and rudder; and square sail flat bottomed boats 'which had to lye bye waiting for a fair wind'. He ended his report with these gloomy words:

> It must be a matter of astonishment to an observer to see, from its present state, the poor progress that has been made in half a century, under several descriptions of bodies that have had the management of the work from time to time, and the expenditure of prodigious sums of Money, and how much remains to bring it to anything resembling a perfect Inland Navigation.

Things were equally bad on the middle Shannon: at Meelick the lower gates had given way two years earlier, 'the timbers of the upper gates are in their places, shut and fixed, the swing beams gone, the sluices broken, and demolished, the sheeting rotten and sticking in pieces, the gates stopped with sods and bundles of potato stalks to retain some water in the upper level of the canal' and the boatmen were forced to resort to using the river, dragging the boats over the falls. The gates were gone at Banagher and Shannonbridge, and boats had to be hauled through the canals against the current; at Athlone the lockgates were gone and the walls warped, the banks of the canal were falling in and, he added, 'this misfortune is much increased by the Publick, here they drive all the cattle to water, here the Artillery horses, Commissary's horses and the horses of the Cavalry have been permitted to ride into the canal, trampling down the banks in a lamentable manner (I saw one man sitting on his horse drive his Car into the Canal thro' one breach and come out at another)'.

On the upper Shannon at Lanesborough he reported: 'the Labour and Straining the Gates of this absurd Lock soon demolished the wooden Work and there is now a rapid free stream through the Canal'; the lock at Clondara was still operational but the lockhouse was in bad repair and, like all Mr Omer's houses, 'smoaks so dreadfully as to be scarcely habitable at some Times'. The lock at Roosky needed new gates and the Jamestown lock also needed gates, there were breaches in the banks of the canal and 'it is apprehended much mischief will be done here in the ensuing winter when the Shannon rises three or four feet higher for there is no person now empowered to lay out a shilling to prevent it'.

The Grand Canal Company had asked William Jessop to re-survey the middle Shannon and estimate the cost of restoring it. With an eye to the navigation fund, Jessop said that the matter should be treated as 'a Great National Concern unfettered by local Considerations or Parsimonious Frugality'. He estimated that it would cost £112,000 to carry out the work, including making towpaths – or £73,383 without. The correspondence continued back and forth between the Directors General and the canal company. In the meantime, work continued: Meelick lock was rebuilt, new locks were made at Banagher and Shannonbridge to replace the single pairs of gates there and Athlone lock had to be taken down and rebuilt. In October 1803 the directors of the canal company said that if they did not receive an assurance within a week that they would be reimbursed, they would not spend 'another guinea in this work, but forthwith remove all our machinery and the materials provided for the completion of it'. The Directors General said that they had never authorised work on this scale, and they continued to press the canal company to reduce tolls on the Grand Canal in return for receiving a grant for the Shannon work which the canal directors equally firmly refused to do. Negotiations dragged on and eventually, in January 1805, the canal directors issued a final ultimatum saying they wished 'to put an end to this tedious and (to us) painful negotiation. . . the period for recommencing the work is at hand – on you alone depends whether the navigation of the River Shannon shall be suffered to languish or be completed within the ensuing year, which great work we are capable of effecting if immediately favoured with a decisive answer'. Finally, on 25 March 1806 an agreement was reached whereby the company was granted £54,634 for the work and agreed to maintain it and charge low tolls on the river, but a reduction in tolls on the Grand Canal was not included in the deal. Friendly relations were established, and the chairman of the Directors General, the Rt Hon. Sackville Hamilton, visited the river and inspected the works, the company marking the occasion by naming the refurbished lock at Meelick Hamilton Lock. All the work was completed in 1810, by which time the company had exceeded the grant by £30,273, but boats drawing up to 5ft 9in. (1.75m) could now pass from Athlone to Killaloe.

At this stage the Limerick to Killaloe navigation was closed to traffic. The Directors General had allocated £6,000 to the Limerick Navigation Company on the strength of Brownrigg's report but when they received no reply to their letters they were told that 'the members who compose the committee for conducting the Limerick Navigation Company are all absent at present, mostly at the different watering places in England'. When a reply was eventually received, the company said that twice this amount would be required. The secretary was summoned to Dublin, the affairs of the concern closely scrutinised and the Directors General decided to take over the carrying out of the work themselves, adding 'that it is with reluctance the Board propose the taking upon themselves the execution of this work which they think should more properly be done by the proprietors but that they have reason to apprehend that unless they undertake it, there is not much possibility of the completing of this very important navigation'. The company had nothing to lose by agreeing to this and received an undertaking that the completed works would be handed back to it before 1 December 1807; in the meantime, the company was allowed to keep any tolls collected for administrative purposes, although these did not amount to much. One month later the company had the audacity to write to 'intimate their astonishment that no attempt has yet been made to forward their works, tho' the season is so much advanced'. The Directors General formally resolved to ignore this letter, 'the Board not being in the habit of using such stile nor disposed to adopt it'.

Work began in July and continued over the next few years but it had to be suspended each winter when the river was in flood, and some traffic was resumed in these months; the most difficult part was the removal of shoals near Parteen. In 1806 Brownrigg explained that he would have to exceed his estimate because 'the prices of materials and labour had risen immediately upon the war and was further increased by the number of men entering the land and sea service'; when he was able to get men to work they went into 'combination' for higher wages. In 1808 the work was officially declared to be complete but the company refused to accept this and, while they were in negotiation, a serious breach occurred in one of the lateral canals at Errina. Brownrigg had to build a dam across the canal to carry out the repairs and this dam was left in position even when the work was completed while the argument continued about further improvements which the company said were needed. The Directors General said they would not remove the dam until the company agreed to repossess the navigation, because boats moving on it might cause further damage, and so all traffic was halted. This ridiculous stalemate continued for five years amidst mounting complaints from the Limerick people and from the Grand Canal Company and despite the intervention of the Lord Lieutenant and the Chief Secretary. Eventually, in 1814, the Directors General decided that the only thing to do was to buy the entire concern from the troublesome company. The agreed purchase price was £17,000, giving the directors and shareholders a much better return on their investment than they could ever have hoped for. The dam was removed and the navigation reopened on 18 June of that year.

The Shannon was now fully navigable from Limerick to Athlone but very little had been done north of Lough Ree. The Directors General had assumed direct control of the upper Shannon but there was very little pressure on them to improve it. The connection with Lough Allen which was to open up the coal trade had never been achieved, the Royal Canal was still scarcely halfway to the Shannon and the only people using the river were a few local traders. No work at all was carried out until 1807, when some of the lockgates were replaced and the navigation was put in 'sufficient order that it may be made use of until it can be fully completed'. The work that was put in hand was badly supervised. A report from Terence McCormick of Roosky spoke of 'flagrant abuse and imposition'. He said that the overseer had removed men to harvest his crops with the sanction of the engineer but the men were still returned as working on the navigation, 'that several others are returned by Murphy who hardly worked at all, that the carpenters do but very little, and that no public business was ever carried on with less attention'. The Board ignored the complaints of traders that there was a total lack of navigation marks and that shallows at old fording places were causing problems. It was said that there was one place south of Tarmonbarry at which there was an annual pilgrimage and the local people 'regularly on that occasion refill the place to make a fordable passage between the two counties'.

The completion of the Royal Canal to the upper Shannon in 1817 put pressure on the Directors General to improve this part of the Shannon navigation. Extensive repairs were carried out on the James-town Canal and harbours were built at Carrick, Dromod, Drumsna and Lanesborough on land donated by local landowners. It was now more important to open up access to Lough Allen and the Arigna coalfields; the government authorised a special grant of £20,000 and work was put in hand in 1818. Tarrant's original scheme to make a lateral canal to the west of the river was abandoned and the Directors General adopted the plan of their engineer, John Killaly, to construct a canal to the east of the river all the way from Battlebridge to Lough Allen, passing through a small lake – Acres Lake – on the way. John Killaly had joined the Grand Canal Company as a young surveyor in 1794, learning his engineering on the construction of the Shannon Line of that canal. He eventually became their principal engineer and when the canal was completed he started working for the Directors General. He was without doubt Ireland's most successful home-trained engineer and he was involved in many undertakings up to his death on 6 April 1832. Denis Hayes and Patrick Kelly, of whom we will hear more anon, won the contract for the building of the Lough Allen Canal and it was completed with commendable speed and opened to traffic in December 1820.

With all parts of the Shannon navigation now in reasonable working order, there was no reason why trade should not improve, but this was a period of economic depression with widespread unemployment and unrest. The banks of the Limerick Navigation were cut three times in 1814, the year in which it had been finally reopened. The breaching of canals became a big problem throughout the country; the purpose of the perpetrators was twofold: to create employment in carrying out the repairs and to slow down the movement of foodstuffs out of the country. Attacks on boats to steal the cargo also became a common practice; these became so bad between Limerick and Killaloe that a convoy system was introduced in 1817 with a military escort. In 1822 all boats laden with potatoes for distressed areas were allowed to pass free of toll. In June of that year one of the lockkeepers near Limerick was dismissed for complicity in an attack 'when a numerous mob stopped four boats with potatoes from Clare'. In July of the same year the Grand Canal Company engineer described how he witnessed hundreds of wretched women and children surrounding a boat which was discharging potatoes at O'Brien's Bridge, hoping to pick up an occasional potato; even when they did succeed they were forced to return them. These were difficult years for navigation employees. John Brownrigg reported an incident on the River Maigue which was also under the jurisdiction of the Directors General and where some limited works had been carried out to improve navigation up to Adare by installing an opening bridge. It was reported that, 'the Rudeness, Wickedness, love of Mischief and inclination to destroy or injure public works is so strongly imbibed in almost every Creature of the lower Class, that it will require the utmost Care in the Bridge keeper to protect his Charge'.

Damage from winter floods was a recurring problem on the Limerick Navigation but by the early years of the 1820s the receipts from tolls were nearly sufficient to meet the cost of the establishment and routine maintenance. On the middle Shannon the Grand Canal Company was enjoying increasing trade, most of it generated to and from the Grand Canal. By 1817 it was reported that there were twenty-six trade boats which operated between Dublin and either Limerick or Athlone. These boats were often delayed for long periods by adverse winds on the Shannon; the plan to make towpaths on the river sections had never materialised. Trade on the upper Shannon was so limited by shallows that no attempt was made to collect tolls until 1822.

Then, in the latter part of the 1820s, trade increased dramatically with the arrival of steamers on the river. Back in 1815 Ringrose Watson had asked the Directors General for financial assistance to enable him to bring a steamer to the Shannon because he was convinced they would be very suitable, 'having witnessed their movements on the River Clyde near Greenock in a high sea'. They were unimpressed by this idea and, although a steamer did arrive on Lough Neagh in 1821, it was not until 1826 that John Grantham brought the *Marquis Wellesley* down the Grand Canal to the Shannon. She was a twin-hulled boat with a paddle-wheel between the hulls and he reported that she had crossed Lough Derg, a distance of about twenty miles, with a slight head wind in six hours. In the same year a new company, the Shannon Steam Navigation Company, brought the *Mountaineer* down the canal to the river. The applications for passes for both these steamers are recorded in the canal company minutes but it was not clear which boat actually reached the river first. In 1828 Charles Wye Williams, of the City of Dublin Steam Packet Company, began to show an interest in the Shannon and he purchased Grantham's steamer and set up the Irish Inland Steam Navigation Company, employing Grantham to run the concern. Williams decided that larger boats would be more suitable on Lough Derg and in 1829 he added the *Clanricarde* to the service, bringing her to the Shannon in sections and reassembling her in Killaloe because she was too large to fit down the canal. In the same year he added the *Dunally* and the *Wye* to his fleet, the latter being used on the Grand Canal. The Shannon Steam Navigation Company seems to have ceased trading at this stage and it is not recorded what they did with the *Mountaineer*, although she obviously left her mark on the river because there is a rock named after her on Lough Derg. In 1832 Williams brought an experimental boat called the *Gazelle* to the river. The German traveller J. G. Kohl has left us an interesting description of this vessel:

> A small steamer, the *Gazelle,* which came alongside our vessel, was making its first experimental trip, and had on board some members of the Shannon Steam Navigation Company (*sic*). It was built on a new plan and consisted of two round boats shaped like cigars and connected above by a common deck. The steam engine was fixed upon the deck and the paddles struck the water quickly but not deeply. The people termed it the 'Cigar Boat'.

James Johnson M.D. described passing through the Limerick Navigation in this boat 'at a very slow rate', adding, 'the quarterdeck being a platform in the place of a forecastle, which was hoisted up perpendicularly, in front of the best cabin, while passing through the locks'. Williams also used this idea in an 80ft (24.4m) horse-drawn boat called the *Nonsuch* which was reduced to 60ft (18.3m) for passing through the locks by raising the bow and the stern sections. Then in 1833 he brought the pride of the fleet to the Shannon, the *Lady Lansdowne*. She was a large paddle-wheeler of 300 tons, 135ft (41.2m) long and 17ft (5.2m) wide, propelled by a ninety horsepower engine. She was built by William Laird in Birkenhead but she had to be shipped in sections and reassembled at Killaloe. The *Avonmore*, a stern wheeler, was added in 1835; she could steam at an average speed of twelve and a half miles per hour. The final steamer to be added to the fleet was the *Lady Burgoyne*, which did not arrive until 1842. Williams also operated steamers on the Shannon Estuary. The most notable of these was the *Garryowen*, which was the first steamer in the world to be fitted with iron bulkheads; these saved her from destruction when she broke away from her moorings at Kilrush during a gale in 1839.

The steamers carried passengers and goods and also towed laden canal boats, the larger steamers operating on the Lough Derg run. This was the first time a regular passenger service was operated on the Shannon, although there is evidence that a passenger boat called the *Speed of Banagher* was on the river in 1823, but without steam it

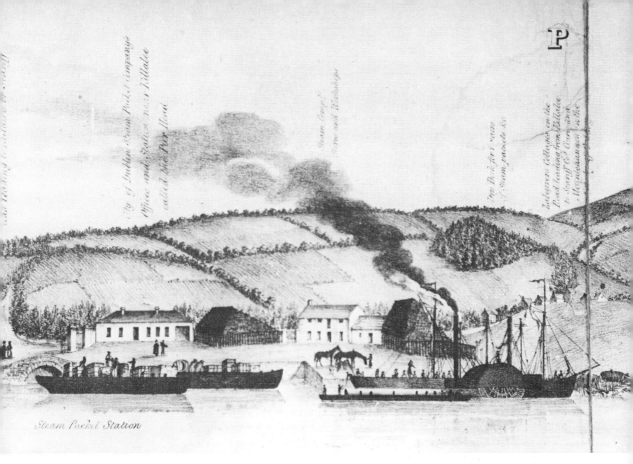

Steam Packet Station

Shannon Navigation: the Lady Lansdowne *at Killaloe drawn by William Stokes for his guide to Lough Derg in the 1840s*

would not have been a very reliable service. All kinds of goods were carried; the *Lady Lansdowne* even carried cattle on her deck and Kohl remarked that he saw 'many packages from the Dublin circulating libraries in which was contained spiritual food for the residents of the country'. He did not add that ordinary food would have been a great deal more welcome at that time.

The steamers made a great difference to the income from tolls received by the Grand Canal Company on the middle Shannon; by 1831 these tolls had increased to over £5,000 per year. There were complaints that the canal company was not fulfilling its obligation to maintain the navigation and it retaliated by pointing to the difficulties experienced on the navigation between Killaloe and Limerick, where the fast flowing river and the shallows at O'Briens Bridge and Parteen were still a constant hazard. The traffic on this navigation had also increased considerably in the closing years of the 1820s. In the early 1820s the income from tolls was between £400 and £500 per year, which just about paid the wages and left enough to carry out routine maintenance, but by 1830 this income had risen to £940. In that year the government agreed to hand over this navigation to a newly formed Limerick Navigation Company on condition that the company would rebuild Baal's Bridge in Limerick and so, once again, a navigation was transferred to private ownership with all the expenses of its restoration paid for from public funds. However, the opportunity to make profits was not great: by 1831 it was reported that 14,600 passengers and 36,018 tons had passed through this navigation, yielding a gross income of £1,514.

On the upper river the Lough Allen Canal had not generated the expected traffic, and the shallow and neglected state of the upper Shannon made it unsuitable for the deeper draft steamers, which did not go north of Athlone, although there was one steamer on the north Shannon owned by Thomas Hughes. It was still expensive to transport coal; the price increased from 7s 6d per ton at the pithead at Arigna to 15s at Carrick a few miles downstream. In 1831 it was recorded that only forty-seven boats had passed through the Lough Allen Canal. Isaac Weld, in his *Statistical Survey of Co. Roscommon,* compiled in the 1830s, remarked on how little the canal was used. He attributed this to the cheap availability of 'sea-coal' at all the ports and to the fact that the imported coal was considered to be of superior quality. He remarked that he saw more Arigna coal going by road to Sligo than down the Shannon.

When tolls were introduced on the upper river in 1822 they were charged on a lockage basis instead of by mileage. They realised a pitiful average of £150 per year in the 1820s and showed no increase in the second half of the 1820s despite the improvement in trade further down the river, which meant that there was not even enough coming in to pay the wages. What traffic there was came mostly to and from the Royal Canal, with about 4,000 tons entering the canal, chiefly corn and coal and about a quarter of this in general merchandise arriving from Dublin. There was much criticism of the state of the navigation and suggestions that it should be opened up into the Boyle Waters and into Carnadoe and Grange lakes. The Directors General did feel that the navigation was having some beneficial effect on the surrounding counties. With reference to the upper Shannon they stated in a report prepared in 1830 'that the agricultural spirit is rapidly extending in the neighbourhood of the Shannon and that in consequence lands have, in the last two years, been applied to tillage, which had not been broken up within the memory of man'.

By and large, however, the Shannonside towns north of Athlone had reaped very little benefit from the navigation judging by receipts from tolls at these stations. On the middle and lower river by far the greatest quantity of goods were being conveyed to and from Limerick and the Grand Canal at Shannon Harbour, more than all the trade handled at Killaloe, Portumna, Banagher, Shannonbridge and Athlone put together. Alexander Nimmo had commented in 1824 about the lack of landing places on the river: 'it is remarkable that, upon the western coast of the broad parts of Shannon, we have not a single landing place. . . . We have no quays or roads to the water at any part of the Shannon except at the bridges'. With the arrival of the steamers on Lough Derg greater use was made of water transport, and a number of stations developed around its shores. The presence of the steamers and the increase in trade on the middle and lower river drew public

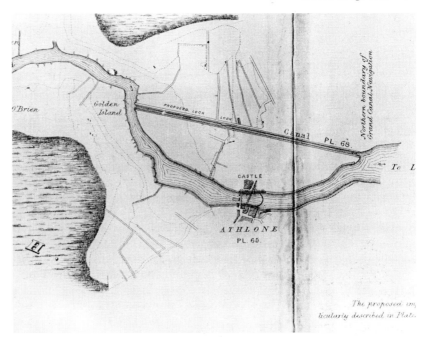

*Shannon Navigation:
one of the plans from
Thomas Rhodes's survey
prepared for the Shannon
Commissioners in the
1830s which shows the
old canal at Athlone and
the original plan to
enlarge this canal and
resite the lock*

attention to the navigation and, in particular, to the poor state of the
upper river. There were reports of long delays in making passages.
One Limerick trader said that it had taken him three months and five
days to bring three boats up the river. Lieutenant John Tully described
a passage he made in 1831 from Killaloe to Jamestown using a steamer
to tow three boats. Although the boats were drawing only 3ft 6in.
(1.06m), he was forced to lighten them in each of the lateral canals
from Athlone upsteam because they had become so silted up. He eventually resorted to offloading much of the cargo on to one boat which
he left behind, then, having completed the journey with the other two,
he had to return with the empty boats to bring up the rest of the cargo.
'Altogether, it was the most vexatious trip that could possibly be,' he
concluded with some feeling. This account was quoted by Charles
Williams in his *Observations on Inland Navigation in Ireland,* published in 1831, in which he called for improvements to the Shannon
Navigation which he considered would help the country's economy
and provide employment for the starving people. He was backed up
by the Directors General, who drew the government's attention to
their dwindling resources and added:

> From the change that has been effected by the introduction of steam and
> the active exertions which are now making for the improvement of trade,
> various works of improvement will soon be called for and required to meet
> the modern system and to assist in developing the incipient resources of
> poor and remote parts of the country. . . and which, as it is unlikely that
> private contributions would be obtained for them are well deserving the
> attentions and support of the legislature.

Finally, in response to all this pressure, the government did establish a commission to report on the condition of the entire river and to make suggestions about what should be done. Steam had revolutionised trade on the Shannon and shown up the deficiencies of the navigation, but that same steam had also led to the introduction of the iron road which was going to make all the proposed improvements of very little use by the time they had been accomplished.

The Blackwater Navigation

The Blackwater, or Munster Blackwater as it is sometimes called to distinguish it from the Tyrone Blackwater, is a natural waterway in its tidal reaches to Cappoquin; its tributary, the Bride, is also navigable on the tide to Tallow. Coal deposits found in the Blackwater valley further upstream tempted the early canal builders to extend the navigation to the coalfields at Dromagh. This was one of the schemes to receive parliamentary support in 1755; a grant of £6,000 was issued and William Ockenden was placed in charge of the works by the Commissioners of Inland Navigation.

Ockenden started work at about the same time as he began work on the Nore at Kilkenny. Once again he did not start at the tidal reaches, but began work some thirty miles upstream at Mallow from where he started to make a lateral canal to Dromagh. Questioned by a parliamentary committee in 1759 he reported that he had made two miles of the canal 'through very difficult ground' and had erected one lock. More money was granted for the work and two years later Thomas Fruin, who took over the works when Ockenden died, told a parliamentary committee that the work had been greatly impeded by severe floods but that five miles of canal were very nearly finished, with two locks. He estimated that he would need another £10,000 to complete the canal to Dromagh, and grants continued until the fall of the Undertakers, making a total of £14,000 in all. When the grants dried up, all work ceased and the canal never extended beyond Lombardstown. It is said that some boats did use the completed canal but as it neither connected with the coalfields nor with the navigable river at Cappoquin, it soon became derelict.

There was one final attempt by the landed proprietors in Co. Cork to establish a navigable link with the coalfields. Their scheme, which was submitted to the Directors General in the early 1800s, envisaged a canal all the way from Cappoquin to Dromagh, a distance of some forty miles. They said that 'skilful engineers have lately been on the spot' and estimated that it would cost £50,000, of which they were prepared to raise one third. This plan received a negative response and nothing further was done.

The complete failure of the Blackwater navigation scheme did nothing for the cause of inland waterways at that time. The Rev. Horatio Townsend in his *Statistical Survey of Co. Cork,* compiled in the early 1800s, suggested sarcastically:

The professed object was, I presume, a communication between Mallow and the Duhallow collieries; the real one, perhaps, more in relation to private than to public emolument. . . . Instead, therefore, of making canals for the purpose of producing affluence, I fear we must wait the arrival of affluence for the purpose of making canals. . . . In considering the subject of canals, I am inclined to think that any great works of this nature are rather above the present circumstances of the country.

It was just about this time that the Duke of Devonshire decided to build a short canal with one lock at Lismore where his estate bordered the Blackwater. This canal enabled boats to come up to Lismore from the sea, extending the navigable waterway a few miles upstream of Cappoquin. The canal was completed about 1814 and was owned and financed entirely by the Duke. It was used as recently as 1922, when railway services between Cappoquin and Lismore were disrupted during the Civil War, but it subsequently became derelict.

Today the only indication that there once was a canal from Mallow to Lombardstown is the name 'Navigation Road' outside Mallow and, concealed behind the hedgerow, the old canal is still visible. Recommendations by both the 1906 and the 1923 commissions on inland waterways that dredging should be carried out to improve the tidal part of the river to Cappoquin were ignored and the replacement of the Youghal Road bridge without an opening span has now restricted headroom to 22ft (6.7m) at high water.

The Nore Navigation

The rivers Barrow, Nore and Suir, which meet together before entering the sea through the Waterford Estuary, are usually known as 'The Three Sisters' despite the fact that Edmund Spenser referred to them as 'the three renowned brethren'. In 1537 an Act entitled 'An Act for the Weares upon the Barrow, and other Waters in the County of Kilkenny' was passed to prevent 'divers wilful persons' from obstructing navigation in the rivers with fishing weirs. The preamble stated that from time immemorial 'Boats, Scowts, Wherries, Clarans, Cottes and other Vessels' had been using the Barrow, Nore, Suir and Rye and that gaps must be left in their weirs to allow boats to pass through with a right of way along the bank for towing boats. This establishes that these rivers were used from early times for small shallow draft boats.

In 1581 the Corporation of Kilkenny agreed to pay Thomas Archer Fitzwalter the sum of £108 6s 8d if he

> shall make or cause and procure that pte of the ryver of the noyer that runneth and extendeth betweene the said town of Kilkennye, to be made passable fitt and servisable for boets of the full ladinge of one toun weight or to towe swyme pase and repasse from tyme to tyme and at all tymes in somer and in wynter to and fro betweene the said townes of Kilkennye and Dourrowe. . . .

In return he was to be given the sole rights of the trade on this stretch

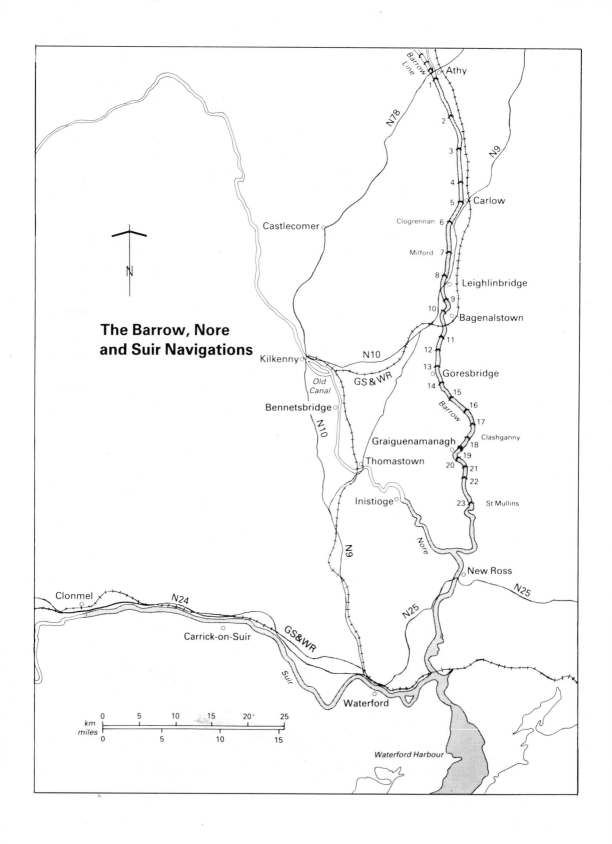

The Barrow, Nore and Suir Navigations

Barrow Line

Athy
1
2
3
4
5 Carlow
Clogrennan 6
Milford 7
8 Leighlinbridge
9
10 Bagenalstown
11
12
13
14 Goresbridge
15
Barrow 16
17
Clashganny
18
19
20 Graiguenamanagh
21
22
23 St Mullins

N78
N9
N10
GS&WR
Old Canal
N10
N9
Nore
N25
New Ross
N25

Castlecomer
Kilkenny
Bennetsbridge
Thomastown
Inistioge

Clonmel
N24
Carrick-on-Suir
GS&WR
Suir
Waterford

Waterford Harbour

km
miles
0   5   10   15   20   25
0   5   10   15

of river. Whether he actually carried out any work is not known but it does confirm that the river was looked upon as an important trading route.

When the public works bonanza began in 1755, the gentlemen of Co. Kilkenny were not slow to petition the Irish parliament for aid to make the Nore navigable from Kilkenny to the tidal portion of the river at Inistioge and it was one of the first schemes to receive a grant. Thomas Omer and William Ockenden both put forward schemes. Omer favoured using the river with short lateral canals by-passing the shallows but Ockenden thought that a longer four-mile canal would be preferable from Kilkenny. His scheme was adopted and the work commenced under his supervision. For the next five years he was directing these works, the work on the Blackwater and on the Shannon between Limerick and Killaloe, receiving a salary of £250 per year for each of the schemes; this was a very sizable sum compared, for example, with the entire cost of the Limerick Navigation Company's establishment some years later, which was about one third of this amount.

In 1759 Ockenden reported to a parliamentary committee that he had spent nearly all of the £10,000 granted to date and he submitted detailed accounts of the expenditure. He said that he had nearly completed the four-mile canal, which would have seven locks and an aqueduct, and that four of the locks were ready with chambers 200ft by 21ft (60.96m by 6.4m). This report encouraged parliament to grant further aid. In March 1761 the following report appeared in the *Universal Advertiser:*

> Kilkenny March 4. Yesterday arrived here for the first time, to the great joy and satisfaction of the inhabitants of this city, three large lighters to take goods for Waterford, which were this day laden with tallow, butter, and marble for exportation; they sailed up and down our new canal, thro' all the locks, gates etc., with the greatest ease and safety. It is with pleasure that we see this great work, begun but three years ago, already become of real use to the public, and will speedily be, when finished, a most useful navigation.

In the light of further evidence, it is difficult to understand this report, but it appears to be a local tradition that this was all part of a scheme to secure the final payment for the work, which was to be withheld until boats could actually pass through from Kilkenny to Inistioge. It is said that the lighters were manhandled upstream with the help of many men and horses and the report was sent to the newspaper with the deliberate intention of deceiving parliament.

In November of the same year it was reported to parliament that Ockenden had died and that five miles of the navigation had been completed, 'all said locks and navigation is fit for use, and that boats have passed up and down through them'. It was further stated that Ockenden's executors had been asked to refund £187 which he had held at the time of his death and that 'plate, goods and effects' had been seized pending recovery of this money. This report was accompanied by a map of the navigation from which the actual works carried out can be traced.

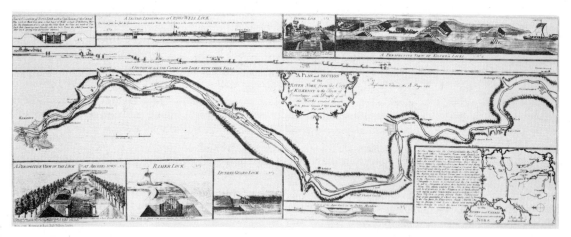

The canal started just downstream of Kilkenny with Scot's lock (no. 1), an aqueduct (no. 2), Crowswell lock (no. 3) and Archerstown lock (no. 4). Here the navigation entered the river but re-entered the next lateral canal almost immediately. This canal was protected by a guard lock (no. 5), with a single pair of lifting gates to be used in time of flood and Kilfera lock (no. 6), which had two chambers. The navigation then crossed the river to the east side and entered another lateral canal which had a guard lock (no. 7) and Dunbel lock (no. 8) at the downstream end. The navigation extended for a total length of about seven miles downstream from Kilkenny. The map also indicated a long length of canal from Bennetsbridge to Jerpoint Abbey on the west side of the river. There are no locks shown, which seems strange, and it is not clear whether this canal had actually been started at this time.

Nore Navigation: the map prepared for the Irish Parliament which conveyed a false impression of the success of these works

The map also contains detailed drawings of the locks which give some indication of how they were constructed. The caption for Scot's lock states:

> The lock in flood time pens fifteen feet of Water, is built of Kilkenny Marble. The foundation of it is cut into the Solid Rock, the Gates are made of Ten Inch Oak Scantling and Plank'd with two Inch Plank the whole framed together in a strong and particular manner.

Archerstown lock is described as having been 'very difficult and expensive as it is laid a great depth under water on a loose Gravel. The Foundation is secured by a strong Frame of Oak timber and piles'. Dunbel lock was 'so difficult it took two Summers to complete'. The legend on the map calls for the 'speedy uniting' of the Nore, the Barrow and the Grand Canal:

> as its banks abound with many useful Commodities much wanting in other Parts, Viz. Corn in great plenty, Butter, Tallow, and Beef, great quantities of which are daily sent by land to the Sea ports for Exportation. Black

Marble (the best in Europe), Coals, Lime, Marle and many other Articles on which the land Carriage rises the Price considerably.

George Smith, the engineer who replaced Ockenden, estimated that he could complete the navigation from Kilkenny to Thomastown for £8,471 and parliament issued a further grant of £4,000.

Reporting to a parliamentary committee two years later, in 1763, Smith said that the navigation to Bennetsbridge was nearly complete, that devastating floods had swept away both the bridges in Kilkenny but 'all the locks erected on this navigation stood the amazing violence of the late floods'. Further grants were authorised in the 1760s, but in 1778 parliament decided to carry out a detailed investigation of the whole scheme. It would seem that by then £22,500 had been authorised for the work since 1755 but that the final grant of £2,750 had never been claimed. All work had ceased, some of the contractors had failed to complete their contracts and Sir William Morres, who had handled the distribution of the grants, was dead with the sum of £786 still held by his representatives.

No further work was ever carried out on this difficult navigation and it is not easy to assess just how much work had actually been achieved. The fact that Ockenden had commenced work at Kilkenny and that these works were never connected with the tidal reaches at Inistioge made the upper stretches useless. There are indications that some excavation was carried out between Bennettsbridge and Thomastown and a by-pass canal was started at Inistioge, but none of these works seem to have been completed. Consequently, the upper reaches of the navigation could never be used and became derelict very quickly. Looking at the locks on this upper part of the navigation today, they seem to have been of a very primitive construction, with the sides of the large chambers formed by sloping banks instead of the conventional perpendicular stonework. Stone piers were erected at either end of the locks on which the gates would have swung but the Kilkenny marble supposed to have been used in the construction of the locks has long since disappeared.

An attempt was made to float a company in the 1780s when the debenture scheme for public works was introduced and William Chapman was asked to inspect the works and put forward a plan and estimate. He suggested that part of the existing works could be used but that the size of the locks should be reduced considerably. He recommended continuing the navigation alongside the river all the way from Kilkenny to Thomastown, crossing the river at just one place and dropping down the 93ft (28.3m) through fourteen locks. From Thomastown to Inistioge he said the river could be made navigable and his estimate for the entire scheme was £30,000. The company failed to attract the necessary capital and the scheme was abandoned.

Interest in making some sort of navigable link to Kilkenny continued and a number of schemes were put forward, including canals which would link directly with the River Barrow. Efforts were made to interest the Directors General in these schemes but they were advised by John Killaly that 'no material improvement was possible' above Inistioge on the river itself. The other schemes also remained 'paper canals', because the Barrow Navigation itself was far from perfect at that time and it was felt more important to improve it.

As recently as 1906 yet another plan was produced which envisaged a canal along the side of the river all the way from Kilkenny to Inistioge, but it had little chance of being adopted in the face of railway and, by that time, road transport competition. Perhaps, if Ockenden had used the original resources to commence work at Inistioge and work upstream, something useful might have emerged instead of a useless stretch of canal which could accommodate boats up to 200ft (60.96m) long but which could not be approached from downstream.

The Barrow Navigation

The 1537 Act, making it illegal to construct fishing weirs without leaving a 'King's Gap' for boats, confirms that the Barrow was used at this time by shallow draft boats. In 1703 a parliamentary committee was set up to bring in a bill to make the Barrow navigable, but no action was taken. Again, in 1709, parliament considered the subject when Colonel Smithwick and others petitioned for aid and it was estimated that it would cost only £3,000 to make the river navigable all the way from Athy to the sea. The Barrow scheme was authorised in the 1715 Act, but no action was taken.

Although the Kilkenny people had been quick to seek a scheme for the Nore in 1755, it was not until 1759 that parliament was petitioned by the 'Burgesses of Carlow and the adjoining Counties' for £2,000 to remove obstructions to navigation in the Barrow from Monasterevin to St Mullins, from where the tidal river was navigable to the sea. This small estimate illustrates the misconceptions surrounding these early navigation schemes and the ignorance about the engineering problems of making rivers navigable. The grant was approved but it still had not been claimed in 1760 and it was not until 1761 that parliament received the first report of the progress of the works.

Thomas Omer was the engineer in charge of the works and John Semple the overseer. They reported that most of the grant had been spent and that another £5,263 would be needed just to complete the first four miles of the navigation from St Mullins upstream to Graig-namanagh, which illustrates how very wide of the mark the original estimates had been. At least Omer was starting from the seaward end of the river, unlike his colleague at Kilkenny, and two years later he reported that he had completed three miles of navigation and 'consid-erable trade was being carried on' but he needed another £2,000 to reach Graignamanagh. In 1767 they were questioned more closely by the parliamentary committee when they came back looking for more money and they still had not even completed the first four miles. Semple explained that in addition to two short lateral canals, each with a lock, a great deal of dredging had been required to makes a navigable channel in the river and it had proved a very difficult stretch of towpath to construct. By this time the public works grants were much more difficult to obtain, but £2,000 was allocated in that session and a further £1,000 in the following session. Thereafter the work had to be financed by the commissioners from their appropriated duties and up to 1783 another £21,000 was advanced from this source, making a grand total of just over £32,000. By this time the navigation had still only been extended to Clashganny a few miles upstream of Graignamanagh. When the commissioners were abolished in 1787 and local commissioners were nominated to administer the navigation, even this desultory work ceased. Shallow draft boats of up to eighteen tons did manage to work their way over the shallows to reach the Grand Canal at Monasterevin, which had been completed by 1785, only to find that they were excluded from entering the canal unless they were carrying a minimum of thirty tons because the company would not waste water passing small boats through the locks.

The Barrow Navigation Company is Incorporated

A number of efforts were made to form a company to take over the works. Eventually a group of subscribers produced a survey by Charles Tarrant and undertook to complete the navigation within ten years if they received a grant of £30,000, which they promised to match with subscriptions. Some of the subscribers asked William Chapman for his advice and he indicated that he considered that twenty more locks would be required in addition to the seven already completed to enable boats of up to eighty tons to navigate the whole river from St Mullins to the Grand Canal. The Barrow Navigation Company was incorporated by charter in 1790 and took possession of the works. By this time the debenture scheme for public works was in operation and the

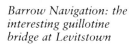

Barrow Navigation: the interesting guillotine bridge at Levitstown

company was allocated a loan of one third of the cost of completing the works, which was estimated to be £60,000. Work went ahead under Chapman's direction, the entire trackway from St Mullins to Athy was completed, ten new lateral canals with locks were constructed and four of the original locks were enlarged so that boats of up to eighty tons could be accommodated.

In 1800 the company approached the newly appointed Directors General and said that it was in financial difficulty. There were further places on the navigation that needed to be by-passed and five more lateral canals would be needed to provide a navigation of 5ft (1.5m) throughout. The usual protracted negotiations commenced and eventually the company was forced to accept a reduction in tolls in return for financial help, thus endangering its future economic viability. The work went ahead and William Jessop agreed to inspect the progress in 1806. He confessed that he had started out with a 'prejudice unfavourable to the navigation' but having viewed the works and those intended he said it had

> completely dissipated with me every shadow of doubt and left me at liberty to say without any hesitation that the River Barrow may be made navigable with a five foot depth of water in every part of it in the driest seasons not only without injury to private property but with considerable benefit to all the existing mills on the river and to the lands on the borders of it.

Barrow Navigation: the lifting bridge at Bagenalstown

Jessop's comments must have encouraged the company, but they were to prove over-optimistic. In 1810 the directors were once again holding out their hands for money, having spent over £120,000, about one quarter of which had come from public funds. There were more inspections, more surveys, more reports and new estimates and eventually the Directors General agreed to meet half the estimated cost of

£60,000 still needed to achieve the five foot navigation. In 1813 the Directors General refused to hand over the final instalment of this grant because the promised five feet had still not been achieved and the company was forced to admit that three feet was the best that could be managed in the dry season. Encouraged by the fact that the Directors General had purchased the Limerick Navigation Company, the Barrow company tried to seek this easy way out, but the offer to sell was turned down and yet another plea for the final instalment of the grant fell on deaf ears.

Despite the imperfect state of the navigation trade did increase, rising from 16,000 tons in 1790 to nearly 60,000 by 1830. The trade up and down the river was fairly evenly divided, and more than half of it was generated by the mills along the banks. The net income from tolls was just enough to encourage halfhearted attempts to improve the navigation; some of the weirs were raised to try to improve levels and a new by-pass canal and lock were constructed just south of Carlow at Clogrennan in 1836. An attempt was made by the company to operate passenger boats between Graignamanagh and Athy in conjunction with the Grand Canal boats, with hotels at Carlow and Graignamanagh but the service was abandoned in 1809. Efforts to run it as a private service also failed even when subsidised by the Grand Canal Company with a bounty of 10*d* for first class and 6*d* for common cabin passengers who transferred to its boats.

The Barrow boatmen stood apart from the Grand Canal men. Many of them traditionally came from Graignamanagh and while they carried their loads through the Grand Canal as well, the canal men seldom ventured on the river. Sails and poles were used in the tidal parts of the river, but the board of the Grand Canal Company banned the Barrow men from carrying their iron shod poles on the canal because of the damage they caused to the banks. In 1835 the Grand directors asked for a meeting with the Barrow directors to discuss the proposed new railroad to Kilkenny but the Barrow board turned down the invitation and said that it did not intend to oppose the railway because the high tolls on the Grand Canal excluded trade with Kilkenny anyway. It may be that William Colvill, one of the Barrow directors, who was later to be chairman of both the navigation company and the Great Southern and Western Railway Company, was already beginning to appreciate the threat the railways were going to pose and was coming round to the 'if you can't beat 'em, join 'em' philosophy.

The Suir Navigation

The third of the three sisters, the Suir, was a fine natural waterway for some forty miles through Waterford and Carrick-on-Suir to Clonmel which needed little more than deepening of the channel in a few places to make it a tidal navigation for deep draft boats. Parliament did issue a grant for work between Clonmel and Carrick in the 1755-7 session but, when the three contractors were questioned by a parliamentary committee two years later, there seems to have been very

little accomplished. Joseph Grubb said that he had been 'obstructed from completing' his contract, Richard Shaw said he could not appear before the committee because he had had a fall from his horse and William Markham begged to be excused on the grounds of his 'age and infirmity'.

The matter seems to have rested there until 1815, when the Directors General carried out an investigation into how the channel could be improved for seagoing vessels up to Waterford. Some question arose as to whether it was within the brief of the inland navigation board to carry out such work, but the matter seems to have been resolved by the Lord Lieutenant, who nominated the Directors General as harbour commissioners for the port of Waterford together with a number of local representatives. John Killaly estimated that the work could be accomplished for £14,588 and the contract went to John Hughes of London, an engineer who it was reported was proprietor of 'a new machine called "an Excavator" worked by steam'. There were some delays in the arrival of the machinery from the Abbey Iron Works in Neath but eventually it was reported that the 'dredging boat' had arrived in July 1817 and the channel was dredged by February 1821.

Killaly had also surveyed the river upstream of Carrick and he esti-

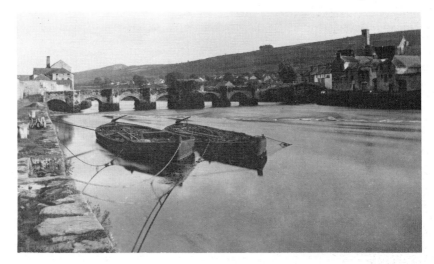

Suir Navigation: the quays at Carrick-on-Suir about 1910

mated that this stretch of river could be improved by dredging and raising and repairing the weirs for the small sum of £2,700. He pointed out that there was a fall of 57ft (17.4m) in the ten and three quarter miles and that what was really needed was a lateral canal with locks because the river was fast flowing and tended to flood and fluctuate a great deal in levels, but he did not think that the potential traffic would warrant the expenditure of this larger scheme. In the event, not even the more modest repairs were carried out either then or later and this was never a satisfactory stretch of waterway. In 1836 the River Suir Navigation Company was incorporated and it undertook to improve the navigation just downstream of Carrick, where a shoal limited the draft of boats. A short canal was excavated through the reef and traffic to Carrick increased, but the company was never profitable and no authority was responsible for the navigation from Carrick to Clonmel, so very few boats used this part of the river.

The Slaney Navigation

The River Slaney was included in the 1715 Act, with authorisation for work for almost its entire length from Baltinglass to Wexford, but no work was ever attempted. In 1795 a more modest scheme for improving the channel to Enniscorthy was suggested, but nothing was done. In 1833 legislation was passed authorising a lateral canal to Enniscorthy but again no work was carried out. The river was not placed under the control of any authority but a little dredging was carried out by the local traders and some quays were build at Enniscorthy. In 1835 it was estimated that some 60,000 tons a year were moving on the river in flat bottomed lighters of fifteen to twenty tons, principally grain downstream and limestone, timber and imported goods upstream. Very soon the Dublin Wicklow and Wexford Railway was to be constructed, running parallel to the river, and this put paid to all future plans to improve the navigation.

4

The Grand Canal

THE 1715 Act reflected the grand concept of that time that Dublin would be linked with the Shannon by connecting the rivers Liffey, Rye, Boyne and Brosna. The failure of the Liffey scheme, however, had illustrated that some rivers were less suitable than others as navigations, and quite a number of surveys were carried out to establish the best line to take. It was accepted that it would be easier to cut a canal for at least part of the way from Dublin, and Stephen Costello, of Liffey navigation fame, and Michael Keating investigated a line through the Bog of Allen in the 1720s. A pamphleteer of that time envisaged the Bog of Allen replaced by 'a vast expanse of meadows' bordered by towns and villages, and John Browne, writing in 1729, spoke of a canal from Dublin to the Shannon 45ft (13.7m) wide which would require only three or four locks and would cost from £10,000 to £15,000. Matthew Peters records that he was instructed by the Commissioners of Inland Navigation to take the levels of such a canal in 1738. Thus, when funds for inland navigation became more freely available in 1755, quite a number of alternative proposals had already been considered.

At this stage the whole matter became the subject of a considerable body of pamphlet literature. Thomas Omer, who, as we have seen, was the commissioners' newly arrived expert, favoured a line to the south of the Liffey in Dublin, crossing it near Sallins, through the Bog of Allen to the River Brosna by which 'there is a certain passage to be had' to the Shannon; this became known as the 'Grand' line. An alternative or 'Royal' line had been surveyed by Thomas Williams and John Cooley. It left Dublin north of the Liffey, joined the Rye near Leixlip and then, using the Blackwater, Boyne, Deel and Yellow rivers, passed through Lough Derravaragh to the River Inny and into Lough Ree. This line was fifteen miles longer and had nineteen more locks and it had the disadvantage of passing through a large lake and of entering the Shannon in the middle of Lough Ree, where the absence of towpaths would cause problems. Omer's opponents on the other hand said that the Bog of Allen would be an impassable obstacle, an observation which was to prove uncomfortably near the mark in the future. These fears were dismissed by yet another pamphleteer who said that he had devised a plan for cutting canals through bog 'and the explanation thereof; and I am sure that he will no longer be afraid of the difficulties so easily avoided'. However, the anonymous author

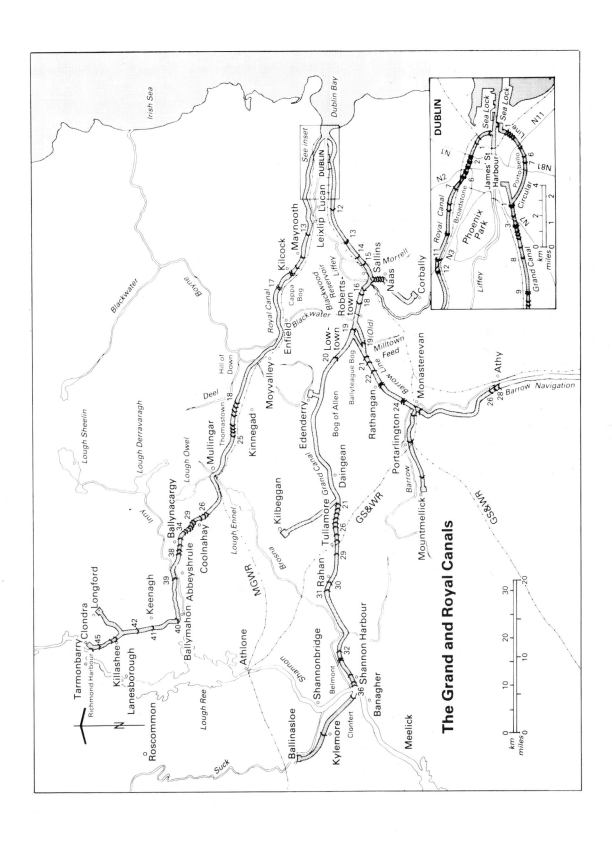

The Grand and Royal Canals

Irish Sea

Dublin Bay

See inset

DUBLIN

See inset

Maynooth
13
Kilcock
Leixlip Lucan
12
Royal Canal 17
Cappa Bog
Enfield Blackwater
Blackwood Reservoir
Roberts- Liffey
town
16
Low-
town
19
18
Sallins
Naas
Morrell
Corbally
15
14
13

20
19 (Old)
Milltown Feed
Monasterevan
Athy
28 Barrow Navigation
26

Ballyteague Bog
22
21
Rathangan 24
Portarlington 24
Bog of Allen
Daingean
Edenderry
Moyvalley
Kinnegad
25
Thomastown
18
Hill of Down
Deel
Mullingar
Lough Owel
Lough Ennel
Ballynacargy
Coolnahay 26
29
34
38
39
Keenagh
Abbeyshrule
Ballymahon
40
41
42
45
Longford
Clondra
Tarmonbarry
Richmond Harbour
Killashee
Lanesborough
Roscommon

Lough Sheelin
Lough Derravaragh
Inny
Boyne
Blackwater

Kilbeggan
Brosna
Tullamore Grand Canal
21
Rahan
31
30
29
21
GS&WR
Barrow
Mountmellick
MGWR
Athlone
Lough Ree
Shannon
Shannonbridge
Belmont
Shannon Harbour
36
32
Banagher
Clonfert
Kylemore
Ballinasloe
Suck
Meelick
GS&WR

Morrell

DUBLIN

Sea Lock
Sea Lock
Liffey Line
N11
N1
N2
N3
Royal Canal
James' St Harbour
Broadstone
Portobello
Circular
Phoenix Park
Liffey
Grand Canal
N81
N7
1
2
3
4
5
6
7
8
9
11
12
km
miles

N

The Grand and Royal Canals

km
miles
0 10 20 30
0 10 20

does not actually say what his plan was. Finally, while accepting that both lines were practical and would benefit the country, the Irish parliament came down in favour of Omer's line and granted £20,000 for the work.

The commissioners lost no time in pressing ahead with the scheme. Omer spent the summer of 1757 taking levels and, in the following season, cut two miles of canal and seven miles of drains in the Bog of Allen and excavated about two miles of canal from the Liffey near Sallins towards Dublin. He explained that he had not begun work in Dublin because there were many delays in assessing compensation for the land-owners. Omer's reports made to parliamentary committees every two years appear in the Journals of the Irish House of Commons. A further £10,000 was granted for the work and in 1759 he said that eight miles of canal were finished from the Liffey near Sallins towards Dublin and that the works west of the Liffey 'have succeeded very well'. He admitted the crossing of the Liffey would be 'attended with much difficulty' but he said this was surmountable. Two years later he told a committee that he would be able 'with ease to carry the line of navigation through every part of the Bog of Allen'. He said that one lock had been constructed near Clondalkin 136ft (41.45m) long which could accommodate a 175-ton boat 'which may be navigated by ten men and six horses. . . such a barge may pass from the Shannon to the city of Dublin with ease in about eight days'. By 1763 he was able to report that he had completed three locks, six bridges and four lockhouses but that he had not been able to acquire the necessary land near Dublin because it was so expensive and he was concentrating on finishing the canal from Clondalkin to the River Morrell, which was to be his first water supply.

At this stage the Corporation of Dublin began to show an interest. If the canal were to terminate near the city basin it could be a useful supplement to the water supply and so the Corporation agreed to put up the money to buy the necessary land to complete the canal from the River Morrell into the city. Parliament agreed to reimburse this money and the pipe-water committee of the Corporation took over the administration of the works. Conceiving that the canal would not only solve their drinking water problems but would also be 'a pleasing recreation as well as a salutory walk to the inhabitants of Dublin, if trees were planted on the banks of the canal', Patrick Edgar was asked to supply 400 trees, 30ft (9.1m) high, 'matched fair and straight at 3s 3d per tree, including all expenses of planting'. Soon the contractors, John Satterthwaite and Barnwell and Tracey, reported that the canal was ready to receive water from the Morrell to Clondalkin, but when it was filled the banks gave way. It had to be emptied and repaired and when it was refilled 'the same disagreeable fatality' occurred. Satterthwaite undertook to carry out repairs and to guarantee a supply of water to the city basin for seven years but it soon became apparent that he seemed unable to overcome the difficulties. After a good deal of accusations and counter accusations, during which the pipe-water committee accused Satterthwaite of 'most daring insolence, paying no regard to his contracts or the orders of your committee', it was decided to advertise for a new contractor.

Although Omer had been asked by the pipe-water committee to prepare the plans and estimates for the canal from Clondalkin into the city, he does not appear to have had any further part in the works. The engineer in charge was John Trail, described as a 'judicious and intelligent person and has received the approbation of Mr Edgar, the officer of the Navigation Board'. Fate intervened in 1768 when it was reported that both John Satterthwaite and his brother Joseph had died and the conduct of the entire works was placed in the hands of John Trail. In the following year he presented an encouraging report to parliament in which he spoke about completing the canal from Dublin to the Bog of Allen and 'from the practice I have had in works similar to this, I am convinced a navigable canal may be made through any part of the bog where the rise and fall of the ground will admit it'. By this time about £77,000 had been spent on the works, but it became obvious that as soon as the pipe-water committee achieved its object of obtaining Morrell water for the city basin, it was unlikely to show any further interest in extending the canal to the west, nor was parliament prepared to go on financing the work. The whole scheme might well have been abandoned at this stage if a private company had not entered the scene.

The Grand Canal Company is Incorporated

In 1770 a group of noblemen and merchants came together to discuss the formation of a company which was prepared to take over the works and complete the canal as a private enterprise. At first some of the members of Dublin Corporation opposed this, fearing that they would lose control of the right to use the water, but good sense prevailed and they decided to offer financial support to the group. Subscriptions amounting to £30,000 were promised and a grateful parliament agreed to the incorporation of the company on 2 June 1772; all the powers, privileges, advantages and authorities of the commissioners in relation to the Grand Canal became vested in the new company. This paved the way for the setting up of other private companies to take over incomplete navigations and subsequent legislation was modelled on this Act.

The company accepted John Trail's proposal that he would complete the canal from Dublin to the River Liffey near Sallins for a fee of five per cent of the expenditure – £300 per annum and the balance at the end of his contract. Work on the city end of the canal commenced in style on 15 April 1773 when the Lord Lieutenant, Earl Harcourt, laid the foundation stone of the first lock at Inchicore to the accompaniment of an army band and a salute from a 'few pieces of Ordnance'. The assembled company then retired to the Rotunda, where Mr Candy of Church Street provided 'an elegant dinner of two courses and a dessert. . . a plan of the intended lock of which the first stone had been

An early Grand Canal Company share certificate

laid was raised in paste and adorned the middle of the table'. This repast cost the company 10*s* 6*d* for each guest, 'excepting Wine, Syder, Spirits and Spa water. . . . The whole was conducted in a manner that gave honour to the judicious contriver, and the evening concluded with harmonious festivity'.

A controversy had arisen over how and where the canal should cross the Liffey. Omer had originally envisaged locking down into the river and up again on the other side but Trail favoured constructing an aqueduct. He said that locking down into the Liffey would create a water supply problem because the water from the summit level would be lost into the river. Charles Vallencey, the well-known military engineer, agreed with Trail but suggested a better location for the aqueduct would be found a short distance upstream where there was a ford, even though this meant making two sharp bends in the canal. The directors decided to seek expert advice about this and other unsettled questions about the route of the canal. One of the directors, Redmond Morres, persuaded John Smeaton, one of the leading canal engineers in England at that time, to come to Ireland to advise the company. Smeaton arrived in the summer of 1773 with his assistant William Jessop, who later became a well-known engineer and acted in a consultant capacity to the Grand Canal Company for many years until 1802.

Smeaton spent fourteen days in Ireland and made a number of significant recommendations which were adopted by the company. He criticised the fact that the line of the canal had been brought through a quarry near Lucan 'but as the difficulty is in great part overcome, it does not now seem proper to depart from it'. He suggested that the dimensions of the canal were unnecessarily large for the Irish trade. Omer's locks were 137ft long by 20ft wide (41.75m by 6.09m), although Trail had already reduced the dimensions of the first first and second locks to 80ft by 16ft (24.38m by 4.87m). Smeaton now recommended a further reduction in size to 60ft by 14ft (18.28m by 4.26m) which would bring about a considerable saving in the overall cost of the canal. Omer's locks were shortened and the gate piers were narrowed, which explains the strange shape of the eleventh, twelfth and thirteenth locks today. Smeaton was very critical of Omer's efforts in the Bog of Allen and suggested a deviation taking the canal along the northern limit of the bog. His criterion was: 'Avoid a bog if you can, but by all means possible, the going deep into it'. The company took his advice and it will be seen that in this instance Omer had, in fact, been nearer the mark with his system of drains, and following Smeaton's advice was going to cost the company dear in the future. He would not commit himself about the Liffey crossing, saying that further site investigation was needed. It was eventually Vallencey's site which was used, but the original line and the excavation for Omer's lock are still visible at the other crossing point downstream.

Trail made good progress but relations between him and the directors became strained. He complained that he was not receiving enough money to pay the men and the directors accused him of carrying out 'exceeding ill executed' work. The final straw came in December 1776 when Trail published a notice of an auction of stores at the Grand Canal storeyard without the board's sanction. The company issued a notice cancelling the auction, there were stormy exchanges and, eventually, Trail resigned, saying he considered he had completed his contract and intended to surrender the works on 'the twenty-first Instant of January at eleven o'clock in the forenoon. . . on the Grand Canal at Sallins'. Ten post-chaises were ordered and eight directors set off with a new engineer, Captain Charles Tarrant, another of those engineers who had learned his trade in military service, and several other men 'of Knowledge in Masonry, Carpentry and Smithswork'. The meeting took place, but the directors refused to accept that the contract had been fulfilled and issued a suit against Trail. The records show that on 16 September Benjamin Matthews was paid £5 5s for arresting him, but his reputation does not appear to have been damaged because he subsequently was knighted for work carried out for Dublin Corporation.

In the meantime, Captain Tarrant's reports confirmed the worst fears of the board that the banks needed raising and strengthening in places and one lock would have to be rebuilt. It was not until August

1777 that the supply of water to the city basin was commenced and the canal was opened to traffic from Dublin to Sallins in 1779. It had taken twenty-three years to complete this first eighteen miles of canal and the cost had been very high. Even now all was not well and Thomas Digby Brooke, the first trader, appealed for a reduction in toll because of constant interruptions 'from various obstructions and the want of water'. He said he was carrying stone, clay and coal into the city and dung from the city streets on the return trip.

In August 1780 the company began a twice weekly passenger service. The journey to Sallins took nine hours and cost 1s 1d in the covered cabin and 6½d in the open portion of the boat. It was laid down that no person 'in liquor' was to be permitted to travel and those behaving 'in an indecent or disorderly manner' could be turned off the boat and forfeit their fare. When the canal was opened to Robertstown in 1784 the passenger service was extended and the company decided to build a hotel at Sallins to cater for the passengers. It was not long before 'houses' along the line began to sell liquor and the crews were sometimes fined for being intoxicated; playing cards with the passengers was also frowned upon. These misdemeanours were exceptions; on the whole it seems to have been accepted by the public as a well run service. A contemporary newspaper reported:

> Water excursions up the Grand Canal are now much in fashion. . . nor can this seem extraordinary, when we reflect on the beauty of the country thro' which the canal passes, the excellent accommodations to be had in the passage boats, and the capital inn at Sallins, fitted up with peculiar neatness and admirably well kept.

A few weeks earlier the same newspaper had recorded that the Marquis and Marchioness of Buckingham had 'made a water excursion up the Grand Canal. . . a coach accompanied the boat along the banks, which was to serve as a retreat in case the passage through the locks should prove disagreeable'.

The Barrow Line

The company decided that it would be more practical to complete a junction with the River Barrow before proceeding with the line to the Shannon, and work began on the Barrow Line in 1783. The first section of this canal passed through bog and it was here that one of the overseers, Bernard Mullins, gained valuable experience about the difficulties of making a canal in boggy terrain. He was later to become one of the partners in Henry Mullins and McMahon, the first major canal contractor in Ireland, and many years later he wrote an interesting paper about the construction of roads, railways and canals in bog in which he described these early works at Ballyteague bog. He explained that 'the water was forced into the canal before a sufficient sectional area was obtained; and it was by dredging at a great expense and loss of time, that an imperfect navigable depth of canal was subsequently had'. This stretch of canal caused so many problems that some fifteen

Athy in the early 1900s

years later it was by-passed by a new canal and the sites of two of the locks were altered.

The canal reached Monasterevin, the junction with the Barrow, in 1785 but the river from here to Athy was so full of shallows that the canal company decided to continue a still-water canal to Athy. As already mentioned in the section on the Boyne navigation, Richard Evans, a very able engineer, had gradually taken over from the aging Tarrant, but his services were soon in demand by other companies and the directors eventually sought an assurance from him that he would devote his full attention to the works on the Barrow Line. When he refused to do this he was dismissed, leaving his three assistants, William Rhodes, James Oates and Archibald Millar in charge. Rhodes and Oates were transferred to commence work on the Circular Line in Dublin in 1790 and it was Millar who completed the canal to Athy. He had worked his way up from the position of overseer and the detailed reports he furnished to the board betrayed his lack of social standing and education. One of his early reports concluded with the words: 'I am much in want of shoes and have no money'. He was very critical of one of the bridge contractors called Dobbins, adding 'an old mason should be frequently eyeing him'. In 1790 he reported that there were 3,944 men working on the line under the various contractors and it is interesting to note that it was not easy to find labourers at this time:

> In obedience to your Orders and agreeably to my appointment, I have been over the Works several times and have given general salutary facilitating instructions which I hope will soon have a good effect, along with proper Instructions the regular supply of Money will I expect in a short time put a new face on the Athy Canal – the thirteen pence per day subsistence mentioned to the Labourers on the Works has opened the Countenance of

every Workman on the Line – that will bring forward a great many more labourers to the Works.

Nearer Dublin wages were higher. A newspaper report in the same year spoke of men 'turning out' for increased wages on the Royal Canal: 'It was found necessary to accede to their proposition and they now receive seventeen pence per day'. The junction with the Barrow at Athy was achieved by 1791 and Millar received a gratuity of fifty guineas as a token of the board's 'approbation and esteem'. He was transferred to work on the Circular Line in Dublin which had begun in the previous year.

The Circular Line

Grand Canal: the fine range of offices at James Street Harbour in 1969

James's Street harbour, beside the city basin, was constructed as the terminus of the canal but there was still a steep drop down to the Liffey to be overcome. Originally, it was intended to lock down from the harbour but William Chapman came up with an alternative plan. He suggested a circular route meeting the Liffey further downstream which would enable boats to avoid the low city bridges on the Liffey and which would also be a suitable site for large docks. In addition, he suggested that his canal would provide a pleasant amenity for the citizens of Dublin. John Macartney and Richard Griffith, two influential directors, supported this more ambitious scheme but Joseph Huband, who owned land at James's Street and was probably hoping to sell it to the company for the canal, opposed it. Huband lost the battle and work began on the Circular Line in 1790. The canal, three and a half miles long with seven locks and extensive docks at Ringsend, was completed in 1796 and a spectacular ceremony was held to celebrate the link with the Liffey and the sea. The vice-regal yacht locked into the basin followed by about twenty barges and pleasure yachts, and 1,000 guests were entertained to breakfast in tents erected for the event. A newspaper report captures the spirit of the occasion:

> The gaiety of the scene enlivened by the number of boats and barges highly decorated and filled with beautiful women, the fury of the cannon, the music and the reiterated shouts of the approving populace – all these impressed the mind with a glow of pleasure and animation scarcely to be described; to these succeeded feelings of a higher order, in the contemplation of the perfection of the workmanship of every part of this noble undertaking, together with the prospect which it gives of the rising prosperity and future opulence of the Kingdom.

DeLatocnaye, the well known French traveller, witnessed the event; the Viceroy knighted John Macartney, chairman of the company, and was then 'rowed from one end of the dock to the other in an elegant barge, followed and preceded by the acclamations of the people. The enthusiasm of the immense crowd surrounding the basin made me fear that many would be crowded into the water, or what I should have liked still less, that I should be pushed in myself'.

The County of Kildare Canal Company

In 1789 the County of Kildare Canal Company had completed a canal from the main line of the Grand Canal near Sallins to Naas, two and a half miles long with five rising locks. It incurred such large debts building the canal that it was finally forced into liquidation and the Grand Canal Company bought the whole concern from the Court of Chancery for £2,250 in 1808. Repairs and improvements were carried out including, unfortunately, the demolition of three early 'skew' bridges designed by William Chapman, who had been the engineer in charge of building the canal. Constructing a typical hump-backed canal bridge to take roads up over the canal, realigning but not raising the approaches, was a straightforward business but Chapman had been instructed that he was not to alter in any way the line of the roads and this involved crossing the canal at an angle which presented problems in designing the courses of the stonework. The Romans had come to terms with the problem centuries earlier but Chapman was the first to build skew humpbacked bridges in these islands. There are two examples of this type of bridge today on both the Grand and Royal canals: Shee Bridge near Robertstown on the Grand Canal and the bridge taking the railway across Ringsend Basin, which was not built until some time later; and Ballasport Bridge, near Hill of Down, and Ballinea Bridge, west of Mullingar, on the Royal Canal. In addition to improving the Naas Canal, the Grand Canal Company extended this canal to Corbally, a further five and three quarter miles. David Henry, Bernard Mullins and John McMahon came together to tender for this work and won the contract, which we have seen was to be the start of a very successful business partnership.

The Shannon Line

In 1789, with work well advanced on the Barrow Line, the directors turned their attention to the completion of the link with the Shannon. We shall see that it was in this same year that the plans for a 'Royal' canal resurfaced and, when all hope of a compromise with this new company failed and the suggestion of sharing a common trunk canal from Dublin to the midlands was turned down, the Grand directors set about continuing their line as fast as possible, maintaining the head start over their rivals that they never lost.

Omer's drainage channels through the Bog of Allen were abandoned and Smeaton's suggested route along the northern edge of the bog adopted. Constructing a canal through bog was not a problem which the canal builders in England had encountred very often and opinion was very divided about how it should be tackled. William Chapman did not share Smeaton's opinion that it was unnecessary to drain the line of the canal first and he said so plainly to the board:

> The declining Surface of a Bog arises not from want of Cohesion but from the greater Desication of its Boundaries and from its small degree of Permeability to water with which the interior part is surcharged and swoln up like a Sponge, which of course occasions its convexity – the great Point therefore undoubtedly is, to have the Level of the Canal sufficiently below the Surface to allow for the Desication and consequent subsidence of the Bog, and what that Subsidence should be in all Cases, I conceive no difficult Matter to be ascertained which when done would be the Acquisition of one of the greatest Desiderata in the Science of Canals.

But Smeaton's views carried more weight. The canal was constructed at the same level as the existing surface of the bog without allowing for a period of drainage and the result was that the land on either side drained into the canal and subsided, leaving the canal confined by high embankments which were to be a constant source of trouble in the future. Jessop devised a method of working: cuts were made along the two outer edges of the proposed line of the canal, these were deepened by degrees leaving a central pyramidal core which prevented the bottom from swelling up until the canal was ready to receive water, then the core was removed. It was a long hard struggle. Captain William Evans was the engineer in charge, with a young surveyor as his assistant. He was John Killaly, who had joined the company in 1794 and, as we have seen, was to become one of Ireland most successful canal engineers.

They were still struggling to complete this five mile long stretch through the bog in the winter of 1795-6. Captain Evans sent in this depressing report:

> The Edenderry Bog has again got into a bad state since the rain, and that what we have done latterly has been of little use, as the Bog has sunk,

Grand Canal: the harbour at Tullamore in the 1890s with its fine range of warehouses which were subsequently demolished

cracked and given way as formerly, so much that I conceive it lost labour to persevere in wheeling Bog Stuff on the bad parts as when the Top weight is added, the bottom gives way.

It was at this point that Jessop advised that a wall of clay should be built some distance from the canal to prevent the tendancy of the embankments to be pressed outwards. This was to prove a very controversial step because it actually was to cause trouble rather than prevent it. Instead of sinking the wall of clay down to firm ground, it was built resting on the crust of the bog, which cracked with its weight causing the ground to split, which in turn made the embankments crack.

The canal was opened to Philipstown (Daingean) in 1797 but in August of that year a breach occurred where Jessop's wall of clay was under construction. Jessop continued to defend his theory and at one stage he described the canal and its banks as floating 'like a huge vessel upon an imperfect fluid below'. The breach was repaired and the canal opened in 1798 to Tullamore, where a harbour was built which was to become the terminus of the canal for the next three years while the directors argued what line to follow to the Shannon. Then, in January 1800, another major breach occurred at the same site and the wall of clay controversy flared up again. It took many months to repair and Killaly, who by that time was in charge of the works, had to strengthen the embankments. Eventually, Jessop did climb down and wrote to the board:

and therefore tho' I feel the strongest impression that a wall of Clay executed according to the true intention of it would be the most probable means of

obtaining security, I feel myself no longer inclined to advise it until any future symptom may make its security, in its present state doubtful.

The wall of clay was abandoned and the canal banks consolidated and remained intact for many years but the structural weakness of the embankments was to cause trouble again in the future.

The Shannon Link at Last

There were three options open to the directors for completing the canal from Tullamore to the Shannon: to lock down into the River Brosna and continue as a river navigation following Omer's original plan; to construct a canal alongside the Brosna and, the third and most elaborate option, to continue the canal on the same level to the south, with

Grand Canal: repairing a breach near Edenderry in 1916 at the old trouble spot. This gives some idea of the height of the embankment which resulted from insufficient drainage in the Bog of Allen and subsequent subsidence

the possibility of an extension to Birr, and then lock down steeply into the Shannon at Banagher. Eventually they decided on the second option, to continue the canal in the valley of the Brosna, which provided a natural route to the Shannon, joining it just north of Banagher at a place described as a 'wild and unfrequented situation' which was to become known as Shannon Harbour. Richard Griffith, one of the directors, who fancied himself as an amateur engineer, accepted responsibility for overseeing the work. This type of 'gentleman engineer' was fairly common at this time and it is interesting to note that he launched his son on a full time engineering career. His son, who was also Richard, had a considerable impact on civil engineering in Ireland and was subsequently knighted and became chairman of the new Board of Works. Richard Griffith senior was lucky in having the now experienced John Killaly as his engineer. Another stretch of bog had to be crossed but Killaly had learnt the hard way on the Bog of Allen and this time he carried out extensive drainage works over a number of years and allowed the land to subside before he attempted to excavate the canal. As they strove to complete the line, over 3,000 men were employed working under twenty-two contractors. There were problems of stoppages for higher wages. Griffith spoke of the 'unchecked spirit of combination among the artificers and workmen of every denomination'. Advertisements had appeared in Irish newspapers for men to cut canals in England. These offered wages of 6s per day, half to be paid at the time and half when the job was completed. This was double the wage being offered in Ireland, and many men set off for England to build navigations, becoming known as 'Irish navvies' and adding a new word to the English language.

With the final stages of the work in progress, in September 1803, Griffith suggested extravagant plans for the opening ceremony. Large numbers of distinguished guests would be brought from Dublin to Shannon Harbour in the fleet of passage boats which now numbered six. Four trade boats would be loaded up with symbolic cargoes in Dublin, Athy, Killaloe and on the north Shannon and would converge on Shannon Harbour at the appropriate time. A military band would play and the usual military salute would be arranged by the artillery. At the last moment the ceremony had to be postponed because there was insufficient water in parts of the canal. Griffith blamed the dry summer but, in fact, some of the levels were leaking badly and further work had to be carried out to staunch them. After a number of postponements, the directors quietly forgot about the grand opening ceremony and it was not until April 1804 that the first trade boat arrived in Shannon Harbour from Dublin, the crew being presented with a suit of clothes each to mark the occasion. Even after that Killaly had to drain and re-puddle the Ballycowan and Rahan levels twice more before the link with the Shannon was permanently secured. The company had succeeded at last but the price had been a heavy one and the debt now stood at over £1,000,000.

It is not easy to assess the exact cost of constructing the canal but

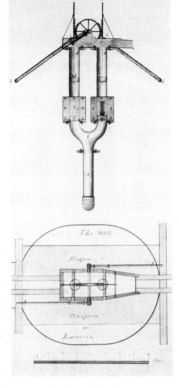

Grand Canal: a pump designed by Israel Rhodes, a Grand Canal Company engineer, to keep the foundations dry while building the aqueduct over the Silver River in 1802

it was something in the region of £877,000, of which about £77,000 had been expended before the Grand Canal Company took over. Unlike many other navigations only about one quarter of the total cost had come from public funds in grants or debentures. The rest was all raised by private subscription. Trade increased rapidly once the canal was opened to the Shannon, rising from about 100,000 tons in 1800 to double that amount by 1810. Revenue from the passage boats also increased rapidly, with a threefold increase to nearly £90,000. Although the company's income was improving, there was not enough to meet the cost of the maintenance and the crippling annual interest on the debt, which amounted to nearly £65,000 in 1810. Despite a shortfall in revenue, an average annual dividend of five per cent had been paid since 1793 to keep the subscribers happy; this dividend payment cost the company over £28,000 in 1810. More money had to be borrowed, therefore, every year and it became obvious that unless some action was taken the debt would continue to rise. In 1810 at the annual general meeting of the company a large group of the old brigade were deposed and a programme of retrenchments was introduced. Negotiations were opened with the Directors General to try to obtain some financial help, even if this meant that tolls would have to be reduced.

At this time the company was also involved in a bitter dispute with the Royal Canal Company about the route of that canal to the Shannon. Eventually, the government decided to carry out a thorough investigation of the affairs of both companies in order to settle the dispute and establish just how the companies stood financially. We shall see that as a result of this investigation the Royal Canal Company was dissolved. The Grand Canal Company, however, under its new board was now faring much better and in 1812, instead of the usual annual deficit, the company had managed to show a net profit of over £5,000. A government grant of £150,000 was authorised to help to liquidate the debt but certain conditions were imposed. The most important of these was the suspension of dividends unless there was a clear profit, and the company had to set aside a certain sum each year towards the liquidation of the debt. The suspension of dividends hit the shareholders badly and one of them, William Blair, was so affected that he applied for the position of lockkeeper on the Circular Line, a position he held until his death. The payment of dividends was not resumed until 1835 and thereafter it averaged about two per cent but never again matched those large dividends which had attracted the early shareholders.

The Passenger Service and the Hotels

Even before the link with the Shannon was established, the company had built up a considerable passenger service and now the fleet expanded to over twenty boats. Roads had greatly improved by this time and coaching establishments had become increasingly strong competitors. This forced the company to keep fares down and to enter

Grand Canal: a unique feature of the canal were the company hotels built in the early 1800s at (clockwise from top) Tullamore (demolished), Shannon Harbour (in ruins), Portobello

(refurbished), Sallins (demolished) and Robertstown (partly restored).

into contracts with coach operators to provide subsidised feeder services. In the early 1800s fares had steadily increasd but by 1816 they had been cut back to even less than the earlier rates. In that year to travel from Dublin to Shannon Harbour, a distance of seventy-eight miles, cost 13s in the state cabin and 8s 8d in the common cabin, and the fare to Athy, fifty-four miles, was 8s and 5s 4d. An average speed of about four miles per hour was maintained, so the journey to Shannon

Harbour took about eighteen hours and that to Athy thirteen hours. It was essential to travel as fast as possible to compete with rival coaches and this affected the company's hotels; passengers preferred to get to their destinations quickly rather than make an overnight stop.

The hotel at Sallins had proved too close to Dublin to be an economic success and by 1805 it was vacant 'with a quantity of fowl feeding in the best parlours'. Four more hotels were built at Robertstown, Tullamore, Shannon Harbour and Portobello in Dublin. None of them proved profitable and the company found it better to lease them to hotelkeepers, keeping the rents low enough to encourage them to stay in business. Some of the hotelkeepers supplemented their meagre incomes in various way. The Whyte family, who leased the hotel at Robertstown from 1815 until 1849, were also horse contractors providing a towing service for the company's passage boats. George Forrest in Tullamore operated a coach connection to and from Athlone. This hotel was later leased by Andrew Morgan from 1815 for over twenty years and it is described in the following glowing terms:

> To such as take the Boat this House claims a decided preference; as it precludes every disappointment; the Apartments are fitted up with neatness and elegance; Beds constantly aired, Good dinners and excellent wines, Carriages and Jaunting Cars and Careful Drivers at reduced prices.

Business, however, declined steadily and by 1830 he complained to the board that he had few customers, 'apart from a few breakfasts'. An example of a typical bill for three gentlemen at Robertstown was as follows:

Dinner for three	6s 6d	Punch	3s 4d
Ale	6d	Beds	3s 3d
Dinner, ale and bed for servant 10d			

Shannon Harbour hotel enjoyed some years of good business in the 1830s and early 1840s when the tide of emigration increased but soon it became a place where canal employees rented cheap rooms. Portobello was the most successful of all the hotels because as soon as it was opened in 1807 the company transferred the terminus of the passenger boats to here from James's Street harbour. A Dublin guide book in 1821 described it as 'fitted up with elegance for the accommodation of families and single gentlemen. The beauty and salubrity of the situation enlivened by the daily arrival and departure of the canal boats, render it a truly delightful residence'.

In all the years there was only one major accident on the canal, although there were a large number of individual drownings. In December 1792 the passage boat for Athy left Dublin with a full complement of people and capsized near the eighth lock with the loss of eleven lives. The *Freeman's Journal* tells the story in the journalise typical of that day:

> Yesterday morning, a melancholy consequence of the drunkenness usual at this season of the year occurred on the Grand Canal. Upwards of one

hundred and fifty people, many of them intoxicated, forced themselves in spite of repeated remonstrances from the Captain, in on the early Athy passage boat. He often, in vain, told them the boat was overloaded, and must sink if many of them did not withdraw; at length, from their numbers and turbulence the boat was overset, near the eighth lock, and five men, four women and two children perished – the rest of the passengers escaped. . . . We are happy to learn that the principal cabin passengers were timely alarmed by the conduct of the unfortunate rioters and drunken people, and all left the boat at the different locks, so that no person of any note, save the Captain, has suffered.

Many accounts of travellers are to be found. John Wesley spoke of fifty or sixty on board, 'many of whom desired me to give them a sermon, I did so, and they were all attention'. Mrs William Leadbeater made frequent references to canal travel in her diaries, which are in the Friends Library in Dublin, and Charles Lever and Anthony Trollope both drew with poetic licence from their practical experience in their novels. Lever described his hero being 'dragged along some three miles and a half per hour, ignominiously at the tails of two ambling hackneys' while Trollope described the 'eternal half-boiled leg of mutton floating in a bloody sea of grease and gravy'. *Duffy's Magazine* of 1862 recalled canal boat travel with a very detailed description of the boats and told how the captain killed two chickens for dinner which were 'plunged still bleeding into the pot containing a leg of mutton' while a second pot contained bacon and cabbage. The minute books of the company contain a great number of references to the passenger service including instances of trouble from attacks of marauding bands in the 1820s, when armed guards had to be carried on board.

With coaching competition increasing in the 1820s, the directors were constantly seeking ways to speed up the service. From the early 1800s efforts had been made to perfect a steam driven boat and the directors observed with interest the performance of the paddlewheeler *City of Cork* which went into service in 1815 between Cork and Cobh. Using steam to propel boats in the narrow confines of a canal proved more difficult because of the size and weight of the engines. A number of 'inventors' had approached the board with novel ideas. In 1807 Thomas Tunks of Hardwicke Street said he had perfected 'a Machine by means of which two men may drive without horses, tacklines or any other assistance from the land Passage Boats at an equal speed at least as that in which they are at present drawn by horses'. He was allowed two trial attempts to demonstrate his invention but he was refused permission to have a third trial and was asked to remove his 'machinery' from the company's boat. Two years later John Maguire sought permission to try out his invention called 'The Nautilus' in which he said 'there are no complex movements, no wheels, no springs, its great power resting on the simplest of all the mechanical principles of force, namely that of the lever, and may be increased to any degree of power, from that of a rowboat to a ship of the line. . .'. The board eventually grew tired of these inventors and resolved it would wait until an invention turned up which was 'reducible to practice. . . and the experience of others shall have proved the usefulness and practicability'. In the end it was not through any form of steam propulsion that the directors were to achieve what they were looking for but through a simple discovery in hydrostatics made, across the water, by an engineer, John Scott Russell.

New Branches

In 1817 the canal company decided to avail of the new loan scheme to enlarge the canal system. The Ballinasloe trade had always been profitable and the company had suggested to the Directors General as early as 1802 that the River Suck should be made navigable while they had men and machinery nearby working on the restoration of the middle Shannon. The river itself presented few problems but it would have been expensive to construct towpaths up the Shannon from Shannon Habour to the junction with the Suck and up along the river to Ballinasloe. It was this expense which prompted the Directors General to turn down the scheme. For this reason the company now decided to construct a canal to Ballinasloe from the point where the Grand Canal joined the Shannon, instead of using the River Suck. If the board had known that steamers were to arrive on the Shannon within the next few years, making towpaths unnecessary, then the river scheme would have been a much better option. As it was, by the time the canal was completed, the steamers had arrived.

In 1822 the loan for the Ballinasloe Canal was approved and it was agreed that repayments would be made from the profits of the new

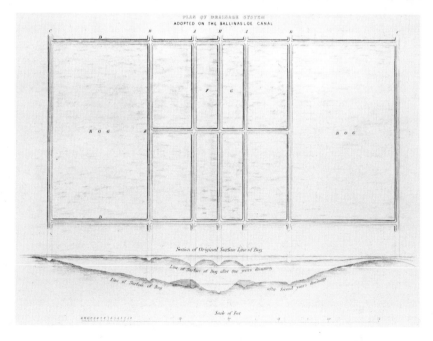

Ballinasloe Canal: Bernard Mullin's drawing which illustrates how the bog was drained in preparation for the canal and to avoid the problems that had been encountered in the Bog of Allen

extension. Three contractors put in tenders: Messrs Henry Mullins and McMahon, Messrs Bergin McKenna and Wood and Messrs Hayes and Kelly, who had just completed the Lough Allen Canal. Bergin McKenna and Woods won the contract but fell out with the company on the question of the levels of the canal and eventually Henry Mullins and McMahon stepped in. The whole question of the allocation of this contract and a subsequent one to construct the Longford Line of the Royal Canal became the subject of a scurrilous anonymous letter which was circulated some years later. The letter attacked John Killaly and suggested that the contracts were awarded because Killaly was the father-in-law of John McMahon. It seems certain that it was Hayes or Kelly who were behind this attack and Henry Mullins and McMahon suggested 'treating the Miscreant Author and his vile hireling Scribe with silent scorn and contempt'. The Grand Canal Company defended the reputation of their engineer: 'In all of which Mr Killaly assiduously co-operated, and the Directors continue of the opinion that the superintendance of these important National Works could not have been confided to an abler or more impartial engineer', a testimony borne out by his many engineering successes.

The Ballinasloe Line proved very difficult to construct because not only was the terrain through bog but there were also problems caused by large numbers of men beseiging the works in search of employment. The canal was eventually opened to traffic in 1829 but it continued to be beset by problems of breaches, sometimes accidental and some-times malicious. Some idea of the extremely difficult conditions of working in this area are revealed in reports from the engineer, John Stokes. On one occasion he wrote:

> The state of the Country here I fear is alarming, the People are decidedly the Governing party – their Law is enforced by a threat of Blood, and no one is willing to contend with them. . . the nearer we approach to a finish, the greater the delay to every movement. . . Mr Seery and your humble servant in a great measure shut up in this abominable and dangerous quarter, that I am really at a loss what to do.

John Stokes had joined the company in 1804 as a supervisor of works and quickly rose to the rank of engineer. He served the company faith-fully in this capacity for over thirty years until his death in 1843 without ever receiving an increase in his salary of £300 per annum, on which he had to rear eleven children. His reports, meticulously transcribed into the company minutes, make fascinating reading whether he is writing from a breach repair, picking his way through snow drifts to look for missing boats or, as on one occasion, writing from his sickbed where he was confined with severe stomach cramps 'occasioned I believe by wet feet'.

Breaches on the Ballinasloe Line continued and greatly hindered trade on this canal. In the end the company refused to employ local labour and enlisted the help of the military to protect the imported workers. Work was at such a premium that Stokes said he was able to reduce the daily wage from 1*s* to 10*d*, 'which has been at once acceded to without complaint'.

A wooden bridge had been constructed to convey the towing horses across the Shannon with an opening span on the east side. Horses had to pull the boats across this exposed river crossing and in bad weather the passengers sometimes opted to make the crossing on foot instead of remaining in the boat. Richard Clooney, one of the passage boat masters, described one crossing on a December evening and recommended using four horses and a stronger trackline. He added: 'When about midway, the waves being heavier than at any other part, she began to heave so much, that the gabouse *(sic)* would, but for the activity of the steerer, have been shifted from its berth'.

In 1824 with the Ballinasloe Line well in hand, the directors sought another loan for an extension from Monasterevin on the Barrow Line to Mountmellick. Once again Henry Mullins and McMahon won the contract and Killaly's son Hamilton was the engineer in charge. This canal, together with an aqueduct over the River Barrow at Monasterevin, was completed and opened to traffic by 1831. The new aqueduct overcame the tedious procedure of locking down into the river and up again on the far side.

The company was also granted a loan for a branch to Kilbeggan. The contractor this time was William Dargan, whose name was to become very familiar as a railway contractor. Although this was just a short eight-mile long canal with no locks, it caused Dargan far more trouble than he had anticipated and it was to be nearly six long years

Grand Canal: the ferry which replaced the wooden bridge in the 1840s for conveying the horses across the Shannon to the Ballinasloe Line

before the company agreed that he had completed his contract. It quickly became obvious that the tolls from the three new branches would never be sufficient to pay back the loans and, eventually, the government agreed to a complicated deal with the canal company commuting the outstanding debt of nearly £100,000 to £10,000 as a sort of quid pro quo for the transfer of jurisdiction over the middle Shannon to commissioners in the 1840s.

Conclusion

The canal had had a significant effect on a number of the towns and communities along its line, with some becoming market and distribution centres for a large hinterland. In the early 1780s Tullamore had been described as 'a very mean village with scarce any better houses than thatched cabins'. Then in 1785 about 100 houses were destroyed in a bad fire when an air balloon caught fire in what is thought to be only the third attempt to make a balloon ascent in Ireland. The fire gave the landlord, C. W. Bury, the impetus to rebuild his town in an improved manner, and the arrival of the canal in 1798 greatly accelerated the growth of the place. A report in the *Freeman's Journal* in 1808 remarked:

> Those who have seen the little village of Tullamore a few years ago, which has now the appearance of a respectable city, can best form an idea of what increase of trade and population may be here in the course of a few years owing to its local situation and circumstances.

By the 1830s it was an important market town and local industries had developed, including a distillery, brewery and brick manufactory. Curiously, Tullamore's development was at the expense of nearby Philipstown (Daingean) which lost its position as assize town to Tullamore in 1833.

Rathangan and Monasterevin on the Barrow Line were examples of towns which benefited from water transport; Monasterevin had a brewery, distillery, malthouse and tobacco manufactory. Towns on the branches all increased in importance as market centres: Ballinasloe, Mountmellick, Portarlington, Edenderry, Naas and Kilbeggan. The canal also created a number a new communities at places like Robertstown, Rahan and Shannon Harbour. On the whole, however, the canal had failed to live up to its promise to bring the industrial revolution to the midlands. Arthur Young, who had not shared the early optimism, was closer to the mark in the 1770s when he spoke caustically of 'ideal navigations through bogs to convey turf to Whitehaven'.

The canal had created a good deal of employment both for company employees and in ancilliary services for those who were lucky enough to be employed, but the standard of living for those who chose to live along its banks was often pathetically low. One traveller, F. S. Bourke, described the scene as he moved along the canal in 1836:

Their habitations are most wretched hovels, constructed of wet sods taken
from the surface of the bog and laid without regard to symmetry or arrangement loosely upon each other. The thatch is generally composed of rushes
or the stalks of the potato sometimes made fast to the roof by a straw rope,
fantastically crossed, but more frequently left, like Nora Creina's tresses,
'free as mountain breezes'. In choosing the sites of these dwellings, a dry
floor or any provision for snug lying seems not to have entered into the
calculations of the architect. The shelter of a turf bank appears in many
instances to have exercised greater attraction than the most tempting
acclivity.

Although the company had managed to put its house in order and
to reduce its enormous debt with government help, the 1820s were
not easy years. The end of hostilities with France had plunged the
country into economic depression, the tonnage carried dropped
sharply and net profits tumbled. The troubled state of the country
caused great problems, the trade boats had to move in convoys to
protect them from marauding gangs and it proved very difficult to
protect the canal works from malicious breaches. John Forrest, the
collector at Lowtown, reported in 1822 that he had been visited by a
large gang of armed men looking for firearms who warned him 'of
the Prophecy which would soon be fulfilled of all the Protestants being
swept away, and that the time is now very near when it would be so'.
There was a high proportion of Protestants employed by the company
in those days as lockkeepers and this much sought after position was
handed down from father to son, the free house and garden being a
valuable supplement to the meagre wage of about 9s per week.

The company had by this time expanded into a large concern. There
were the passage boat crews, the masters, steerers, stopmen (so named
because they operated the rope used to stop the boats as they entered
the locks) and boys. The masters received as little as one guinea per
week in wages but they were allowed to supplement this with the
profits on the food and drink served abroad; this service was operated
by the wife of the master and it was their responsibility to pay the
serving girls. The steerers were paid 15s per week, the stopmen 10s
and the boys did not receive any wages. Some of the masters seemed
to incur the board's displeasure for 'irregularities' more often than
others. Captain Weekes so angered the directors that he was twice
demoted but on each occasion they relented and reinstated him. After
many years service he was appointed to be the first hotelkeeper at
Portobello but he died before he could take up the appointment.
Richard Clooney made himself so unpopular with the passengers on
the Mountmellick boat that he had to be transferred to the Ballinasloe
boat. He was subsequently dismissed for gambling with passengers,
drunkenness and other breaches of the rules but he too was reinstated.
Sometimes fines were imposed on them, for example they were fined
for allowing the crew to throw rubbish overboard in Portobello harbour which at one time it was reported 'amounted to a heap above
the bottom of the canal about four feet high'; the citizens of Dublin
had to drink the water from the canal untreated up to the middle of

the nineteenth century. With the tide of emigration on the increase there were times when the master's job was not an easy one. Richard Clooney described how his boat was besieged by a large mob in Shannon Harbour in 1834. He managed to reach Belmont but the mob had followed him on foot:

> notwithstanding that the Soldiers and Police had their Bayonets to the Country People, they found their way thro' the ones formed and literally dashed their luggage down on the Boat when little better than half raised in the Lock and leaped on board in numbers after it, they then forced the Boat out of the Lock. . . .

Eventually the Riot Act was read, the soldiers were ordered to open fire and he managed to remove the non-travelling people and proceed on his way under military protection. There was also an inspector of passage boats, a position at one time held by James Butler, Lord Dunboyne, who received one and a half per cent of the revenue from fares.

In addition to the fifty-six lockkeepers there were fourteen collectors handling the company's business at stations along the line, about fifteen staff at James's Street harbour in Dublin and an engineer, overseers and men employed on maintenance work. The company also employed a staff of about fifty at its colliery near Castlecomer together with colliers who worked on a casual basis. The board had decided to become involved in the coal business in the early 1800s in an attempt to encourage the coal trade on the canal and a coalyard was built at Lowtown as a distribution centre. The colliery proved a costly and disappointing venture and took up a great deal of the board's time. Eventually, in 1831, the directors decided to cut their losses and managed to surrender the lease by sacrificing the coal on bank, the machinery and rents.

Apart from the company employees a large canal community had become established. There were the men who operated and manned the trade boats, the horse contractors and their drivers. It must have been a hard life but it had its lighter moments. On one occasion it was reported that boats were delayed at the twenty-sixth lock because stones were thrown into the chamber jamming the gates:

> One of the crew, a man named Keogh, has a brother in Tullamore, who keeps, I understand, a very irregular public house, it is the haunt of almost all Boatmen, and he himself is the terror of the entire Canal. . . the crews of all, I was informed yesterday, met at said house, and were dancing the entire of the night.

Then there were the staff who ran the hotels and the coach operators and carters who ran feeder services. The company's business extended over a wide hinterland. By the end of the 1820s trade had begun to pick up and the company even managed to pay a small dividend from clear profits in 1836. If it had not been for its crippling debt the company would have had a thriving business and it was without doubt the best equipped of all the navigation companies to face the impending threat from the railways.

5
The Royal Canal

THE story begins in 1755 when the Grand and the Royal lines were under scrutiny by the Commissioners of Inland Navigation and were the subject of much public controversy. The Grand line eventually won the day but the Royal surveys were to resurface again some thirty years later in a manner which has fascinated canal historians ever since.

It is said that one of the directors of the Grand Canal Company took umbrage, feeling himself to have been insulted by his fellow directors, and walked out of a board meeting vowing that he would build a rival canal. Samuel Smiles in his *Lives of the Engineers*, published in 1874, tells this story but does not mention the man by name, referring to him instead as 'a retired shoemaker'. All the evidence points to John Binns as the principal promoter of the Royal Canal Company but he remained a director of the Grand Canal Company for several months after the incorporation of the Royal Canal Company, attending board meetings when the matter of the new company was being discussed – nor does he appear to have had any connection with shoemaking. There was another Grand Canal Company director called William Cope who was a director for only one year, attending nine meetings, and he was a director of the Royal company from its beginnings until 1802. There is evidence of Copes in the shoemaking trade, and William Cope himself was in partnership with John Binns in a wholesale silk merchant's business in Dame Street. He would seem to be the more likely candidate as the insulted shoemaker, although it was undoubtedly his stronger friend Binns who engineered the setting up of the new company.

A letter read by John Macartney in the Irish House of Commons some years later from the engineer John Brownrigg stated that he, Brownrigg, had been asked by Binns for his opinion about the Royal surveys, which were 'ideas from some old materials that fell into his hands that had been used about forty years ago in Parliament'. Brownrigg added that he had acted under Mr Binn's authority alone and that the latter had dismissed all difficulties saying that 'things that were lions in other men's way were but little dogs in his'. These early surveys, as already shown, were for a route using rivers and lakes to join the Shannon at Lough Ree. It is not quite clear how much surveying Brownrigg actually carried out. However, when the company was incorporated it was authorised to construct a canal from the Liffey to the

Shannon at Tarmonbarry, north of Lough Ree, which bore no resemblance to the original Royal line. The fact that parliament agreed to the new canal at all seems very strange when by this time in 1789 the Undertakers had been deposed and the navigation board wound up. John Binn's grand nephew, an American journalist of the same name, said that his grand uncle and his friend Napper Tandy 'were influential, indeed leading members, in opposition to those who were supporters of every measure proposed by those who, from their obedience to every behest of the English government, were called "Castle Hacks"'. This makes it even more surprising that he was able to summon enough support for the bill of incorporation. It is possible that they were just lucky that their efforts coincided with the introduction of the debenture scheme to encourage public works, and in accordance with the terms of that scheme the new company was granted £66,000 in four per cent debentures to match the £134,000 promised by subscribers.

At this stage the Grand Canal board, accepting that the Royal Canal Company was a reality, made the very reasonable suggestion that the new canal should commence in the midlands at Kinnegad, about ten miles north of Edenderry, and serve the north Shannon, sharing a common trunk canal from Dublin. This would have saved much time and expense in cutting a parallel canal from Dublin and have enabled the two companies to work in co-operation rather than in opposition. It should be remembered that at this time the Grand Canal Company was well advanced with its work on the Barrow line and had just turned its attention to starting the Shannon line; an extension up to Kinnegad could have easily been incorporated into the plans. The Royal directors turned down the offer as 'inexpedient' and it is of interest to note that John Binns was at the Grand board meeting when this reply was read. The minutes of that meeting give no indication of the tension that must have existed, but Richard Griffith, the Grand director and a member of the Irish parliament, subsequently referred to Binns as a 'jobbing demagogue' in a speech to the house in 1790, saying that he had endeavoured 'by all means in his power (and he is a man of resource) to prevent the subscribers of the Royal Canal from coming to a clear understanding with the Grand Canal Company'. In any event the gauntlet had now been thrown down and for many years there was absolutely no contact between the companies.

Work began in 1790 and in the same year the company asked parliament to sanction a deviation in the line of the canal. It is possible that it was only at this stage that proper surveys were actually carried out. The deviation was allowed but it was stipulated that the new canal must not approach the Grand Canal closer than four miles after reaching a point fourteen miles from Dublin. Two years later it was reported that eighteen miles of canal had been completed and a second issue of debentures amounting to £23,000 was authorised to enable docks to be built where the canal entered the Liffey; parliament was told that 'from thence to Mullingar the line will be completed in less

Royal Canal: the 6th lock in Dublin about 1890

time and with less expense and trouble, the country being flat and few locks will be required', an indication of the sketchy nature of the survey work at that stage. In the following year, 1793, the company itself instituted an inquiry into why progress was so slow and the expenditure to date so high.

This inquiry turned into a personal battle between John Brownrigg and the engineer in charge of the works, Richard Evans. Brownrigg was very critical of the line and claimed he had only had a very cursory part in the preparation of the original line and estimates. The investigating committee recommended that Evans should be dismissed but this was not done. There was more mud slinging in the next year between the two men when they were giving evidence before a parliamentary committee set up to investigate why the debentures allocated for the building of the docks had not been used for this purpose. The committee heard evidence of contractors being dismissed, levels proving faulty, two bridges collapsing killing six men and the location of one of the locks, a triple chambered lock at Ashtown, being sited 'to the fancy of the mason'; this lock was subsequently altered to a double chambered lock and an additional lock inserted. English experts, William Jessop and Thomas Hyde Page, were consulted but seemed reluctant to become involved, and Evans continued as engineer.

In 1796 Evans presented a progress report to parliament in support of a petition for more financial aid. The cutting through Carpenterstown quarries, Clonsilla, had proved difficult and expensive, costing £4,968, much of it for gunpowder. The Ryewater embankment had been equally difficult and costly; the final figure for it was £28,231, not the £7,500 originally estimated by the contractor. Several writers of the time suggested that neither of these difficulties need have been encountered if a more sensible route to the north had been adopted, but that a deviation to the south had been made to bring the canal through Maynooth to please a wealthy subscriber, the Duke of Leinster. However, Evans did report that the canal was now virtually ready from Broadstone in Dublin to Kilcock, and parliament reluctantly agreed to a further advance of £25,000 because it was felt that this was the only way to protect the interests of the many small shareholders. A warning was issued that no further advances would be made until the canal was completed to Thomastown, near Mullingar.

By 1801 the company had managed to avail of only about half of the last issue of debentures because it had not been possible to raise the required two thirds contribution from new subscribers. The link with the Liffey had been completed but without the docks and the harbour at the Broadstone was still unfinished. To the west, the canal was still ten miles short of Thomastown and had reached the place where it crossed the River Blackwater. The Directors General were now the board responsible for navigation grants and they sent their engineer – who, ironically, was John Brownrigg – to prepare a full report of the works. He could not resist criticising the line of the canal:

> Whether the Canal from the Broadstone up to Kilcock and thro' the Bog of Cappa was in the first instance fairly and impartially laid out for the public benefit or the advantage of the Canal Company, or whether the money was well expended is no part of my present enquiry. It being now reported a navigable Canal I shall notice its present Condition and the probability of its becoming a useful and effectual mode of conveyance of persons and properties for the public accommodation.

Of the line proposed from the Blackwater he remarked it was 'as bad and as expensive as can be imagined'. He referred to the 'great difficulty, the disappointments, the accidents, the losses and vast expense attending the Cut through the Bog of Cappa [which] has frightened so many of the Directors of the Royal Canal that they are willing to engage in any danger, delay or cost in hard Ground rather than face a bog again'. The line chosen by the company went through Kinnegad, bringing it back to within eight miles of the Grand Canal at Edenderry, and Brownrigg put forward a plan for a straighter line to Thomastown. In that same year William Cope was declared a bankrupt and his £150 shares were sold for £70. John Binns retired from the board in the following year a broken man and died two years later.

The Directors General agreed to make a grant of £95,866 to the company so that work could recommence. This was the estimated cost of completing the canal, using Brownrigg's route, to the end of the summit level west of Mullingar, building the docks at the Liffey and completing the harbour and aqueduct at the Broadstone in Dublin. In return, as usual, the company had to agree to charge a low rate of toll on the completed canal and undertake to finish the work by 1812. Richard Evans had died and the company called in the English engineer, John Rennie, as a consultant. He said that the estimates were nearly £30,000 below the figure he would have put on the work. The Directors General chose to ignore this information, saying 'whether they employ one gentleman or another to be their engineer, or whether their calculations be correct or not, are indeed matters of considerable importance to the company, but have no relation to their contract with this Board'.

Thomastown was reached in 1805 and ahead lay a rise through eight locks, bringing the canal up to the summit level, then a 'laborious, hazardous and slow work through quarry near Mullingar, the expence being extraordinarily heavy'. Mullingar was reached in 1806, according to the *Freeman's Journal*, and the passenger boat, the *Countess of Granard* made the trip 'with a number of passengers of distinction. . . . It being a novel sight a number of spectators assembled and the band of the Sligo Militia ushered it in with appropriate music'. The number of boats trading on the canal increased and the passenger boat fleet was expanded but business was only about one third of that on the Grand Canal, which was now open to the Shannon.

By 1809 the canal had been completed to Coolnahay at the western end of the summit, three years ahead of its scheduled completion date with the Directors General. The tonnage carried on the canal in 1810

Royal Canal: the rules governing the lock-keepers and boatmen in 1813

ROYAL CANAL.

RULES
To be observed by LOCK-KEEPERS.

If a Lock-Keeper be absent from his Lock without Leave, he shall be liable to a Fine of Two Shillings and Six Pence.

If a Lock-Keeper has not his Upper-Chamber full, and his Gates open to receive the Packet-Boat the Moment she arrives on her Passage to Dublin, he shall be liable to a Fine of Two Shillings and Six Pence.

If a Lock-Keeper leaves the Chamber of his Lock full of Water for Half an Hour, except he gets Leave so to do, from the Inspector, on account of a Scarcity of Water, in order to let one Boat down upon the Water of another, he shall be liable to be fined Two Shillings and Six Pence; but if he leaves it full all Night, or by Neglect or Laziness he suffers it to remain full for two or three Hours by Night or Day; or that by any Chance he lets or leaves a Sluice playing, by which his upper Level lower than it ought to be, or leaves it running all Night, he shall be fined Five Shillings: but if, by any such Neglect and bad Conduct, he Level be found to be so low as to prevent the Packet and Trade Boats from plying, he shall be fined a Month's Pay, or dismissed, with Orders never to be employed upon the Line again, upon any Account whatsoever.

If a Lock-Keeper permits a Boat through his Lock, without said Boat having a regular Pass, the Lock-keeper shall, for such Offence, be dismissed from his Situation, and rendered incapable of ever again serving upon the Line, as a Lock-Keeper.

If a Lock-Keeper refuses or neglects to attend any Trade or Lumber Boat, whenever she comes to his Lock, having a proper Pass, he shall, upon a proper Complaint of such Conduct, be fined according to the Nature of such Neglect or Time delayed.

If a Lock-Keeper suffers a Trade or Lumber Boat to pass through his Lock by Night, without an Order from the proper Officer, he shall be fined Five Shillings.

Every Lock-Keeper is to inspect the Marks of each Boat, and ascertain that the Draught of Water corresponds with that marked in the Pass of the Boat; and should there be any difference, he is to report to the Inspector what that difference may be, with the Number of the Boat, and the Master's or Owner's Name; in Neglect of so doing, he shall be liable to a Fine of Two Shillings and Six Pence.

If a Lock-Keeper be detected in letting his Racks fall, without winding them down, by which Means the Sluice Rods, Paddles or Loggerheads, may be materially injured, he shall be fined Five Shillings.

If by any Accident the Foot-Boards, Gates, Machinery or Locks, should be damaged by Packet Boats or others, the Lock-Keeper must immediately report to the Inspector, by what Boat such Injuries have been done, so as that Reparation may be instantly made, at the Expense of the Masters or Owners of said Boats.

Every Lock-Keeper shall send to the Secretary, an Account of the State of the Water on his Upper and Lower Cills, at least Once a Week, in Times of Scarcity of Water, and if by Neglect or Accident, his Level be reduced, his Account must be immediate, and the Cause fully stated therein.

Any Lock-Keeper leaving his Key neglected, so as that it can be come at or made use of by any Boatman or others, to the Waste of Water or Injury of the Works, shall be fined Half a Crown.

If any Boat shall be sunk in any Part of the Canal, the Lock-Keeper in whose Level it has occurred, shall immediately report to the Officers nearest to him at the time, in order that such Boat may be raised without delay.

The Lock-Keepers are to report to the Inspector of the Line, any Neglect or Disobedience of the Boatmen, to the Rules published for their conduct, while Trading on the Line.

By Order of the Directors General of Inland Navigation,

SAMUEL DRAPER,
SECRETARY IN THE ROYAL CANAL.

ROYAL CANAL HOUSE, BROAD STONE,
October 7, 1813.

RULES
To be observed by BOATMEN trading on the Line.

No Trade or Lumber Boat whatsoever, shall attempt to go through any Lock, without a regular Pass, under a Penalty of £2.

The Passes of all Trade and Lumber Boats are to be carried by the Drivers, for the convenience of their being examined by the Inspectors and Lock-Keepers, under a Penalty of Five Shillings; and no Lock-Keeper is to permit any Boat to enter the Chamber of his Lock, until he shall first have seen such pass.

Any Lumber Boat or Trade Boat stopping, damaging, or delaying the Packet Boat or Trade Boats, shall be detained in the Harbour, if laden with Goods or otherwise, and not suffered through a Lock, until the Amount of all such Damage shall be paid; and also fined, from Five Shillings to a Guinea, according to the nature of the Offence.

Any Trade or Lumber Boat that shall be found in the Quarries, except well moored and close in a Lie-by, at the Hours and Times that the Packet Boats are expected, shall, upon such Offence being reported, be detained until such Trade or Lumber Boat pay a Fine of Five Shillings.

Any Trade or Lumber Boat attempting to pass through a Lock, must not be allowed to do so, except the Lock-Keeper sees that she has a good Stop Rope on Board, as well as a Track Line free from Knots.

No Trade or Lumber Boat shall be allowed to go through a Lock, unless provided with two good Iron Pins, and Rings fastened to them, with short strong Ropes or Iron Chains, to moor her with, wherever said Boat shall have occasion to stop.

If Stones be found fastened to Ropes, for the purpose of mooring Boats with, the Boatmen to be fined Half a Crown.

Any Trade or Lumber Boat doing Damage to Locks, Banks, or any other Parts of the Canal whatsoever, shall be detained until the Amount of all such Damage, or Repairs, occasioned thereby, shall be paid for.

If any Boatman behave in a disorderly or disobedient manner to Officers or Lock-Keepers, the Boat to which such Man belongs, shall be prohibited from plying on the Canal, until ample Recompence for such Offence shall be made, by Fines or otherwise.

Any Boat suffered to drift on the Canal, or suffered to remain on the West Side, between the Broad Stone Harbour and the Fifth Lock, at the Times of the Packet Boats either coming in or going out of said Harbour, shall be liable to a Fine of Five Shillings.

If any Boatman shall attempt to go through a Lock in the Night, except upon some extraordinary occasion, and in that case, the Inspector must sign his consent, he shall be fined Five Shillings.

No Boatman to attempt deceiving the Lock-Keepers or Collector, by false Passes or false Marks, under the Penalty of Forty Shillings on the first Detection, and on the second, of being excluded from ever working a Boat again upon the Canal; nor shall any Boatman make alterations in the Boat's empty Marks, by Weights which can be taken in or out occasionally, under the Penalties aforesaid.

If any Trade or Lumber Boat be suffered to lie loaded in the Quarries, One Hour by Day, except lying by for the Packets, without emptying or moving, the Boat shall be fined One Shilling for every Hour so neglected; but if suffered to lie loaded by Night, in any part of said Quarries, between Blanchardstown Road and the Harbour at Clonsilla, the Boat shall be liable to a Fine of One Guinea.

Any Boat sunk in the Canal, (except in the fourth Level, and there only with the approbation of the Dock-Master,) to pay a Fine of Forty Shillings; and if not raised immediately by her Owner, she is to be weighed by the Inspectors or other Officers, and to be detained until all Expenses incurred therein, as well as the Amount of any Damage done to other Boats, or the Expences of Passengers, occasioned thereby, shall be discharged.

All Irregularities, Neglects, or Disobedience of the above Rules, by the Boatmen, are to be reported to the Inspectors of the Line, by the several Lock-Keepers.

By Order of the Directors General of Inland Navigation,

SAMUEL DRAPER,
SECRETARY TO THE ROYAL CANAL.

ROYAL CANAL HOUSE, BROAD STONE,
October 7, 1813.

PRINTED BY J. AND J. CARRICK, BACHELOR'S-WALK, DUBLIN.

was 52,643 tons; grain, potatoes, turf, dung, coal, building materials and general merchandise made up most of the cargoes. The company's debt now amounted to £862,000; it had never been able to declare a dividend and by the time the interest on the debt and the cost of the establishment were deducted, there was insufficient income to undertake any further construction work. Even if the money to continue the canal could have been raised, the company was locked in a bitter confrontation with the Grand Canal Company about the line of the canal to the Shannon. This company had reacted sharply to the suggestion that the Royal Canal Company should be allowed to alter its authorised route and lock down into the River Inny, entering the Shannon in Lough Ree instead of further north at Tarmonbarry which would pose a threat to the Athlone trade. It was at this stage that the government decided to carry out detailed investigation into the affairs of both companies. The Royal Canal Company did make one last despairing effort to reorganise its affairs but finally, in 1813, a parliamentary committee recommended that it should forfeit its charter and that the concern should be handed over to the Directors General for completion at the public expense. It was the government's intention to try to alleviate as much as possible the hardship caused by the winding up of the company to the many small shareholders, loanholders and creditors by allocating shares in a new company when the canal was completed; this was eventually done, allowing £40 shares for every £100 formerly held stock or loan.

The Directors General Take Over

The navigation board was instructed to complete the canal according to the authorised plan, and John Killaly surveyed the line. Henry Mullins and McMahon contracted to build the entire extension for £145,000. It was a very big undertaking for a single contractor; it was only five years earlier that these three men had come together to build the Corbally extension of the Naas Canal. In addition to the engineering problems, they had to cope with the very unsettled state of the country. They reported instances of workers being 'carded' and receiving 'thrashing notices', that is, receiving warnings from marauding bands that they had incurred their displeasure and would be attacked. On one occasion they reported that 'forty men armed with guns, swords and pistols had carded eight men more in a shocking manner and that the workmen were afraid to continue in their employment'. In the end an entire regiment of men was needed to protect the workers along the line. It was a big operation. £10,000 was spent in laying down 'oak, pitch, pine and other timber, horse waggons, drays, machinery etc.', and lime kilns, stone cutters' sheds and forges were built along the twenty-five mile length of the canal. Despite all the problems, the contract was completed on time on 26 May 1817 with only minor adjustments in the contract price. Twenty-one locks, thirty-eight bridges, one large aqueduct and several harbours and quays were constructed. The cost worked out at about £8,000 per mile, which compared very favourably with the £20,000 per mile which the first part of the canal had cost and it was just a little higher than the £6,000 per mile which was the average cost of the Grand Canal system.

The New Royal Canal Company

With the canal completed and all its debts wiped out, the shareholders of the New Royal Canal Company looked forward to some return on their investments at last. The government took the precaution of appointing a Board of Control to monitor the company's financial affairs and decisions such as the declaration of the half yearly dividend had to be sanctioned by it. Sharp differences of opinion arose as to the extent of the jurisdiction of this board and the directors greatly resented its interference. The company found it hard to match the performance of the well established Grand Canal Company in the 1820s. The tonnage carried built up slowly but the completion of the western end of the canal did not produce the expected boost. Even when the Lough Allen Canal was opened in 1820 the anticipated coal trade did not materialise. To a certain extent this was due to the defective state of the north Shannon; in 1825 a boat leaving Lough Allen with twenty-five tons had to lighten her load in twelve places and

Royal Canal: an attempt by the government to apprehend the people who were breaching the canals in the 1820s

By the Lord Lieutenant and Council of *Ireland*,

A PROCLAMATION.

RICHMOND, &c.

WHEREAS We have received Information upon Oath that several evil-minded Perfons, at prefent unknown, did at different Periods lately, wilfully, and maliciouſly cut through the Banks of the Grand and Royal Canals at ſeveral Places, whereby the Water has been let off from the ſaid Canals, and that other wanton and malicious Acts of Mifchief and Damage have been done to the Works on the Line of the Grand Canal, by which Acts much Injury and Lofs has been fuftained by the Proprietors of thofe Canals, and the Communication by Means of ſaid Canals with the Metropolis, and the Conveyance of Provifions thereby, maliciouſly endeavoured to be interrupted:

NOW We the Lord Lieutenant and Council being fully determined, as far as in Us lies, to have all ſuch atrocious Offenders difcovered and puniſhed according to Law, do hereby publiſh and declare, that if any Perfon or Perfons ſhall, within One Calendar Month from the Date hereof, difcover all or any of the Perfons who have at any Time fince the 28th Day of *February* laſt been concerned, or aiding or aſſiſting in fo wilfully and maliciouſly cutting through the Banks of the ſaid Canals, or either of them, or committing any other wanton and malicious Damage to the Works of the ſaid Canals, fo as that fuch Perfon or Perfons ſhall be apprehended and convicted of the ſaid Offences, or any of them, fuch Perfon or Perfons fo difcovering ſhall receive, as a Reward, the Sum of ONE HUNDRED POUNDS Sterling for each and every of the firft Three Perfons who ſhall be fo profecuted and convicted thereof.

reached Richmond Harbour carrying only five tons. The principal cargo carried towards Dublin was corn, potatoes, pigs, cattle and turf from the midland bogs and, ironically, one of the principal outward cargoes was imported coal, with general merchandise making up most of the rest of the tonnage. Most of the movement of goods was to and from towns along the canal, very little was Shannon trade for transhipment at Richmond Harbour, unlike the Grand Canal, which carried on an extensive trade with Limerick and Athlone. At least the Royal shareholders were able to enjoy a small dividend in the 1820s; the Grand shareholders had to go without while their company struggled to pay off its debts.

The Royal Canal Company suffered even more from malicious breaches and attacks on boats in the 1820s than most other navigations. Well organised combinations for higher wages among the horse drivers were supported by armed gangs. The company and traders were afraid to dismiss drivers because the lives of those who took their places were threatened. The company passage boat inspector reported, 'that latterly the Ribbon system got to such a head, he had no power or control whatever over his drivers, as those that were correct and attentive were unmercifully beat and turned off the canal, and those that remain do as they please'. In 1821 the engineer recommended that watchmen should be placed to guard the vulnerable banks in the vicinity of the Blackwater aqueduct 'until the Frost is gone, as there is no employment in the Country, and the People are very viciously inclined'. He had to summon the help of a sixty-strong company of the 44th Regiment from Naas to guard the men repairing a breach. Workmen had to be brought in from other places to stop the practice of breaching the canal to create local employment. Mr More O'Ferrall, a local landowner, raised a force of police to guard the canal in this area but there was even trouble among the guards. On one occasion some of them had to be dismissed because they were reported to be intoxicated and they were firing their guns indiscriminately and were 'using irritating expressions on Religious subjects, which is by no means proper in the present state of the country'.

The Passage Boats and the Hotels

The new Royal Canal Company extended the passenger service to Richmond Harbour and a fleet of about ten boats was in operation. The speed achieved by the boats was similar to the Grand Canal Company boats; it took just over twelve hours to reach Mullingar, a distance of fifty-three miles, and another eleven hours to travel on to Richmond Harbour, thirty-seven miles further. In 1819 the fare was 8s 6d state and 4s 10d common cabin to Mullingar and 13s 6d state and 7s 8d common cabin to Richmond Harbour. These prices were really quite high when set against the weekly wage of a lockkeeper at that time, which was just 10s per week plus a free house and garden.

The food provided on board seems to have been much the same as on the Grand Canal boats. One passenger complained to the board that they had to sit down to 'a leg of mutton, nearly raw – a piece of carrion salt beef – a small bit of good bacon – three fowls – the port bad – the cider like vinegar, the porter was good'. The same passenger complained that he was not even allowed to have 'a small lap dog' in the cabin with him. The captain, however, produced evidence on his own behalf from another passenger who said, 'I never saw a better dinner in my life' and that the dog was 'a very disagreeable kind of large size cur dog who greatly annoyed the other passengers'. The clergy seemed to head the list of those complaining. The Rev. Henry Wynne of Killucan said that the decks leaked, a pane of glass was missing from one of the windows and the tablecloths were dirty. The Rev. Arthur Hyde complained that he had to wait for a knife and fork 'until a gentleman lent him those he had', the boat was knocked about in the locks, the crew were drunk, and Captain Farrell 'made an attempt on the female attendant in the Bar Room during the time my daughter was asleep in the Ladies Room next door and would have effected his purpose but for a second cabin passenger'. Captain Farrell was dismissed forthwith, but the unkindest cut of all came from another gentleman who said that the captain was 'more like an inmate of Hawkins Street than Captain of a Canal Boat and he was shocked at the manner everything was conducted when he considered how different it was in the Grand Canal Passage Boats'.

Not to be outdone by the rival company, the Royal Canal directors built two hotels on their line, one at Broadstone Harbour (part of which survives today as no. 1 Phibsborough Road) and the other at Moyvalley, about a third of the way along the canal from Dublin and on the main road to the west. The Moyvalley hotel was opened in 1807 and run for the company by hotelkeepers. John Brownrigg,

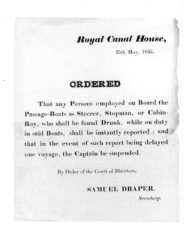

Royal Canal House,
25th May, 1835.

ORDERED

That any Persons employed on Board the Passage-Boats as Steerer, Stopman, or Cabin-Boy, who shall be found Drunk, while on duty in said Boats, shall be instantly reported ; and that in the event of such report being delayed one voyage, the Captain be suspended.

By Order of the Court of Directors.

SAMUEL DRAPER,
Secretary.

Royal Canal: the company's attempt to curb drunkenness among the crews

Royal Canal: the hotel at Moyvalley opened by the company in 1807, later adapted as a hydropathy establishment in 1848 and recently demolished to make way for road widening

during one of his inspections, remarked, 'It is said to be the best building of its kind and the best kept of any in Ireland'. When the New Royal Canal Company assumed control, the board decided to try to lease the hotel because business had declined, but it became increasingly hard to find tenants. By the 1820s it had ceased to operate as a hotel and the building was used for a time by Mr O'Ferrall's police force. It was eventually purchased in 1848 by John Wright Switzer, who set up a very successful hydropathy establishment there.

About 40,000 passengers a year were travelling on the canal by the 1820s, many of them emigrants. There were many instances reported of trouble caused by the great crowds of people who came to see them on their way: 'that they act in some instances in a most outrageous manner, and insist on being allowed to go in the Boats Free of any Charge, and that if opposed, they strike the Master and Crew, also throw stones at them'. In 1819 one of the captains reported that a pane of glass had been broken in an attack, 'the injury had been done by some persons that frequently assembled in two Public Houses at Coolnahay kept by Thomas Cormick and Walter Walsh which frequently remained open at improper hours'.

The company encouraged coach operators to run feeder services by offering them bounties for passengers, and by the 1830s canal and coach services were providing efficient transport to many places. When the steamer services began on the Shannon and the Grand Canal system with its feeder services was operating passengers could reach places as far away from Dublin as Limerick, Sligo and Ballinasloe with ease.

The Longford Line

It is a measure of the confidence felt by the directors of the Royal Canal Company that they began to investigate extending their system by building branches to Longford and Roscommon. They approached the Exchequer Loan Commissioners for a loan to build the short branch to Longford, seeking the same terms as the Grand Canal Company had obtained for the Ballinasloe Canal – that is, with repayments from the net profits of the new canal. The commissioners very unfairly refused to offer them the same terms and insisted that they would have to mortgage the profits of the entire canal, effectively making the payment of any dividend out of the question for many years. Rather than accept this, the directors decided to risk building the canal using their own financial resources.

The same 'miscreant Author' who had criticised the way in which the contract for the Ballinasloe Canal had been awarded, drew the attention of the Directors General to the jobbery involved in the granting of the contract for the Longford Line. Certainly, there would seem to have been some justification in the accusation. John McMahon, the father-in-law of John Killaly who drew up the plans for the branch, withdrew from his partnership in the firm of Henry, Mullins and McMahon, resigned from the board of the Royal Canal Company and was awarded the contract by the board on which his two former partners were principal directors. The tender of Denis Hayes and P. Kelly was turned down because it was slightly higher, but McMahon would have had the advantage of inside knowledge of the figure they had quoted. It seems very likely that Hayes and Kelly were behind the anonymous communication and the board protested to the Directors General:

> We cannot avoid expressing our deep regret that a dastardly assassin should find facilities in Departments of the Government for the propagation of falsehoods effecting the Characters of Individuals which he could not with impunity disseminate in any other way.

Although only five miles long with no locks, this canal was much more difficult to build than McMahon had anticipated, and he incurred very heavy losses on the contract. The canal was opened on 19 January 1830 and the company's engineer, Mr Tarrant, described the scene:

> On the arrival of the Packet, which was attended by a vast Concourse of People, amounting to, as near as he could guess, six or seven thousand, the Band of the First Regiment of Dragoons, that are stationed at Longford, met the Boat about a mile from the town and after her arrival in the Harbour, Mr Williamson entertained them at the hotel – that next day on the Boat returning, she proceeded as far as the Junction, but in consequence of the Strong Ice she was obliged to put back.

There had been a great deal of opposition to the new branch from the people of Kilashee and Richmond Harbour, who feared that they would lose traffic, and the company placed watchmen along the canal to protect the embankments because of threats that the banks would be breached. Four days later the banks did give way, but it was never established whether it was a malicious or accidental breach. The company made Longford the terminus of the passage boats and much of the trade was transferred to the new harbour, so the worst fears of the people west of the junction were quickly realised.

The company's second and more ambitious plan to construct a canal from the Shannon at Tarmonbarry to Roscommon ran into the same difficulties with the loan commissioners, who once again asked for the tolls on the whole line to be put up as collateral. The canal would have been ten miles long with a 45ft (13.7m) rise and so the company decided that the expense would be too great and shelved the idea.

The Royal Canal had undoubtedly helped the towns along its route to prosper, although Mullingar, Longford and Ballymahon were already busy market towns before its arrival. Smaller places like Kilcock, Maynooth and Ballynacargy benefited to a much greater extent and became important distribution centres. Trade picked up in the 1830s; the tonnage carried had more than doubled from the early years to over 80,000 tons per year, and the number of passengers increased steadily. It was, therefore, with a degree of optimism that the company faced the future, unaware of the giant that was about to swallow it up.

PART TWO

6
The Waterways
and
The Railway Age

THE onset of the Railway Age caused the government to look back and review the role that waterways had played in the country's economy in order to decide what part should be taken in the development of the railways. There was no shortage of advice from commentators of the time. George Lewis Smyth, writing in 1839, advocated 'private enterprise and penetrating and tenacious self interest'. He summed up the events of the Canal Age as 'a history of government interference with private enterprise, and complete consequent failure impeded by government boards and commissions'. The Railway Commissioners, set up to advise the government, found that despite a large expenditure of public money on navigation schemes, not a single canal company could be adjudged to be enjoying prosperity. In the event, railways were allowed to develop in much the same haphazard manner as the waterways, with some financial assistance from the government but administered by private companies.

The new Board of Works had an immense task to perform. It was government policy to discourage free handouts and so it fell to the board to organise public works schemes to provide employment. Soon the years of the Great Famine were to add to the plight of the people and, indeed, by the time some of the schemes were in hand, famine and emigration had so decimated the population that it became difficult to find sufficient men to carry out the work.

It is easy now to criticise the continued expenditure of public money on navigation works and to question why the impact of the railways on inland transport was so slow to be realised. Remarks found in the records of the Grand Canal Company illustrate that people were by no means convinced that a new age was at hand. When the Dublin-Kingstown railway was mooted in 1825 the canal company placed a counter petition before parliament for a ship canal along the shore, concluding with the words:

> We pray that your Honourable House will not mar these splendid prospects by sanctioning an insignificant railroad, which will require a heavy expenditure to make and defend, and without materially benefiting the public, will be a nuisance to the inhabitants along the coast and an obstacle to a ship canal.

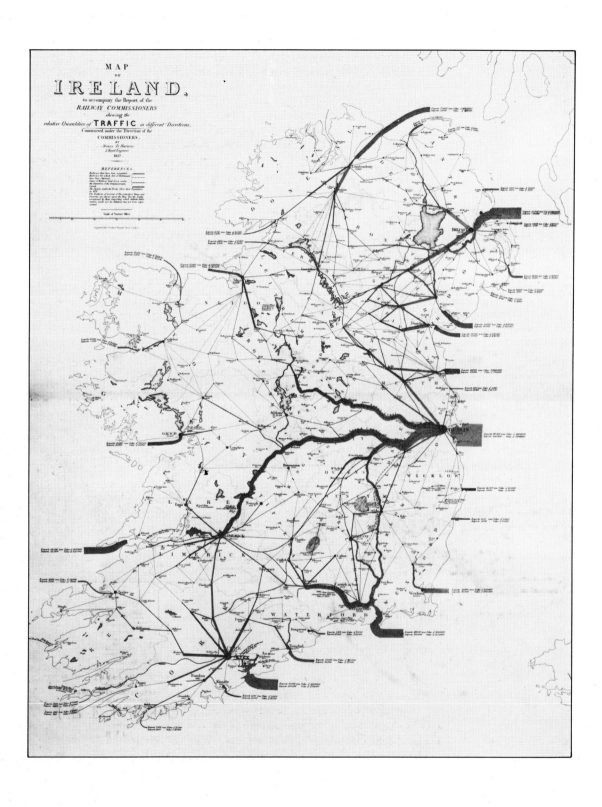

MAP
OF
IRELAND,
to accompany the Report of the
RAILWAY COMMISSIONERS
shewing the
relative Quantities of TRAFFIC in different Directions.
Constructed under the Direction of the
COMMISSIONERS.
BY
Henry D. Harness
Lieut. Royal Engineers
1837

It was said of another railway scheme that it would 'probably prove ultimately unsuccessful', and with reference to another scheme it was minuted: 'at this period when railways are not found so advantageous as was once anticipated and when experience has proved that they are attended with more danger and expense that the proprietors were led to expect. . . .'

Four major navigation schemes were undertaken at this time: the Shannon navigation works; the Bann and Lough Neagh scheme; the Corrib and Mask works; the Shannon-Erne link. These were to prove the last occasions when public money would be spent on large scale navigation works, because it soon became apparent that the railways were here to stay and further expenditure on waterways no longer made sense.

A flowline map of Ireland prepared for the Railway Commissioners in 1837 to illustrate inland transport density at that time

Another aspect of these works which is very open to criticism was the concept of combining navigation and drainage schemes, which frequently led to a conflict of interest to the detriment of both aspects. A tendency to underestimate costs was also the cause of much friction. Landowners who benefited from the drainage had a vested interest in seeing that expenditure was controlled because they had to pay a small proportion of it and they also had to pay for the schemes indirectly through their rates; the counties adjoining the works had to pay about half the cost and the government granted the rest. In the 1850s influential proprietors began to question the way in which the Board of Works was operating, and the government instituted a number of inquiries which led to a curtailment of expenditure where estimates had been exceeded. Disagreements between Richard Griffith (son of the Grand Canal Company director), who was a civil engineer and one of the commissioners, and William Thomas Mulvany, who was responsible for arterial drainage schemes, led to unpleasantness and, ultimately, to the departure of Mulvany for Germany.

In 1845 the curious anomaly in the law which had prevented canal companies from acting as carriers on their own canals was removed in an effort to allow the companies to compete with the railways and encourage the lowering of rates. For many of the waterways the early years of the Railway Age had been the best years in terms of tonnage but railway competition forced rates to be lowered and reduced profitability. There is no doubt that well into the next century the waterways played a significant role in keeping down railway rates wherever water and rail transport were in direct competition. Rates agreements were usually short-lived and for most of the time it was outright war; for passenger services the battle was lost at a very early stage.

The closing decades of the nineteenth and early twentieth century saw a number of commissions set up to consider the waterways. A great deal of evidence was heard, providing much useful material about the condition of the waterways, but although sensible recommendations were made, the government's response was completely negative. The 1880 commission was set up under the chairmanship of Lord Monck to inquire into the system of navigation connecting Coleraine,

Belfast and Limerick – in other words, to advise the government what should be done about the Bann, the Ulster Canal and the Ballinamore and Ballyconnell Canal. The commission concluded that there was insufficient prospect of traffic to warrant the expenditure of public funds restoring the parts of these waterways which had been allowed to deteriorate but that nothing further should be allowed to happen to them which might hinder their restoration at a later date. The Allport commission on public works in 1887 and the Binnie commission on arterial drainage in 1905 both recommended the setting up of a government department to administer every aspect concerning the waterways; drainage, navigation, fisheries and water power. Then, in 1906, a commission was set up under the chairmanship of Lord Shuttleworth to examine the whole question of the future of water transport in the British Isles. Over the next four years a very thorough investigation into Irish waterways was conducted. The evidence of witnesses revealed that the condition of most of the waterways was deteriorating rapidly but that they were still playing a significant role in keeping down railway rates. The commission agreed with the recommendations of the Allport and Binnie commissions that what was needed was a 'Water Board', not a 'Waterway Board', which would deal with every aspect including navigation. It was strongly recommended that all the waterways in Ireland should be taken under state control but, while major expenditure was recommended for the British waterways, 'such moderate expenditure as may be necessary to keep alive inland navigation' was suggested for Ireland.

The frustration from ineffective commissions is summed up by a member of a sub-committee on transport in 1918: 'It is widely thought that everything that needs to be known about Ireland is known, and that what is wanted is not more inquiries but more action'. The political situation, however, ruled out action at this stage. The 1914-18 war had little direct effect on the waterways apart from some subsidisation of wages but in 1922 the first commission established by the new Free State government was the Commission of Canals and Inland Waterways. This commission stressed the vital importance of the waterways to the national economy, suggested certain modernisation schemes and repeated earlier recommendations that the waterways should be placed under state control. This government, like those before it, chose to ignore the findings; and the condition of most of the waterways continued to deteriorate. In Northern Ireland the waterways suffered an ever more rapid demise under the administration there and by the end of the 1950s the Erne, the Lower Bann and the Newry ship canal were the only survivors. In the Republic there was a brief revival of traffic in the Emergency Years, when the scarcity of fuel brought horse-drawn water transport into its own again. After the war, road transport quickly asserted itself, posing an increasing threat to both the waterways and the railways.

The 1948 Milne Transport Inquiry recommended the setting up of a national transport authority and suggested that the Grand Canal

Grand Canal: Mr De Valera visits James's Street Harbour in 1942 to discuss canal transport

Company should be merged with this new semi-state body. This was implemented in 1950 but, although none of the waterways now remained in private control, administration was still divided between the semi-state Córas Iompair Éireann (CIE) and the Office of Public Works. The 1957 Beddy Transport Inquiry hammered home another damaging blow by recommending that CIE should be permitted to abandon its commercial fleet. This was done by 1960 and some of the waterways were declared closed to navigation. Some said it was the end of an era, and most people neither knew nor cared about the waterways that remained. A handful of people did care, however, and they fought hard to save what was left of this great national heritage. Thanks to them a new chapter was just about to begin in the long history of the waterways.

7
Northern Waterways
and
River Navigations

Newry Navigation

THE government decision to hand over control of the Newry Navigation to local interests in 1829 proved a wise one. The waterway had never prospered under the administration of the Directors General; even after its restoration, toll receipts had failed to improve. From the time the Newry Navigation Company took over, however, traffic increased considerably and by the 1850s had risen to an average of 120,000 tons per year, more than double that carried in the best years under the navigation board, which produced a gross income of about £4,000. But in 1852 the final section of the Belfast to Dublin rail link was completed and this line ran parallel to the waterway for much of its course. Although the completion of the new ship canal in 1850 had greatly increased the traffic through the port, not only did the inland canal not seem to benefit from this increase, it actually suffered a sharp decline in trade. This situation became even worse in 1865 with the completion of the rail link between Newry and Armagh, and more and more traffic was routed to the railways so that by the 1880s, although there was over 300,000 tons being handled in the port, the tonnage carried on the inland canal had fallen to under 40,000 tons, less than a quarter of the amount carried in its peak years. By this time the shipping of Tyrone coal, which was to have been the canal's principal cargo, had completely ceased and imported coal was travelling up the canal instead. The Ulster Canal connecting Lough Neagh with the Erne had failed to generate the expected increase in trade. By keeping rates low, water transport did manage to compete with the railways along its line but the Newry lighters could not fit in the Ulster Canal and all the goods had to be transhipped, which greatly increased handling charges.

Heavily encumbered with debts from the major engineering works on the ship canal, the company was unable to pay any dividend until 1876 and with the profit from the inland canal reduced to under £500 by the 1880s there was little incentive to carry out more than the minimum of maintenance, which in turn discouraged traffic. By this time the increasing size of coastal vessels had once again outstripped the facilities of the port and despite further expensive dredging and widening operations carried out to the approach channels, Newry port continued to lose trade while Belfast increased in importance. Local interests in Newry grew dissatisfied with the performance of the company and it became increasingly obvious that it did not have the finan-

Newry Canal: the quays at Newry about 1910

cial resources to improve the situation. In 1901 the company was dissolved and the Newry Port and Harbour Trust was established to administer both the port and the inland canal, so once again they were in the hands of a public body. The trust did make strenuous efforts to improve the condition of the canal but traffic continued to fall and the expenditure soon outstripped the income, making the inland canal an increasing liability. The income from tolls had fallen to just over £200 in 1934 and it ceased to make sense to spend money on maintenance. The last recorded commercial journey was made in 1936, the canal became derelict and, in line with its overall policy towards inland navigation, the Northern Ireland administration issued a warrant for its abandonment in 1949, although it continued to have certain drainage functions. Fixed bridges erected over the canal where it passed through Newry permanently severed its connection with the sea and, finally, even the ship canal was closed in 1966 when it was decided to develop Warrenpoint as the port for Newry. The Trust itself was dissolved in 1974 and a liquidator appointed to wind up its affairs.

The Tyrone Navigation

The Tyrone Navigation did not fare any better. Traffic was boosted for a time by the opening of the Ulster Canal and by improvements on the Upper and Lower Bann in the 1840s and 1850s but it soon declined rapidly in the face of railway competition. The navigation remained in public control, passing to the Commissioners of Public

Works when the Directors General were dissolved in 1831. By the 1880s the commissioners were very anxious to be rid of it and the Lagan Navigation Company agreed to take it over in the hopes of improving business and thereby increasing trade on the Lagan. This company dredged the canal so that deeper draft boats could use it and trade did increase from about 20,000 tons to over 36,000 tons in 1900, which produced a modest profit of £355. Most of the trade was between Coalisland and Belfast, and with steamers towing the lighters on Lough Neagh the service became a great deal faster and more reliable. The goods carried from Coalisland stemmed from its local industries, which had sprung up because of the ready supply of coal: bricks, tiles, pottery, fireclay goods and agricultural products. Grain, hardware, foreign timber, general provisions and, ironically, some imported coal were the principal goods carried up the canal. While the total tonnage carried remained fairly constant up to World War I, a greater amount was carried up the canal than from Coalisland, and the cargoes became more bulk cargoes with the manufactured items finding their way to the railways for more rapid transit. More and more imported coal was coming into the area as the local coal workings declined and sand for building became the principal cargo down the canal. For a short period in the 1920s under the Northern Ireland administration there was actually an increase in trade on the canal but before long road transport began to have an increasing effect on the amount of goods being carried by both rail and water. World War II made very little difference to this decline, commercial traffic ceased in 1946 and the navigation was officially abandoned in 1954. Responsibility for the canal as a drainage channel passed through several government departments to the Department of Agriculture (N.I.) in 1967.

The Lagan Navigation

Despite the problems which still existed on the navigation, traffic continued to improve in the 1830s to an average annual figure of 40,000 tons. The company was under increasing pressure from road transport, which was always at its most competitive on the shorter hauls and, because a great deal of the Lagan trade was on the short run between Belfast and Lisburn it was particularly vulnerable. Water transport, however, continued to operate competitively for bulk cargoes even on the short trip because many of the industries were located on the river. In the early 1840s the 1814 Act expired and the future of the company came under review. There were those who favoured a take-over by the new Board of Works, already controlling the neighbouring Tyrone Navigation, but a strong body of local interests felt that the navigation had the potential to become more successful once the Ulster Canal, linking the Erne and Lough Neagh, was opened and longer-haul traffic increased. Once again the full implication of rail competition does not seem to have been appreciated because in 1842, in the same year in which a rail link was established between Belfast and Portadown, a parliamentary committee advised the government that the Lagan Navigation should be left under the control of a private company. Legislation was passed creating a new Lagan Navigation Company, but a price was imposed on its continued independence. Under the watchful eye of the Board of Works the new company had to pledge to spend £12,000 on improvement works over a period of four years and at the end of that time, in 1848, an annual rent of £300 would be imposed. If at any time the Commissioners of Public Works considered that the company was failing to fulfil its obligation to preserve a well maintained navigation then the company could forfeit the concern. These seem harsh terms, but the company did manage to comply with them and to continue a steady improvement in trade, although the shareholders did not benefit because all the profits went back into maintaining the navigation.

The Ulster Canal proved a disappointment. It was difficult for traffic to remain competitive against road and rail on the eagerly awaited longer hauls because the locks on the Ulster Canal were not large enough to accommodate the Lagan lighters, and this led to expensive and time consuming transhippping of cargo. The Board of Works took over the Ulster Canal in 1865 and carried out some improvements and, in an effort to overcome the problems of transhipping, W. R. Rea, the secretary of the Lagan company, established a new carrying company with a specially built fleet of forty-five ton lighters which could operate on both waterways. At this stage someone in the Board of Works conceived the bright idea that the Lagan company might like to take over the Ulster Canal and the Tyrone Navigation so that the system could be operated as a whole. By this time the province of Ulster was very well served by a network of railways and neither the Ulster Canal nor the Tyrone Navigation had much of a future, but after considerable pressure the Lagan company was persuaded that it would be in its own interests to administer the Ulster waterway network. The government made three unsuccessful attempts to introduce the necessary legislation for the transfer but the bill was defeated on each occasion because there were local interests who resented a private company receiving two publicly owned navigations for nothing. Eventually, the Lagan company itself introduced a bill which was passed by the House of Commons, but the Lords insisted on deleting the clause which gave the company power to close navigations after a period of ten years if they did not prove viable. The matter dragged on for so long that the Lagan company wearily agreed to the deletion even though it meant that it was saddling itself with two navigations in perpetuity regardless of whether they were economically viable. The commissioners must have been delighted to have got rid of these two troublesome waterways in one fell swoop.

It was to prove a fatal mistake for the Lagan company. It was immediately faced with the expenditure of putting both navigations into good repair and, with the Ulster Canal, it was committed to an annual expenditure for maintenance with no prospect of an adequate return; the canal continued to be operated at a loss of about £500 per year. It was a great pity that it had allowed such a millstone to be imposed on it because the Lagan Navigation itself continued to prosper. By 1898 the tonnage carried had risen to over 170,000 tons, a fourfold increase on the 1830s, and the net profit was averaging over £5,000 a year. Coal represented about two thirds of the total traffic, all of it imported through Belfast and moving upstream, a sad reflection for a navigation which its originators had expected to be carrying Tyrone coal downstream. The other upstream cargoes were grain and general merchandise, while downstream most of the lighters returned empty or carried building materials – sand, bricks, native timber and fireclay goods.

Although steamers were used to tow the lighters across Lough Neagh, the traffic on these waterways was all horsedrawn. May Blair, in her fascinating book *Once Upon the Lagan*, has given us a very good description of what life was like for the men who worked on the navigation, the lightermen, the haulers (or horse drivers, as they were called), and the lockkeepers. The boats that worked the Ulster waterways were always called 'lighters' and not 'canal boats', the term used elsewhere in Ireland. Another unique feature was the fact that the families travelled on board, as they did on the English waterways, until well after the turn of the century. The haulers had a hard life, paying a licence fee of 1*s* per year to enable them to offer their services to the lightermen. They would receive £2 for hauling a boat right through the Lagan Navigation from Belfast to Lough Neagh, a two day journey if all went well, but only 10*s* if the boat was light, which took twelve hours. In the summer they slept on deck, using their bag of corn for the horse as a pillow, and in the winter the lighterman would let them stretch out on the cabin floor.

The tonnage carried on the Lagan remained fairly constant at about the 160,000 ton mark for the first years of the new century. During World War I the upstream traffic in coal was halved, and this reduced the total tonnage carried to under 100,000 tons, but the government considered it was important to maintain waterway traffic and so subsidised maintenance and wages. After the war, traffic picked up again and with an increase in tolls the company managed to make a net profit of about £8,000 per year. Three quarters of this came from the operation of the Lagan, one quarter from the Tyrone Navigation and other sources, such as rents, while the Ulster Canal was still a constant drain on resources. The company made strenuous efforts to get permission to abandon this canal but with the setting up of Northern Ireland as a separate political unit the question of the Ulster Canal became even more involved because it straddled the border.

The Northern Ireland administration showed little interest in encouraging water transport and traffic fell away rapidly. With increasing competition from modern road transport, by the early 1940s traffic on the Lagan had fallen to under 30,000 tons. Faced by fuel shortages during World War II, the government decided to subsidise the Lagan

Lagan Navigation: the quays at Lisburn

company again to keep this line of transport in operation. Grants were made to carry out quite extensive repairs, and the company's annual deficit was made up from public funds, but the actual tonnage carried continued to fall during the war years. By 1947 all traffic upstream of Lisburn had ceased and in 1953 the government, which had continued to subsidise the company, decided that it was no longer practical to keep open a navigation that was not being used. By the Inland Navigation Act (N.I.) 1954 the Lagan Navigation Company was dissolved and the Ministry of Commerce assumed control with permission to abandon the navigation from Lisburn to Lough Neagh. The last lighter delivered a load of coal at Island Mill quay in Lisburn in 1954 and where in the early years nine quays had been in constant use, all now fell silent. The abandonment of the remaining section from Lisburn to Belfast passed virtually unnoticed in 1958 and in the 1960s any chance of restoring the Lagan Navigation was lost for ever when the new M1 motorway obliterated about eight miles from Union locks near Lisburn to Moira. The final chapter of this interesting waterway had been ended. Despite its engineering drawbacks, it had enjoyed a greater commercial success than most Irish waterways and deserved a better fate.

The Boyne Navigation

When the Boyne Navigation Company was forced to forfeit the lower navigation in 1835 and the river came under dual control, it greatly lessened its chances of remaining a viable waterway. In its first year as the administrator of the lower river, the Board of Works reported that 10,000 tons were carried, the gross tolls were £707 and the expenditure was £1,985. In the years that followed, the same situation arose each year with an annual subsidy needed to meet the expenditure,

*Boyne Navigation: the
Ros na Righe passing
under the rock arch near
Slane in about 1910 and
the same scene today.*

which was increased by the need for extensive repairs to the navigation. Deprived of the profitable two thirds of the navigation, the Boyne company had neither the incentive nor the money to carry out anything more than minimum maintenance work. The railway and the roads attracted more and more of the traffic, and by the 1890s the toll receipts of the Board of Works had shrunk to under £200 per annum.

Despite this gloomy outlook there were those who saw a future for the navigation. A new company was incorporated in 1894 and the government agreed to vest the lower navigation in this company so that the whole navigation would be under single control again. Safeguards were written into the deal to ensure that work would be carried out to restore the navigation to full working order with a reasonable depth throughout. The Drogheda Steamship Company was involved in the new company as well as local millers and merchants and their efforts were so successful that the railway company was forced to reduce its rates to win back trade.

In 1902 James McCann, the active chairman of the Grand Canal Company who had connections with the Boyne area, conceived a very ambitious plan to extend the navigation from Navan to Lough Ramor up the River Blackwater. He established the Meath River Navigation Company and leased the entire Boyne concern for a period of seven years from 1902. He improved trading facilities considerably on the existing navigation and activated its tourist potential by establishing passenger trips to the celebrated Boyne valley sites like Newgrange. Unfortunately, he died two years later, and without his drive and initiative the extension plan was dropped and the concern went into decline again, reverting to the Boyne Navigation Company at the end of the lease in 1909.

Problems of silting and lack of water on the bar at the entrance to the estuary had seriously reduced trade to the port of Drogheda and there were increasing complaints about the tidal stretch of the navigation from the town to the first lock at Oldbridge, which boats could negotiate only at high water. The Royal Commission in 1907 heard evidence that traffic had steadily declined and plans for a new tidal lock were drawn up by Charles Oliver and recommended by the commission, but no action was taken. The passenger trips continued in the summer months but by 1912 the total receipts from tolls had dwindled to £31 and the company went into liquidation in the following year.

This might well have been the end of the story but John Spicer and Company, owners of the Boyne and Blackwater Mills in Navan, had themselves a number of boats, and were reluctant to see the navigation abandoned. This firm purchased the entire concern for £500 but with the obligation that it must be kept in proper working order. Mr Spicer tried to interest the local authority in granting money to carry out improvements, pointing out the low cost of waterborne transport, but the council saw no future in such an investment. Spicers continued to use the navigation and in 1923 they reported to the commission, set up by the Free State government, that they had two boats in operation which could use the navigation about eight months of the year; for the rest of the year there was either too much flow in the river in the winter or too little depth of water in the summer. Steamers had been tried without much success because of the narrow section of the canal, and so the boats were still horse-drawn. It was emphasised to the commission that the Great Northern Railway Company feared the competition from the navigation even in its rundown condition because goods could still be moved by water for half the cost. Nothing came of the recommendations for improving the navigation and shortly after this Spicers withdrew their boats and ceased to carry out any further maintenance. The navigation, already in a poor condition, quickly became completely impassable. Parts of it were purchased from Spicers by local landowners and in 1969 John Spicer donated the remaining stretches to An Taisce. Some efforts have been made to open up the towpaths for walkers and there have been suggestions that the navigation has potential as an amenity for canoeing and water activities. It is possible that this interesting navigation might still have some future.

The Shannon Navigation

The commission set up in 1831 to report on the condition of the Shannon was made up of Colonel Burgoyne, chairman of the new Board of Works, Captain Mudge, an Admiralty surveyor, and Thomas Rhodes, a civil engineer and relative of the explorer Cecil Rhodes. Captain Mudge was charged with surveying the tidal part of the Shannon, and Rhodes the rest of the river from Limerick to the source. Over the next two years Rhodes carried out a careful survey and recommended enlarging the lateral canals and locks and opening up the Boyle Water into Lough Key. A select committee of the House of Commons was set up to consider the reports and it recommended that the whole navigation should be placed under a single authority and funds should be made available to implement the scheme.

With commendable speed the Shannon Navigation Act was passed in 1835, appointing five Commissioners for the Improvement of the River Shannon. Burgoyne and Rhodes were joined by Harry Jones, William Cubitt and Richard Griffith. Their brief included drainage as well as navigation; winter flooding had always been a problem and nothing had come of earlier drainage investigations in the 1820s. The commissioners decided to carry out further surveys and it was found that some of the lateral canals could be dispensed with by dredging out a channel in the river. Rhodes had been involved in perfecting steam bucket dredgers on the Caledonian Canal and he saw the advantages of opening up the river in preference to enlarging the canals. Because of the low volume of traffic on the Lough Allen Canal it was decided that no enlargement works would be carried out on it and the commissioners also baulked at the idea of reconstructing the Limerick to Killaloe navigation. The end result would be a navigation large enough to take the larger steamers from Killaloe upstream but they would still be unable to gain access to Lough Allen or to the sea at Limerick.

The commissioners were authorised to take possession of the whole navigation. The recently formed Limerick Navigation Company was paid £12,227 compensation but the Grand Canal Company was not so fortunate. The commissioners considered that the company had done well out of its period of control of the middle Shannon, taking in an average of £5,000 per year once the steamers had commenced operations, and had spent little maintaining the works. They awarded a nominal sum of £5 to the canal company, which naturally provoked an outburst from the directors. When the day for handing over the navigation arrived, the company's engineer, John Stokes, was instructed 'to avoid any act which could on the one hand be construed with or have the appearance of a voluntary surrender or abandonment of the company's rights in respect of the navigation or on the other of any opposition or interruption to the proceedings of the commissioners'. He handled the situation most diplomatically. He met one of the commissioners, Major Jones, at Athlone lockhouse and

> remonstrated that it could not be surrendered unless that kind of force was applied to mark the proceedings against my consent, whereupon the Major applied his hand to the shoulder of the lockkeeper, his wife and child and also your humble servant and closed the door upon us outside. He immediately re-admitted the whole party and matters went on as before.

This charade was repeated at the other lockhouses, but the commissioners did assume control of the middle Shannon and the company eventually accepted the award. However, as already mentioned in Chapter 4, this became part of a complicated deal with the government whereby the outstanding loans for constructing the branches, amounting to nearly £100,000 by this time, were commuted to £10,000.

With the whole navigation now in the hands of the commissioners, work commenced in 1840 and annual reports were made to the government detailing the works accomplished, the money expended, the number of men employed and the trade figures for the navigation; traffic continued to move for most of the time with temporary closures of sections from time to time. The Scarriff river was dredged and banked and a harbour constructed near the town. At Portumna a new bridge replaced Samuel Cox's wooden structure. A completely new canal was made at Meelick with a very large lock, 142ft (43.3m) long, nearly double the size of the old Hamilton lock and large enough to accommodate Williams's *Lady Lansdowne*. The lateral canal was abandoned at Banagher, a channel was dredged in the river and a new bridge erected. At Shannonbridge the canal wall and lock chamber were removed and the old canal became the navigation channel in the river; the gate recesses of the old lock are still visible on the shore side under the navigation span.

At Athlone a major change in the original plan was adopted. Instead of enlarging the old canal it was decided to run the navigation up the river bed. Athlone needed a new bridge badly, as the old bridge was

Shannon Navigation: the large lock at Meelick built by the Shannon Commissioners in the 1840s to accommodate the large steamers

very narrow and obstructed by three mills. It was described as 'not merely a discredit to the town alone, but a positive stigma on the nation'. If a new bridge had to be constructed it seemed more practical to make a channel for the navigation at the same time. It was a big undertaking; the bridge supports were erected using caissons and a giant coffer dam was used for the construction of the new lock. When the bridge and lock had been completed, major difficulties occurred with the construction of the weir, which became undermined. Eventually it was decided that the only way to cope with the problem was to completely dry out the river bed and divert the water down the old canal by erecting a temporary dam right across the river. Critics were later to ask why this had not been done in the first place and the works carried out in comfort in the dry river bed, but in fairness to the engineers it was not considered practical to try to hold back the river for more than a very brief period. Plans were carefully laid and large numbers of men were standing by for the day when the river would be dry. It was decided to remove some troublesome shoals and the remains of the old bridge at the same time as repairing the weir wall. The local newspaper reported the day when 'the long promised period of employment' arrived and added that 'in consequence of a report which had been spread through the country some thousands of poor creatures crowded into the town'. On 14 July 1849 some 1,000 men

Shannon Navigation:
Athlone lock about 1910

were put to work in the river bed, 'which is completely dry, and which as far as the eye can reach is filled with workmen and horses, miners and engineers etc.'. It must have been a remarkable sight, but the worst fears of the engineers were realised and the dam did give way. There is no record of loss of life so there must have been some warning, but one of the engineers, W. Forsyth, subsequently gave this graphic description:

> During the execution of the work they were troubled with water because the bottom was so low it would scarcely run out, so they opened the gates of the new lock to allow the drainage water to pass it there. However the water rose until it burst the dam and the whole flood and the damming up of Lough Ree came down upon us. I was sent down from Dublin to get the gates of the new lock shut, and with a great deal of difficulty we got them shut at last.

At Lanesborough the canal wall was removed, a channel was dredged out and a new bridge was erected. At Tarmonbarry and at Roosky the lateral canals were abandoned and a channel was dredged in the river with a lock, weir and new bridge erected at each place. The Jamestown Canal was enlarged and straightened with a new lock constructed nearer the downstream end of the canal. The Carnadoe Waters were opened up into Grange and Kilglass lakes and a new bridge was erected at Carrick. The Boyle Water was opened up into Lough Key with a new lock and the bridges at Cootehall and Knockvicar were replaced. Many shallows were removed in the bed of the river using four steam dredgers, patriotically named *Victoria, Albert, Prince* and *Princess Alice*. The new bridges were fitted with opening spans to a design by Thomas Rhodes but by the time the works reached the Jamestown Canal funds were running low and fixed bridges were built from here upstream. The locks became smaller as the works moved upstream; Athlone was 15ft (4.6m) shorter than Meelick and north of here they were 40ft (12.2m) shorter. The work continued over a period of ten years with an average of 2,000 men employed at any one time. There were few problems with the men, who were grateful to be employed, and there was no longer any trouble from armed gangs who had harassed earlier canal workers. The third report in 1842 stated:

> It is satisfactory for us to state that with the exception of two or three attempts for an increase in wages, the mechanics, labourers etc. employed on the several works, have conducted themselves in a very orderly manner, and have willingly applied themselves to the use of the improved tools and machinery introduced by the contractors and which cannot fail hereafter to prove highly advantageous to the individuals themselves as well as the community at large. We have also been partially successful in introducing piece-work; and it is to be hoped from the known advantages gained by the parties who undertook it, that the system will, during the ensuing summer, be favourably received, and extend itself throughout the entire of our works.

By 1847 there was less resistance to piece-work. For example, the men were divided into gangs of ten or twelve and paid from *5d* to *7d* per cubic yard for excavation, and found that they could earn more than the daily wage. Considering that the country was in the grip of the Great Famine there are surprisingly few references to the condition of the people, except for an occasional comment such as this reference to the works at Tarmonbarry: 'Work has been of the greatest possible service in relieving the lamentable distress which exists here in common with most parts of the country'.

In 1850 the commissioners presented their eleventh and final report. They stated that they had substantially carried out all the works as specified and within the original estimate; any deviations had received the approval of the government. The estimated cost had been £584,805 17s 9½d, about half of which was a grant from public funds and the rest levied on the adjoining counties with a small contribution from landowners whose lands were adjudged to have been relieved from flooding. Detailed accounts had been submitted with the annual reports and one of the accountants who had been found to have embezzled over £8,000 was convicted and sentenced to seven years transportation. But the sad truth was that even before the works were completed there were signs of the impact the railways were going to have on the trade.

In 1840 it had been reported that a total of 18,544 people had embarked at the various stations along the river between Athlone and Limerick, but in the 1849 report a reference was made to the opening of the railway between Dublin and Limerick. This had forced the carrying trade to introduce freight reductions and 'the passenger traffic may be considered as totally annihilated'. The number of passengers embarking in that year was reduced to 4,033 and the services were cut to running on alternate days.

There are quite a number of descriptions of voyages on the steamers at this time. John Forbes, in *A Physician's Holiday*, published in 1852, described the variety of people on board the crowded steamer on Lough Derg: 'bankers, merchants, doctors, county squires, farmers, fishers with their rods, sketchers with their tablets and professors with their pupils' together with about twenty emigrants, the majority heading for the United States, 'going out on funds supplied by their friends who had preceded them'. He gave a vivid description of the scenes on the quay as families made their last farewells:

> And when the final orders were give to clear the ship and withdraw the gangway, the howl of agony that rose at once from the parting deck and the abandoned pier, was perfectly overpowering. 'Oh Mary!' 'Oh Kitty!' 'Oh Mother dear' 'Oh Brother!' 'Oh Sister!' 'God Bless You!' 'God preserve you!' 'The Lord in Heaven protect you!' and a thousand other wild and pious ejaculations. . . amid the crowds of people on the pier, swaying to and fro as they shouted aloud and waved their hats and handkerchiefs, several women were seen kneeling on the stones, kneeling and weeping, with their hands raised fixedly above them.

As if the competition from the railways was not enough, in 1858 the Midland Great Western Railway Company (MGWR) brought two steamers from Scotland and put them into service on the Shannon. The vessels, the *Duchess of Argyle* and the *Artizan*, had to be cut into sections and reassembled in Athlone because they were too large for the locks on either the Grand Canal or between Limerick and Killaloe. They operated in conjunction with the railway at Athlone and were very fast, making the run from Athlone to Killaloe in under six hours. For a time there was cut-throat competition, the railway company is even said to have carried some passengers free, but in 1859 the railway company and the City of Dublin Steam Packet Company came to terms and agreed to share the traffic. In the following year the MGWR decided that the boats were uneconomic and sold them to the Great Southern and Western Railway Company, who operated a summer service for a couple of years. By this time even the steamer company was attracting very few passengers and by 1868 it was reported that all the fine steamers were laid up and 'rotting at Killaloe'. There they were allowed to sink, too large to leave the river, and the fine locks which had been built to accommodate them a few short years before were soon dwarfing the boats that were using them. The hull of the *Lady Lansdowne* lay for many years under water in Killaloe, where she had been allowed to sink, but it was later broken up by marina development works.

With the works completed, the Shannon Commissioners had been dissolved and the navigation handed over to the Office of Public

Shannon Navigation: an excursion trip aboard the Lady Betty Balfour *at Athlone quay in the early 1900s*

Works. While the works were in progress, and in the years that followed before railway competition began, the tonnage carried on the river continued to rise to over 100,000 tons per year, but by the 1880s, with Athlone and Limerick served by railways, the tonnage fell to half this figure and the income was rarely sufficient to meet the expenditure. Almost half the total traffic was still generated by the Grand Canal and only about five per cent of it was on the upper Shannon. Steam tugs had replaced the passenger steamers for towing the boats, and in 1897 the Board of Works agreed to subsidise the reintroduction of passenger services. The Shannon Development Company purchased the *SS Fairy Queen* in Scotland and had three new steamers built there, the *Countess of Cadogan,* the *Lady Betty Balfour* and the *Countess of Mayo.* The Duke and Duchess of York lent royal patronage to the venture and the artist for the *Illustrated London News* vividly captured the scene on board with the royal party well muffled up against a typical damp Shannon day. Four routes were operated, providing services from Killaloe to Carrick with two further steamers, the *Olga* and the *Shannon Queen,* joining the fleet. The Duke of York Route became a popular tourist round trip with rail connections to and from Dublin. The venture was not a success and after a few years the regular services were suspended but some of the vessels continued to ply in the summer months up to the outbreak of war in 1914.

Shannon Navigation: the Duke and Duchess of York's trip aboard the Shannon Development Company's Countess of Mayo *as portrayed by the* Illustrated London News.

The works carried out by the Shannon Commissioners failed to come to grips with the problems of flooding, and in the early 1860s disastrous flooding reopened the question. After innumerable public inquiries, surveys and reports, some work was carried out which improved the situation but did not solve it. Sluices were fitted to the open weirs at Killaloe, Meelick, Athlone, Tarmonbarry, Roosky and Jamestown which ensured better control of the levels, but flooding continued and was the subject of more surveys and reports. Later it became something of a political football with parties making electioneering promises to do something about it. An American expert, Louis E. Rydell, summed up the whole problem very well in a report in the 1950s:

> The problem of the Shannon River flooding has been the subject of much study over the past 150 years. Because of the flat terrain through which the river flows, the almost imperceptible gradient of the stream with its series of lakes and connecting channels, and because of the large volume and long duration of flooding, no simple or obvious solution has heretofore

The Shannon Electric Power Syndicate, Ltd.

INCORPORATED UNDER THE COMPANIES ACTS, 1862 TO 1890.

The liability of Shareholders is limited to the amount of their Shares.

CAPITAL, £12,000.

Divided into 12,000 Ordinary Shares of £1 each.

No. 36

This is to Certify *that* John Alexander Wilson Esq

of 36 College Green Dublin

is the Proprietor of Two Hundred *Ordinary Shares of*

One Pound *each, Numbered* 7871 *to* 8070 *(both inclusive) in*

The Shannon Electric Power Syndicate, Limited,

subject to the terms and conditions set forth in the Articles of Association and Regulations of the Company, and that on each of such Shares there has been paid up the Sum of **One Pound Sterling.**

Given under the Common Seal of the Company this 8th *day of* June 1900.

} Directors.

} Secretary.

Offices— 22 NASSAU STREET, DUBLIN.

NOTE.—No Transfer of any portion of the Shares represented by this Certificate will be Registered until the Certificate has been deposited at the Company's Office.

Shannon Navigation: a share certificate which shows that attempts were made as early as 1900 to set up a company to harness the hydroelectric power of the Shannon

It is extremely unlikely that any of the radical schemes proposed will ever be undertaken now because of the effect they would have on the river's ecology and tourist potential, particularly in the light of modern thinking on the efficacy and cost effectiveness of major drainage schemes; even in Ireland there is a limit to the amount of water that should be speeded on its way to the sea.

In 1901 the Shannon Water and Electric Power Act was passed, authorising the development of a hydro-electric scheme for the river.

It was not implemented, however. Investigations continued and eventually a young Irish engineer, T. A. McLaughlin, succeeded in attracting the interest of the German firm Siemens-Schuckert. A report was submitted to the government in 1925 which won approval from the Dáil despite determined opposition. The work took five years and had a number of significant effects on the navigation. The Lough Allen Canal, which was rarely used by this time, was abandoned and Lough Allen became a storage reservoir with sluices to control its flow into the river. The weir was removed at Killaloe, creating an artificial lake downstream, the old navigation canals were abandoned and a new head race, which also served as a navigation, was constructed. Most of the water was diverted by a dam at Parteen down the head race to the power station at Ardnacrushna, where a double chambered lock was constructed with a fall of 100ft (30.5m). The opportunity to make this lock to the same dimensions as Meelick and Athlone locks was not taken, probably because the volume of traffic on the river at that time did not seem to warrant the additional expenditure. The works, financed by the government, were carried out by the German firm; the workers, thankful to get employment, worked in appalling conditions for low wages.

Shannon Navigation: CIE's St Brendan approaches Athlone lock on her inaugural trip on 26 June 1955. Her arrival on the river ensured that adequate headroom would be preserved at the bridges

The tonnage carried on the river over a period of fifty years from the 1880s had remained fairly constant at an average of about 70,000 tons, giving the Board of Works a small operating profit. It had become almost exclusively dependent on the Grand Canal trade and there was very little traffic north of Athlone. In the 1950s traffic began to fall and a new threat to the navigation appeared in 1954 when it became necessary to replace some of the opening bridges. An effort was made by the local authorities to bring in legislation to allow fixed spans, which in the case of Tarmonbarry and Roosky would have effectively strangled the navigation. The Inland Waterways Association of Ireland (IWAI) was formed in that year by a small group of enthusiasts who sensed the impending danger and appreciated the potential of the river for tourism. There was little public interest in the river at that time but a turning point in the campaign came when the Tanaiste, William Norton, was persuaded to encourage CIE to put two passenger launches on the river. These boats required a minimum headroom of 14ft (4.3m) and this became the accepted clearance required at the bridges.

It was only just in time because in 1960 when CIE withdrew the canal boats from the Grand Canal and Shannon, traffic fell to its lowest ebb. The IWAI continued to insist that the river had potential, despite the gloomy report of a well known Norfolk Broads operator who said that it had no future unless a large umbrella could be erected over it. Today the Shannon is a great success story and some of the founders of the IWAI can be forgiven for looking back with a certain nostalgia to the days when they had the river all to themselves.

The Barrow Navigation

By 1830, despite the unsatisfactory state of the navigation, the tonnage carried on the river had risen to 58,100 tons and the company declared a dividend of two per cent. Complaints continued and the company did investigate the possibility of constructing a sea lock south of St Mullins so that boats could pass over the shallows known as the 'Scars' and enter the navigation at all states of the tide. The company's own engineer, Humphrey Mitchell, had produced a scheme for this in the early 1800s, Thomas Rhodes drew up a similar plan in 1841 and in the 1850s yet another engineer, Christopher Mulvany, drew up plans. The company was reluctant to finance such a scheme and those engaged in the carrying trade were happy to wait for the tide rather than incur the additional toll of a new sea lock.

When the statutory restriction to operating as carriers on their own navigation was removed in 1845, the company built up its own fleet and for a time, with the assistance of the chairman, William Colvill, who was also chairman of the competing Great Southern and Western Railway Company (GSWR), a rates agreement enabled the company to retain traffic at a reasonable profit. In the 1870s dividends of up to six per cent were declared, but relations with the Grand Canal Company were not good and in 1878 the Barrow company decided to restrict its trading to the river because of the high rates being charged on the Grand Canal. When the influence of Colvill was removed, railway competition began to increase and the tonnage carried on the river fell back. Negotiations were opened with the Grand Canal Company to sell the entire concern to that company, but the asking price of £54,000 was rejected and a counter offer of £48,000 was turned down by the Barrow company. Negotiations became so protracted that the worsening state of the company's finances eventually forced

Barrow Navigation:
constructing a harbour
for the Sugar Company
at Carlow

it to sell at the much lower figure of £30,000 in 1894. By this time the railway company had taken over a great deal of the Barrow valley trade. One of the greatest difficulties of the navigation had been the heavy current in winter, and the Grand Canal Company moved towing steamers to the river to try to alleviate this problem.

Both the Shuttleworth Commission and the 1922 Free State inquiry highlighted the many defects of the navigation but no action was taken to remedy them and matters were made considerably worse in 1935 when a drainage scheme on the upper river greatly increased the problem of silting in the lateral canals and led to an even greater current in certain sections of the river. The Grand Canal Company eventually accepted £18,000 compensation and put a more powerful steamer on the river with winches on the shore at the places where the current was most severe, but nothing could be done to prevent silting. Traffic below Carlow gradually declined, but the establishment of the Carlow Sugar Company's factory boosted trade between Carlow and the Grand Canal at Athy. The navigation was transferred to CIE together with the rest of the Grand Canal system in 1950, and when commercial traffic was withdrawn in 1959, the works were allowed to deteriorate.

In recent years, with the resurgence of interest in the waterways as a tourist and recreational amenity, pressure was brought on CIE to restore the navigation to full working order. This was done but the same deficiencies which had always dogged the navigation still persist: there is too little water in the summer for trouble-free boating, and there are problems of silt and weeds in the lateral canals and a heavy stream at other times of the year. No long term solution is possible except the costly one of installing control sluices on the open weirs. The fact that this is one of Ireland's most attractive waterways may eventually make this a cost effective proposition, and the fine navigation which Jessop had predicted 178 years ago might be finally achieved.

The Nore and Suir Navigations

No further work was ever undertaken on the Nore but the tidal portion of this river to Inistioge is now a popular stretch of waterway for pleasure craft, offering scenery unequalled on any waterway in the world. No further improvements were made to the Suir Navigation and recommendations from various inquiries were ignored. The Shuttleworth Commission heard evidence that there was quite a considerable trade in the early 1900s, with over 100,000 tons a year moving between Waterford and Carrick and about 28,000 tons up stream of Carrick to Clonmel, but the income from tolls was nominal because only sea-going craft paid any toll. Between Carrick and Clonmel there was an insufficiency of depth, a rapid current and poor towpaths. It was said that eleven or twelve horses were needed to tow even lightly laden boats upstream. C. D. Oliver, an engineer giving evidence to the commission, painted a vivid picture of this: 'the spectacle of twelve powerful horses struggling against this (6 mph) current at the rate of perhaps two to three miles an hour, while a great wave moves upstream in advance of them, is a most remarkable one'. He suggested the installation of a power haulage system by means of a cable from the towpath, but this sort of expenditure was not felt to be justified and traffic upstream of Carrick declined and eventually ceased. It was pointed out to the 1922 Inquiry that railway rates had increased as soon as water competition was withdrawn and this was considered a good reason for suggesting that the navigation be improved to force railway rates down again. Once again no action was taken and over the years the traffic even as far as Carrick declined.

8
The Grand
and Royal Canals

The Grand Canal

IN October 1832 the board of the Grand Canal Company sent
Andrew Bagot, the inspector of passage boats, to Scotland to
inspect the new fast boats which were in service there. The theory
behind the new boats was based on experiments carried out by an
engineer, John Scott Russell, who had proved that, up to the speed of
seven and a half miles an hour, the resistance of the water increased
as the square of the velocity of the boat, but at eight and a half miles
an hour the resistance decreased because the boat mounted on its own
bow wave instead of pushing it ahead, thereby diminishing the necessary traction. Using this theory, William Houston had constructed
boats of a very light displacement, using thin iron plates and making
the cabin of a wooden framework covered in oilcloth. Towed by two
horses, one behind the other, with the leading horse blinkered and the
rider sitting on the second horse, he achieved a speed of nine to ten
miles per hour. The Grand Canal Company directors were impressed,
some 'Scotch boats' were ordered and the new service was brought
into operation in May 1834. The new boats, which were referred to
as 'fly boats', averaged speeds of six to eight miles per hour including
locks, cutting running time by half and presenting a new challenge to
the coach operators.

The new service was not without its problems. The horse contractors
complained bitterly about their new schedules and the heavy fines
imposed on them for running late. One of them said he needed sixteen
horses to operate his fifteen mile stage because the horses had to be
changed so frequently and this required new stabling facilities. Great
damage was inflicted on the banks by the galloping horses and the
great surge from the fast moving boats which swept right over the
banks. John Stokes, the company engineer, estimated that the damage
and loss of water far outweighed the increase in revenue from the
greater number of passengers. The 'Scotch boats' were altered to suit
the Irish conditions, and wooden cabin structures replaced the oilcloth
coverings. The boats were about 65ft (19.8m) long but only 6ft (1.8m)
wide and could accommodate twenty state and thirty-two common
cabin passengers. Conditions were very cramped and passengers had
to remain seated while the boat was in motion to preserve the balance.
There were no longer any cooking facilities but 'snacks of cold meat
and a limited allowance of the usual liquors' were available.

The introduction of the faster services encouraged coach operators

Grand Canal: the hull of a flyboat, the Hibernia, *salvaged from the canal by the late Father Murphy for Robertstown canal museum*

to offer feeder services rather than compete for passengers. In 1836 Charles Bianconi approached the company and agreed to operate coaches to meet the boats on a number of routes if he was paid a bounty for each passenger he supplied. By 1844 he was receiving over £900 per year and a total of over £700 was being paid to other coaching establishments. Fares, however, had to be kept so low to compete with rival coaches that although the numbers of passengers increased to a peak of 120,615 in 1846, the profits from the operation did not reflect this.

Whether the service would have survived for long with the increasing competition from faster and more efficient coach operators is uncertain. In the event, neither coaches nor boats could compete with the fast growing railways. The end came very quickly; by the end of the 1840s the canal company was forced to withdraw some of its services. Attempts were made to reach agreement with the GSWR, whose line followed the canal out of Dublin. The canal company suggested that it would start its services at Sallins because the heavy lockage out of the city made it impossible to travel this stretch from Dublin quickly. The railway company was very uncooperative and put uncovered waggons on its trains for the boat passengers, 'thereby exposing the Passengers to all the inclemency of the weather'. This was in the month of January, so the canal company protested in the strongest possible terms and covered waggons were supplied after two weeks.

Bianconi reacted in characteristic manner to the new threat. In his biography, written by his great grand-daughter, Molly O'Connell Bianconi together with S. J. Watson, it is recorded that he attended a conference of proprietors of canal and coaching establishments at the Imperial Hotel in Dublin. This had been called to protest about the findings of the Drummond Commission on Railways in 1838. When it came to his turn to speak he addressed the meeting as follows:

> I think I know as much of the country as any gentleman in this room, and I look upon it to be as foolish to try to prevent the establishment of railways as to try to stem the Liffey. My own loss by the establishment of the railways would be greater than that of any gentleman here present – I may say greater than the combined losses of all the gentlemen here present. . . . Still I see that railways must be made; and I not only do not oppose them, but I have taken shares in the undertakings.

He was soon providing feeder services at the new rail heads while the canal company, in one last despairing effort, decided to build two twin screw passenger boats. These were much heavier than the fly boats and were unable to match their speed so they never went into service. By this time the new railway to the west was competing for the Ballinasloe passengers, which had always been the company's most successful route. The unequal struggle was abandoned and the last boat was withdrawn on 31 December 1852. A colourful period in the canal's history had come to an abrupt end: after eighteen years the galloping horses and surging fly boats were a thing of the past.

War With the Railways

The impact of the railways on the carrying trade had not been equally disastrous. The tonnage carried had been increasing steadily and, although there was a decrease in 1846 and 1847 because of the Famine, trade soon picked up again and topped the 300,000 tons mark by the end of the 1850s. The convoy system had to be introduced again for the worst years of the Famine and troops were stationed along the line of the canal; less corn was carried into Dublin in this period and there was an increase in food supplies out of the city but it was 'clogged and encumbered with so many difficulties and embarrassments that it has been found impossible to carry it out to the extent which the wants of the country require'. There were two factors which helped the company at this time. In 1848 permission had been given to consolidate the company's stock and loan holdings, and this enabled a small dividend to be declared again in the years that followed. The company also took advantage of the removal of the restriction preventing it from acting as a carrier and it began to build up its own fleet, buying out some of the traders.

It was inevitable that a rates war would commence with the railway companies but the company did manage to negotiate a rates agreement with the GSWR in 1852. Both this company and the MGWR showed an interest in buying out the Grand Canal Company, and the directors accepted the MGWR offer. The GSWR obstructed the required legislation and the MGWR agreed to lease the tolls and duties of the canal for seven years from 1853-60 while the legislation was being enacted; a rent of £19,564 per annum was agreed, which represented the annual net profit of the company at that time. A bitter struggle had developed between the two railway companies and the canal company now became a pawn in this battle even though the issue of water transport was one very small element in the confrontation. In the end both railway companies decided that they did not want the canal and the MGWR handed it back at the end of its lease and said it was no longer interested in the purchase. The Grand Canal directors, who had already cut back board meetings to once a week and who thought they would soon be finished with the canal, were furious, but they were advised that they had no legal right to enforce the agreement to purchase.

In the years that followed, agreements were made with different railways companies from time to time and in between bitter rates' wars developed. By using towing steamers on the Shannon, the canal company was able to offer a regular service to Limerick and Athlone but experiments with the use of steamers in the canal proved unsuccessful. It was found impossible to design a boat which would have sufficient room for cargo in addition to the heavy and bulky steam engines. Steamers were used for a time on the long levels to tow trains of boats, but even this led to long delays for some boats waiting for the others to assemble. By the 1880s traffic had begun to decrease but the company was still making a profit. By this time more than half of the tonnage was being carried in the company's own boats, and the trend towards a reduction in the number of bye-traders continued. James McCann became chairman in 1891 and his drive and initiative put the company into a much stronger position in the closing years of the century. He worked towards more permanent rates agreements with both the GSWR and the MGWR, and the acquisition of the Barrow Navigation Company in 1894 extended the company's network. Trade figures improved and the company was able to increase its dividend

Grand Canal: in 1975 there was a bad breach on the long level east of Daingean (Philipstown)

to an average of four per cent in the first decade of the new century.

The development of the Bolinder diesel engine overcame the size and weight problem and in 1911 the company started converting its horse-drawn fleet, which greatly increased the efficiency of the service. Industrial unrest in the years leading up to the Great War, and a serious breach in the old trouble spot near Edenderry, caused some problems and from 1917-20 the government subsidised maintenance costs and paid war bonuses to the employees. During the Civil War stores were burned and boats attacked but the boatmen refused military protection because they felt that this would endanger their lives. The rates agreement with the railway companies had all terminated again by 1920 and, with railways amalgamations in 1924, the canal company found itself struggling against the new Great Southern Railway (GSR) network. Economic depression had led to an overall reduction in traffic, the trade unions were becoming much more organised and demanding better wages and conditions for their members and, in addition, there was increasing competition from road transport.

Grand Canal: one of the wooden G-boats under construction. These were built to transport turf to Dublin during the Emergency Years

Railway and canal companies were precluded by law from operating road services until 1927 but when this restriction was removed the canal company built up a fleet of lorries at the larger centres to provide a door-to-door service. The tonnage carried by water continued to fall in the 1930s and dividends were reduced to an average of one and a half per cent. Stringent restrictions on road transport during the Emergency Years brought about a temporary return to water transport, and horse-drawn haulage came into its own again with the company building a fleet of boats made from native timber, known as the G-boats to distinguished them from the M-motor driven boats. It was only a temporary respite; road traffic recovered quickly after the war years and by 1948 the company's own road services were accounting for twenty-seven per cent of its total income. The tonnage carried by water

*Grand Canal: the middle
harbour at James's Street
in the 1940s*

in that year was only 143,000 tons but the company was still making a good profit and paid out a dividend of three per cent. The directors strongly resisted the government decision to merge the company in the new transport authority, CIE, but, despite their protests, the merger went ahead and on 1 June 1950 a total of £702,500 in government guaranteed transport stock was issued to shareholders on a pound for pound basis. The long history of a private company which had survived so many ups and downs for 178 years was at an end.

Inevitably, CIE routed traffic to the struggling railways and drove the bye-traders off the canal by increasing tolls. The Beddy commission on internal transport in 1957 suggested that CIE should be allowed to withdraw its waterborne services, and this was done in December 1959, although a few boats remained in service in the following year until Messrs Arthur Guinness, who by this time was the principal user of the canal, had made alternative arrangements in Limerick. The withdrawal of the trade boats sealed the fate of some of the branch lines because there was virtually no pleasure traffic at that time. A clause had been inserted in the 1958 Transport Act, as a result of pressure from the IWAI, which restricted the closure of waterways to those which had not been used for three years. It is an indication of the extremely low ebb of the Grand Canal system that even this clause was not sufficient to save the branch lines but it did at least ensure that the main line to the Shannon, the Barrow Line and the Barrow Navigation remained open.

The End of an Era

The abandonment of the commercial traffic marked the end of a long line of canal boatmen and led to the cutting back of the staff who had kept the canal in working order. James McGreevy, a bankranger from Sallins, summed up this concept of a canal community in an interview recorded in *Canaliana* in 1980:

> Well, you see, the way it is with the canal, it's an old job that falls from generation to generation. My father was on the job, my grandfather, my great grandfather. . . . They never worked only on the canal. We came with the canal.

There were also weedcutters, dredger drivers, inspectors and lockkeepers. The position of lockkeeper in particular stayed with the same family through several generations. The house and garden were the attraction because the wages were very poor; the Barrow lockkeepers were still getting as little as 11s per week in 1930 and the others not much more. The hours were very long, as boats had to be locked through at all hours of the day and night. On one occasion Thomas Murphy, lockkeeper at Lowtown, was asked by the chairman of the company how long he had worked in the service of the company and he received the reply, 'A hundred years, fifty by day and fifty by night'.

The boatmen were also drawn from the same families. They often started as young as fourteen years old as 'grazers'; the greaser not only had to grease the engine but acted as cook and general factotum. He could work his way up from greaser to deckhand to engineman and eventually possibly skipper. It was a hard life and poorly paid. The four men lived in the tiny cabin in the bow, conditions were very primitive and they often shared their meagre meal from a communal enamel basin. Until 1946 they were expected to travel night and day, with twenty-four hours a week off on Sundays. Many of them came from counties Kildare or Kilkenny and had their homes along the line of the canal. If they were lucky they might hit off Sunday at home. There were also casual labourers, known as 'webs' because they tried to stick to a boat, who would be taken on in a temporary capacity. It took about three days to make the journey from Dublin to Shannon Harbour with another day on to Limerick and about four days from Dublin to Waterford. It could take as little as four minutes to lock a boat through. Steering and locking on a dark night was a skilled job; the Bolinder diesel had to be stopped to put it into reverse and so a stop-rope was used instead to slow down the boats. The steering position on the stern was very exposed and the men usually worked in pairs, sharing six-hour stints. In 1946, in an early example of a productivity deal, the men agreed to man the boats with only three men and work a sixteen hour day. This gave them more opportunity to get home because they could stop over and make up the time by travelling through the night. Holidays of one week were also introduced for the first time, with maintenance work being carried out on the boats while the men were on holiday. The men did all their own

Grand Canal: a canal boat powered by a bolinder diesel engine approaching the 9th lock, Clondalkin

loading and unloading but there were 'bulkers' to help with this at James's Street harbour, the terminus in Dublin.

Every hour spent travelling and every item of cargo aboard had to be carefully accounted for to the agents of the company, but there was one unwritten concession which seems to have become accepted. The boatman would carefully extract porter from the casks they carried for Guinness's Brewery. The trick was to tap up the hoop and make a small hole with a gimlet. In hot weather the precious black liquid would flow freely from the cask but in colder weather two holes were needed and sometimes a redhot poker had to be inserted in the cask to liven up the stout. It was recognised that a sweet-canful could be extracted from a firkin and a biscuit-tinful from a hogshead, and the men filling the casks at the brewery made careful provision for the needs of the canalmen by adding a few extra pints. Messrs Guinness might have thought that they had put an end to this practice when a metal container known as an 'iron lung' was introduced, but it did not take the men long to learn how to deal with this new challenge.

There were special terms used; for example, the port side of the boat was called the 'stoprope-side' and the starboard side was the 'scuttle-side', the scuttle being the companionway to the cabin. The boats were 'canal boats', not 'barges', and the men 'canal boatmen', not 'bargees'. There were many accidental drownings over the years. At one time the unfortunate widows received as little as £10 compensation, which the company was careful to point out was an *ex gratia* payment and not an admission of liability. It was not until 1900 that any form of insurance was negotiated for the men. These accidents sometimes led to the places becoming unpopular places to tie up for the night in case the spirit of the unfortunate man was still about. The thirteenth lock was also avoided because it was said that it went through the site of a graveyard which had upset the occupants. There was also a mysterious companion who used to accompany the horse drivers along the

Shannon Navigation: an assembly of converted canal boats at Jamestown Canal in 1972 en route to carry out work at Leitrim

towpath near Hazlehatch in the old days. The old canalmen enjoy talking about their days on the canal; for most of them its seems to have been a hard but a good life and it is sad that this canal community is no more.

The Royal Canal

The number of passengers increased steadily in the 1820s, but the directors of the Royal Canal Company were very conscious of the need to maintain a fast and efficient service if they were to compete successfully with coach operators. They were approached by the customary 'inventors', some of whom were allowed to demonstrate their ideas, but they did not prove practical. One of them, Henry Eager of Baltinglass, said that the force required in his plan was 'neither steam, wind, men or horses' but he claimed that he could move boats 'with a power equal to twenty horses, by means of water wheels and a succession of pullies'. Some correspondence was carried on with a firm in Liverpool in 1831 which was experimenting with a twin-hulled steam boat which was guaranteeed to travel at a speed of six and a half miles per hour. In Dublin, William and Robert Mallett and John Marshall were also carrying out experiments with iron steamers but none of these boats proved satisfactory in the narrow confines of the canal. In July 1832, four months before the Grand Canal Company

Royal Canal: an engraving of a flyboat from Hall's Ireland

took any action, the Royal directors dispatched their dockmaster, Thomas O'Neill, to view the remarkable 'Scotch boats'. When he returned he reported his amazement at seeing the boats rising up twelve inches as they travelled along at speeds of up to twelve miles per hour. He explained how important it was to build the boat of light displacement with no top hamper or deck weight, and the passengers 'must be obliged to sit down equal on both sides'. Efforts to build a similar boat in Dublin were not successful, and a boat was ordered from Scotland which arrived in August 1833. The board was delighted with it and a second boat was ordered immediately with 1ft (0.3m) more beam and 6 ins (0.15m) more draft to improve its stability in the locks. The new service went into operation in December of that year, about six months sooner than the Grand Canal fly boats.

   The report of the very first trip was an indication that there would be problems. She was scheduled to make the journey to Mullingar, a distance of fifty-three miles, in eight hours, cutting four hours off the time of the old boats, but it was reported that 'the rudder caught under a paddle at the twelfth lock, a horse dropped down dead at the thirteenth lock, head winds and the delay in striking off the line in the locks occasioned about twenty-five minutes delay'. The captains were also greatly troubled by the large numbers of well wishers who came to see off the many emigrants; this problem was greatly increased with the new unstable boats. In 1845 there were two serious accidents. The evening passage boat from Dublin struck a rock on the side of the canal in the narrow cutting at Clonsilla, the boat keeled over and filled, drowning sixteen people. It was later established that the regular steerer was not at the helm and the boat was being steered by a company employee who was travelling on the boat. The second accident happened in Longford harbour, when a boat full of emigrants capsized and twelve people drowned.

In 1831 the board had approached 'Mr Bianci' of Clonmel to supply the company with one of his specially designed two-horse cars. Bianconi, never slow to seize an opportunity, waited on the board and persuaded the directors to allow him to run feeder services to Athlone and Boyle. These services began in 1832, four years before he began feeder services for the Grand Canal. Before long he was complaining about the late arrival of the boats: 'if regularity in the arrival and departure of the boats was not strictly adhered to, the Royal Canal Establishment must suffer materially'. By 1835, with the fly boats in service, the company was paying him more than £300 a year in bounties on these two routes alone and a considerable amount to other coach operators as well. It was not long before the railways were to have a devastating effect on these services, and in an even more direct way than on the Grand Canal.

The Midland Great Western Railway Company

The Royal Canal Company had continued to show a clear profit in the 1830s, but the tonnage carried on the canal never rose much above 80,000 tons, with only a little over one quarter of this west of Ballymahon; the tonnage passing to and from the Shannon at Richmond Harbour was about 15,000 tons. This was not at all what had been anticipated when the canal was specifically planned to join the Shannon at a northerly point to facilitate the Leitrim coal trade. The company seems to have had much greater problems than the Grand Canal Company in the 1830s, with malicious breaches, attacks on boats and combinations among the horse drivers. Boats with food supplies were particularly at risk 'from the dearness of provisions and the general distress felt by the poorer classes'. In October 1833 the board sent a memorial to the Lord Lieutenant seeking more protection:

> That a spirit of Turbulence and Outrage pervades the entire Class of the working persons employed in the carrying Trade throughout the whole Line of the Royal Canal, alike destructive of the interests of the Company, the Traders and the Public at large. This Spirit has assumed a tone of menace and insubordination of so formidable a character that if not timely checked, its influence upon the Peace of the Country must be productive of extremely pernicious consequences. The cases of outrage are too numerous to detail, but they are now so organised and they have arisen to such a Pitch that the Dictum of the Combinators supercedes the authority of the law.

No response was forthcoming from the government, and the continuing problems were not an encouragement to trade, although the tonnage carried in the early 1840s did rise to over 90,000 tons. However, this was less than half the amount carried on the rival canal.

It is not surprising, therefore, that the directors were not slow to recommend the acceptance of an offer from the newly incorporated

MGWR in 1844 to purchase the entire concern for £298,059, which represented forty per cent of the capital holdings. The government agreed to the take-over even though it was known that the railway company intended to lay its line alongside the canal for part of its route to the west, thus saving the long and expensive business of acquiring land. A statutory obligation was imposed on the railway company to maintain the navigation to the satisfaction of the Board of Control but the decline of the waterway was inevitable from the day it was taken over. The railway company proceeded to lay its line alongside the canal to a point some miles west of Mullingar. By 1848 it was completed to this town, and three years later across the Shannon at Athlone to Galway.

At this stage the railway company was still interested in developing trade on the waterway in conjunction with its rail services, but the passenger services were obviously uneconomic and were wound up within a few years. It has already been seen that it even contemplated purchasing the Grand Canal in the early 1850s, leasing this canal for a few years. The tonnage carried on the canal rose to 112,181 tons in 1847, its highest ever level, despite the impact of the Famine, and maintained a figure of just under 100,000 tons through the 1850s and 1860s. In 1871 the railway company decided to commence its own carrying trade, and in 1873 Spencer Dock was completed where the canal entered the Liffey; this was the dock which the canal company had received money to construct but had never succeeded in carrying out the work. A handsome and imposing building had been erected at the Broadstone terminus of the railway, combining an Egyptian and Grecian style of architecture, and in 1877 the harbour of the Broadstone Canal was filled in to make a forecourt for the station.

All this was only a temporary reprieve for the canal. The tonnage began to fall, Spencer Dock became a useful railway distribution centre, and the carrying trade venture was abandoned in 1886. By the end of the 1880s there were only about forty boats moving on the canal and the tonnage had fallen to just over 30,000 tons. Inevitably, despite the protests of the traders and the admonitions of the Board of Control, the condition of the waterway was allowed to deteriorate. In the early 1900s the Shuttleworth commission heard evidence that the canal was in a very neglected condition, although this was strenuously denied by the owners. The commission chose to believe the report of Dudley Fletcher, the Board of Works engineer in charge of the Shannon Navigation, who confirmed the need for dredging and weed cutting. It recommended that the canal should be removed from the control of the railway company and restored so that it could operate in competition with the railways and act as a means of controlling rates. Like all the other recommendations of this commission, the suggestion was ignored, the railway company remained the owner and little was done to maintain the canal which in turn led to a further fall in trade. By the 1920s the tonnage had dwindled to about 10,000 tons, about one third of which was porter from Guinness's Brewery and empty barrels

Royal Canal: the 39th Draper's lock; when the canal was closed to navigation the western end was de-watered and the condition of the canal works deteriorated much faster than the eastern end which remained in water

being returned to Dublin. The 1922 commission was told that the number of boats on the canal had fallen to thirteen, all horse-drawn, and it repeated the recommendation that the canal must be removed from the control of the railway company if it was to survive. Once again no action was taken by the government and, when the railways merged in 1938, ownership passed to the new GSR. There was a very brief revival in the turf trade in the early 1940s when fuel was scarce, and in 1944, seemingly irrevocably attached to its railway companion, the canal became part of the even larger national transport authority, CIE.

Tom Rolt travelled the canal in 1946, a journey described in his classic book on the Irish waterways, *Green and Silver*. He reported that there were only two boats trading on the canal and the last bye-trader, Leech of Killucan, ceased to operate in 1951. The last boat to be issued with a permit to pass through the canal was Douglas Heard's *Hark* in the spring of 1955. I was on that memorable trip, and we encountered very few problems although the western end of the canal showed most signs of deterioration. The canal was officially closed to navigation on 6 April 1966. CIE placed a dam across the canal west of Mullingar, cutting off the main supply of water west of this point, and local authorities were given permission to put low level culvert bridges across the canal from Mullingar west. Everyone, including the IWAI, wrote off the Royal Canal, but one man, Ian Bath, would not accept this defeatism and his enthusiasm and dedication to the restoration of the canal was to prove sufficient to pull it back from the brink of extinction.

9
Nineteenth-Century Navigations

The Ulster Canal

As Ireland's waterway network developed, it was a logical step to envisage an ultimate through route from Belfast to Limerick. The Lagan Navigation had reached Lough Neagh in 1794, the Shannon was being improved and all that was needed were the two final links between Lough Neagh and Lough Erne and between Lough Erne and the River Shannon. In 1814 the Directors General of Inland Navigation instructed their engineer, John Killaly, to investigate 'in general terms' the first of these two links, a canal from Lough Neagh to Lough Erne.

Six months later Killaly presented his report and pointed out with enthusiasm the great benefits such a waterway would produce: 'a door would be opened to the English market from the north-western parts of Ireland, agriculture would be encouraged; the comfort of the poor increased and a check put to the spirit of emigration, at present so prevalent in that part of the Kingdom'. Killaly envisaged a canal thirty-five miles long with twenty-two locks built to the same dimensions as the Royal Canal (now nearing completion), which would cost about £223,000. At the same time he produced estimates for a canal of reduced dimensions which would cost less. It is strange that an engineer of Killaly's experience should have even contemplated such an idea. Already the locks on the Royal Canal were 1½ft (0.4m) narrower than the smallest lock on the Newry, Tyrone and Lagan navigations. There would seem to have been little point in trying to establish a network if boats could not move freely from one system to another. There was one further observation in Killaly's report which might have sounded a warning note. He said that he had been able to find only one practical source as a water supply for the summit level, 'which I have strong hopes would be found a sufficient supply', but he suggested making the summit level deeper than usual to make sure of enough water down the line.

Despite considerable support for the scheme from local landowners and from the Lagan Navigation Company, the Directors General, with their dwindling resources, did not feel justified in proceeding with it, and the scheme was shelved. Seven years later, in 1822, renewed efforts were made to reactivate the project, and a plan was put to parliament based largely on Killaly's original surveys. The petitioners stressed that it would be a useful undertaking at this time when unemployment and near famine conditions existed:

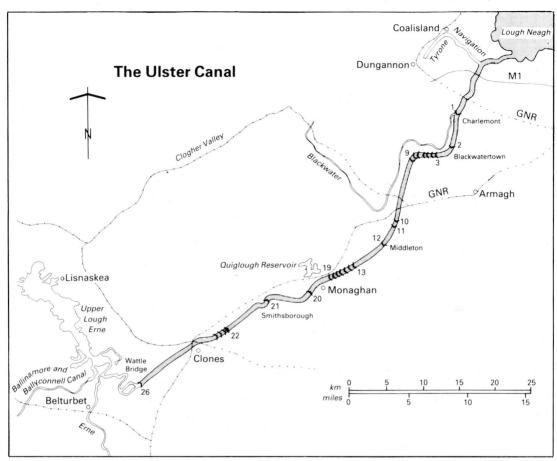

The present is indeed a favourable moment for commencing public works to give employment both to the peasantry of north and south. Such measures would do more to tranquilise the disturbed districts of Ireland than can ever be effected by military coercion.

Loans were being made available through the Exchequer Loan Commissioners for such schemes, and parliament agreed to the incorporation of the Ulster Canal Company to carry out the plan.

The Ulster Canal Company

With no prospect of getting a grant from the navigation board, the company sought ways to cut the cost of the scheme to reduce the amount that would have to be borrowed. Killaly produced a revised estimate, reducing the number of locks to sixteen by making them deeper, which brought the cost down to £160,050. The company euphemistically estimated that the net profits of the canal would be £14,000 per year. This figure was based on the tonnage carried on the Grand Canal, the most successful navigation in the country at this time, and, before agreeing, the loan commissioners sent their consultant engineer, Thomas Telford, to inspect the plans. The tender of Henry Mullins and McMahon was accepted and a start was made with land purchases. Some time later Telford advised against making such deep locks, and recommended increasing the number to twenty-six. The contractors were asked for a revised figure for the work and then Telford queried the amended cost, saying it was much higher than his estimate. Utterly frustrated, the contractors withdrew from their contract. By this time over six years had elapsed but eventually, with the guarantee of a loan of up to £120,000, work began again; this time William Dargan was one of the principal contractors.

We have already seen that Dargan had contracted to build the Kilbeggan Branch for the Grand Canal Company in 1830, a job which he had thought he could complete within a year, but it was to take him four long years and he was still struggling with it when he took on the Ulster Canal work. Killaly had died in 1832, and Telford in the following year, so it was yet another engineer, William Cubitt — who, like Dargan, was to become a railway man — who acted for the Exchequer commissioners while the work was in progress. In the end there were twenty-six locks on the canal and, whether it was the decision to increase the number of locks again or the reduction in the loan that prompted the company to try to cut back costs, at some stage the decision was made to build the canal to smaller dimensions. The smallest lock was only 11ft 8½ins (3.6m) wide, the narrowest lock in the country, which meant that none of the lighters from the other Ulster navigations could pass through it. It is difficult to understand how the company could have justified this extraordinary decision.

The canal commenced at Charlemont on the River Blackwater, a

Ulster Canal: 1st lock, Charlemont, where the canal enters the River Blackwater. Note the small dimensions of the lock

couple of miles upstream of the point where the Coalisland Canal connected with the river. It passed up through nineteen locks to the summit level near Monaghan; this included a staircase of seven locks in the space of three quarters of a mile cut into the side of a deep limestone gorge alongside the swiftly flowing Blackwater, which proved a difficult and expensive part of the canal to construct. The summit level at Monaghan was short and was fed by a small lake which was embanked to increase its capacity and was controlled by a regulating sluice. The small reserves of water held in this Quiglough reservoir, combined with the short summit level, were to provide a very inadequate supply in the summer months, bearing out Killaly's original doubts on this score. From the summit the canal dropped down through seven locks to join the Upper Erne at Wattle Bridge. The work was completed by 1841 at a total cost of £230,000, so the company had been forced to raise nearly as much again as the guaranteed loan.

The first ten years were a great disappointment. Because many of the lighters were too large to pass through, most goods had to be transhipped; this caused delays and added to the freight costs. The inadequate water supply was felt from the start in the summer months, particularly west of Clones where it was found impossible to maintain water levels; imperfect puddling which allowed seepage added to this problem. The anticipated traffic failed to develop; as yet, there was no direct rail competition but the canal failed to attract business away from the roads. The final link in the great through route from Belfast to Limerick was still just a 'paper canal' at this stage; the connection between the Erne and the Shannon still remained to be undertaken. Maybe the company still hoped for better things if this was achieved; the vision of this great water highway through the country seems to have been held by many people, but time was running out for the Ulster Canal Company. It became obvious that there was not the slightest chance that the company would ever be able to meet the loan repayments and so in 1851 the Board of Works took possession of the canal and the company was wound up.

Board of Works Control

After carrying out some minor repairs, the Board of Works leased the canal to William Dargan at an annual rent of £400. He had built up a fleet of boats and was already the principal carrier on the canal; having built the canal he was determined to try to make it successful. He was on bad terms with the Lagan Navigation Company and so he concentrated on building up trade between Enniskillen, on the Erne, and Newry via the Newry Canal. He succeeded in establishing an efficient service; goods leaving Enniskillen on a Wednesday evening arrived in Newry on Friday and could be transhipped and delivered in Liverpool by the following Monday. The tonnage passing through the canal, however, was not sufficient to encourage any expenditure on the works and, anticipating the new threat which would be posed by the extension of the Ulster Railway Company's line from Armagh to Monaghan and Clones, Dargan surrendered his lease to the Dundalk Steam Navigation Company in 1858. It is difficult to understand the motives of this company in taking on the canal; Sir John Macneill advocating the construction of more railways in that part of the country in 1861 had remarked about the canal: 'the only plan. . . by which any return at all can be obtained from the undertaking. . . is to take off all the lock gates, drain the canal and convert its bed and slopes into grassland which may be let for grazing'.

It was little wonder that the shipping company showed no interest in renewing the lease in 1865 and the Board of Works had to assume control. By this time the long awaited route from Belfast to Limerick had at last been achieved with the completion of the Ballinamore and Ballyconnell Canal and so a decision had to be made either to write off the Ulster Canal, which was not yet twenty years in existence and which had been built with the help of public money, or put it into proper working order. It is easy now to see which of the options should have been taken. The Ulster Railway Company's line ran parallel to the canal and this, combined with its engineering defects and its small locks, did not point to a very hopeful future. But writing off the Ulster Canal also affected the recently completed Erne-Shannon link, and a great deal of public money had been spent on this navigation. Was the through route from Belfast to Limerick to be severed within a year or two of its achievement? Rightly or wrongly, the decision was made to restore the Ulster Canal.

The canal was closed for eight years while major works were carried out and efforts were made to improve the supply of water to the summit and prevent seepage; the cost of the work was £22,000. By the time the canal was reopened in 1873, the Ballinamore and Ballyconnell Canal had proved a dismal failure and it soon became obvious that despite all the work, the water supply on the Ulster Canal was still very inadequate. In the first three years after its reopening the average annual income from tolls was £163 and the annual maintenance bill was over £1,000. In 1878 an inquiry into the affairs of the Board of Works heard evidence that the canal was navigable for only eight months of the year because of water shortage in the summer and that only forty boats had passed through it in the previous year, paying £68 in tolls. Spokesmen for the Board of Works made it clear that they would welcome the transfer of the canal to a private company and that any further government expenditure would be unjustified.

In 1882 the government set up a commission specifically to inquire into the Belfast-Limerick through route so that some decision could be made about the future of both the Ulster and the Ballinamore and Ballyconnell canals. This commission was told that traffic on the Ulster Canal had increased slightly with the establishment of W. R. Rea's Inland Carrying Company, with its specially built fleet of smaller light-ers; eighty-one boats had passed through and the income had risen to £87. It was estimated that it would take about £10,000 to put the canal into good repair with a depth of five feet at all times of the year. The importance of cheap water transport as a curb to railway rates was stressed and once again it was suggested by the Board of Works that a private company might like to take over the navigation. These hints were obviously aimed at the Lagan Navigation Company, of which Rea was secretary, and this time the company took the bait and entered into negotiations to take over the canal.

The Lagan Navigation Company's Millstone

It was perhaps understandable that this company wanted to see the link with the Erne maintained, and it was obvious that the Board of Works would soon abandon the canal if it was left in its control. It has already been shown that the Lagan company eventually agreed to accept the canal even though the clause allowing it to abandon it if it was uneconomic was deleted from the legislation. After six years of negotiations it was understandable that the directors should make this unwise concession out of a feeling of frustration and it had also been agreed that government assistance would be given to carry out the necessary works to improve the canal. Over the next few years £12,000 was spent, a little over one quarter of which was granted from public funds, but the problems in maintaining water levels persisted.

In the 1890s the average annual receipts from tolls rose to about £700, but this was still not enough to meet the cost of maintaining the canal. Profits made on the Lagan and Tyrone navigations were eaten up by the Ulster Canal, which became a millstone weighing down a company which otherwise might have been reasonably successful. Repeated efforts were made to rid itself of the encumbrance, but even when the Shuttleworth commission in 1906 recommended that the canal should be taken over by the government again, no action was taken. Refused permission to close the canal, the Lagan company just quietly allowed it to close itself and, when it became divided by the Border in 1921, neither government showed any interest in enforcing the company's statutory duty to maintain it. The last lighter entered the canal on 29 October 1929 and, after much legal wrangling and local opposition to its abandonment, it was finally closed officially in 1931 and some of the property sold off.

The Ballinamore and Ballyconnell Canal

'It is one of the most shameful pieces of mismanagement in any country' – hard words, spoken by one of the trustees of the navigation, J. G. V. Porter, before the Monck commission set up in 1880 to investigate the through route from Belfast to Limerick. It would be fairer to say that this navigation was as much the victim of circumstances as mismanagement.

Upper and Lower Lough Erne, like all the larger lakes in Ireland, were used extensively from early times as a trading route. It was always envisaged in the overall plan for an Irish waterway network that the

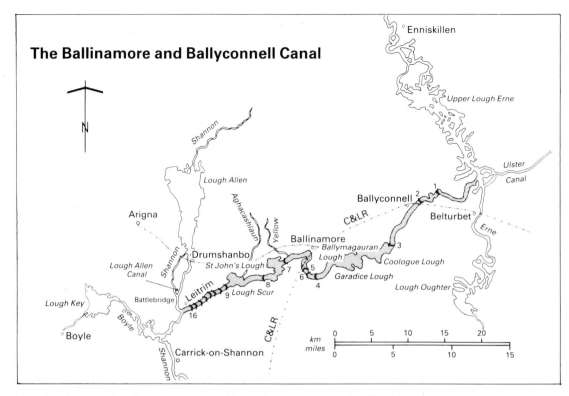

The Ballinamore and Ballyconnell Canal

three systems, the Shannon, the Erne and Lough Neagh should be linked together with access to the sea at Limerick, Ballyshannon, Belfast, Coleraine and Newry. A first step was taken in the 1780s to achieve the link between the Shannon and the Erne when a lock was constructed by Richard Evans at Carrowl on the Woodford river where the first obstruction to navigation occurred after leaving Lough Erne. This work was financed by a parliamentary grant of £1,000, but when no more money was forthcoming the work ceased. In 1790 a company was formed to link the Erne with the sea. This involved making the River Erne navigable from Belleek to Ballyshannon, which was a distance of only five miles but with a very steep fall. The Ballyshannon Company intended to avail of the debenture scheme for public works in operation at that time and it was allocated £5,100 in four per cent debentures to match the £10,200 which it intended to raise in subscriptions. Work began at Belleek on the first of the twelve locks that would be required but the scheme was abandoned through lack of support when just £2,059 had been expended.

William Chapman surveyed the Woodford river in 1793 and estimated that a navigation could be achieved into Garadice lough from the Erne for £5,000, from where an extension westwards to the Shannon would be possible, and in 1801 the Directors General asked Richard Evans for a new estimate for both navigations, the Woodford river and the Belleek to Ballyshannon schemes. Evans did produce an estimate of £48,000 but no action was taken and it was nearly forty years later before the Woodford river navigation was to be considered, while the making of a connection with the sea at Ballyshannon was never attempted again.

In 1838 the newly appointed Commissioners of Public Works were investigating schemes which would provide employment, and they instructed William Mulvany, a young engineer who had been engaged in ordnance work and was also engaged in survey work on the Shannon, to investigate possible routes for a navigation from the Erne to the Shannon. Now that work was in progress on the Ulster Canal, this would be the final link in the great through route from the north east to the south west of the country. It was not until 1842, when the commissioners were given wide powers to carry out schemes for the public good such as navigations, drainage and water power works, and pressure was exerted by the Ulster Canal Company, that a decision was made to proceed with the scheme. Local landowners were pressing for works to improve drainage in the area to prevent flooding, and John McMahon, one of the Board of Works engineers, was instructed to draw up plans for combined drainage and navigation works. He produced an estimate of just over £100,000 and work began in 1846.

The Link is Forged

There were a number of disadvantages to the concept of a combined drainage and navigation scheme. To begin with, in some instances there was a conflict in the works required and in the end neither proved satisfactory; if a still-water canal had been made for the entire distance and an independent drainage scheme carried out on the Erne and Woodford catchment area, it would have been much more practical from an engineering point of view. Another difficulty arose because the funds for the two schemes had to be allocated and accounted for independently and the work was sometimes held up because of delays in receiving money in one area or the other. Problems were also encountered with millers who had water rights and with owners of eel fishery rights.

Work continued through the 1850s and, ironically, some delays were reported because labourers could not be found in sufficient numbers; over 7,000 men had been employed initially but this number fell to about 2,500 and the shortage of manpower prolonged the time taken to finish the work. Steam dredgers were used to deepen the channel in the six lakes through which it had been decided to bring the navigation, and costly weirs were constructed at each of the locks on the Woodford river, where work was often impeded by floods. The last five miles from the summit level at Lough Scur down to the Shannon at Leitrim village involved turning the small Leitrim river into a canal with eight locks requiring a considerable amount of excavation. As work progressed it became obvious that the estimates were hopelessly wrong; by 1852 even a revised estimate of £127,276 for the combined drainage and navigation works had been exceeded by

Ballinamore and Ballyconnell Canal: 1st lock on the Woodford River near Ballyconnell

some £40,000 and the work was still far from complete. It was in that year that the Board of Works came under scrutiny for a general failure to keep within estimated costs, with W. T. Mulvany, who had been responsible for the plans and estimates for this scheme, becoming the scapegoat. Stringencies began to creep in. The original plan had envisaged a depth of 6ft (1.8m) throughout; this was abandoned for a depth of 4ft 6ins (1.4m), but even this was not actually achieved. On the other hand, towpaths which were very expensive to construct were made along the canal sections even though steam towage was established on the Shannon by this time and the fact that part of the navigation passed through lakes made horse towage impossible.

There is evidence that some boats began to pass through the navigation in the late 1850s and in June 1858 an official trip took place. The Ulster Canal Company made a lighter available which was loaded with goods for destinations on the upper Shannon and, on the return trip, coal for the steam dredgers working on Lough Garadice was brought from Lough Allen. J. B. Pratt, the Leitrim county surveyor, was authorised to use a screw steamer on the navigation in the same year, and a double bend in the river below Ballyconnell was widened 'to prevent accident to the fan of the screw steamer, which with the Board's permission, had been running between Carrick-on-Shannon and Belturbet since the previous month'. This suggests that Pratt was endeavouring to establish a service.

With work nearing completion, it was decided to set up navigation trustees elected from the adjoining counties with a second body of drainage trustees to look after the drainage aspects: dual control by conflicting interests. In 1859, with the navigation almost ready to be handed over, a dispute arose as to who was responsible for the sum of over £150,000 by which the estimates had been exceeded; the final total was £276,992, more than double the estimate, about one sixth of which related to drainage. The landowners who had benefited directly from the drainage works were responsible for a percentage of the cost and the rest was to be paid by the counties adjoining the navigation and the government in the same way as the Shannon navigation works had been financed. The counties disputed their liability to pay anything over their share of the original estimate and this claim was sympathetically received at a public inquiry. In the end the counties' contribution was assessed as £30,000 for the navigation works and the government paid the balance. The reasons given for this decision are interesting:

> The prospects of advantage, however, and of a remunerative return which the project was originally considered to hold out, have we believe, been materially interfered with and lessened by the altered circumstances of the country at large and the general extension of railways.

It should be pointed out that at this stage there was not as yet any direct competition from railways in the area, but the expansion of railways in the country had reduced the value of a waterway route from Belfast to Limerick. On 4 July 1860 the navigation was officially handed over to the twelve navigation trustees. The through route had at last been accomplished but the question now arose as to whether anyone would want to use it.

Within five months of the transfer J. P. Pratt, who had been appointed secretary and engineer to the trustees, prepared a report listing many deficiencies in the works. He said that in some places there was less than 3ft 6ins (1m) depth of water, some of the banks in the canal sections had caved in, water was leaking through the stonework of the locks and there were numerous other problems. The Board of Works refused to accept responsibility for putting right any of the defects and nothing was done about them. Whether this was because there was no traffic or whether trade failed to develop because the navigation was so unsatisfactory is debatable. By this time the Ulster Canal was also in a poor condition, trade on the upper Shannon was very limited and there appeared to be no incentive to develop the Lough Allen coal trade. The official records were subsequently reported to have shown that only eight boats passed through the navigation from 1860 to 1869, paying a total of £18 in tolls – a poor return for a waterway which had cost nearly a quarter of a million pounds. Other boats may have used the navigation without paying tolls and there is evidence that some private boats passed through.

Information about the so-called working years and subsequent decline of the navigation can be gleaned from the evidence heard before two inquiries. The first of these was the Crighton Committee of Inquiry into the activities of the Board of Works in 1878 and the second was the Monck commission which was set up as a direct result of the earlier inquiry specifically to investigate the through route from Belfast to Limerick. Pratt explained that he had done his best to keep the navigation operational until 1865 but because there was no traffic there seemed little point in maintaining it after that time. J. G. V. Porter, who was a trustee for a period and who had fought hard to try to have the navigation maintained, related his experience when bringing a steamer, the *Knockninny*, through from the Shannon to Lough Erne in 1868:

> . . . only through the kindness of the people and Mr Pratt, the engineer, was I able to get through the canal. They took the greatest trouble to get the water from one reach to another to float me down. But my coming through is no proof for it took me three weeks to get through.

One of the last boats known to have made the passage through the navigation was the *Audax*, a yacht owned by W. R. Potts.

In 1887 the Cavan and Leitrim Railway Company's line, which ran from Dromod on the MGWR Dublin-Sligo line, to Belturbet on the GNR's Belfast line, was opened. A tramway extension from Ballinamore to Arigna was opened in the following year but the final extension to the mines was not opened until 1920. The railway thus served the same area as the navigation but the fact that the navigation was well and truly disused by the 1880s is indicated by the action of the railway company in placing low bridges across the channel confident that it would never be asked to raise them. It is perhaps worth noting that the railway was not a great success and became a heavy burden on the local ratepayers.

The Shuttleworth commission looked into the whole question of the navigation in some detail in 1906 and suggested that steps should be taken to repair the upper gates of the locks to prevent water gushing through and damaging the masonry in case the navigation was ever restored in the future. Funds were not forthcoming for this work and the navigation trustees did little, except for minor repairs to bridges to satisfy landowners and the local authorities. The navigation trustees ceased to function after 1948, and the local authorities were obliged to take over responsibility for the bridges. Flooding continued to be a problem, and local farmers have always considered that restoring the navigation would compound these problems.

In recent years this waterway came into the news again when its restoration as a cross-border scheme was considered. The Board of Works has carried out a detailed survey, and the cost of restoration, according to a recent report by the Regional and Development Section of the Economic and Social Committee of the EEC, would be about IR£3.5 million. This committee recommended the use of community funds to restore the navigation as a 'priority project', and added that it saw no conflict on any scale between the project and arterial drainage plans for the Erne catchment area; it was suggested that the work should be carried out independently of drainage but fitting in with subsequent drainage proposals. This suggestion that the restoration should proceed in advance of drainage works was welcomed by the IWAI. The growth in pleasure boat activity on both the Shannon and the Erne in recent years has given a new sense of purpose to this unwanted waterway and there is no doubt that the linking of the two systems would give Ireland a cruising waterway unrivalled in the world.

The Erne Navigation

It has already been shown that efforts to provide access to the sea through Ballyshannon and a link with the Shannon by way of the Woodford river in the 1780s and 1790s were singularly unsuccessful but, although isolated, the two lakes connected by the River Erne through Enniskillen had at all times provided a natural waterway forty miles long from Belleek to Belturbet, covering over forty square miles of water. In the early days flat bottomed cotts, some as long as 55ft (16.7m), had been sailed and rowed on the lakes and the lakes had also been the scene of naval battles in Viking times. There is evidence of pleasure boating on the lakes in the eighteenth century. William Henry, writing in 1739, described 'pleasuring yachts and other boats' lying at anchor at Belturbet and he said, 'it is usual for company who have been pleasuring on the lough to retire for their entertainments' to Knockninny. The Lough Erne Yacht Club was founded in 1820 and many of the families living around the shores had boats which competed in regattas; Lord Ely had a 'smart little yacht – a sort of half-decked vessel – and a large well built barge or cutter for rowing'. John Barrow, an English visitor, described the traffic he saw on the lakes in the 1830s:

> Cotts – like our coal-barges on the Thames, square at each end, flat bot-
> tomed, drawing little water, and rigged with one large gaff sail; and seldome

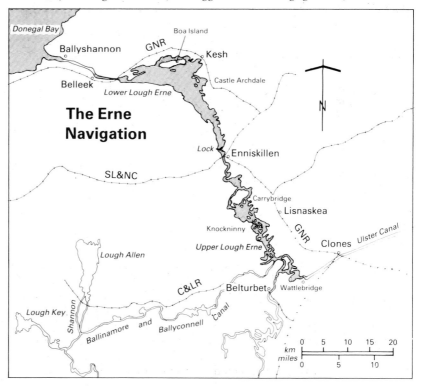

exceed the burden of ten or twelve tons. The natives who manage them are miserable sailors, who, with the least breeze that blows may be seen skulking under the lee of one of the islands. Their chief employment is carrying turf from the bogs near the shores of the lake to Enniskillen, stones and sand for building, and slates and coal from Belleek which have been imported at Ballyshannon.

In his book, Barrow quotes a letter written by Lieutenant Beechey to his brother when he was on board the cutter *Eagle* surveying the lakes with Lieutenant Wolfe in 1835. The *Eagle* had been carrying out survey work off the north-west coast and had been brought from Bally-shannon to Belleek by road 'with no small difficulty'. They were caught in a sudden storm and the letter to his brother is headed: 'Eagle – hard and fast, bumping on a lee shore off Roe *(sic)* Island'. Beechey wrote that he did not consider their lives were in danger but that he was writing the letter to keep his mind off their predicament:

> Wolfe is very anxious about the work and the instruments, of course, and they are all in readiness for the first chance. We came on shore dragging two anchors at 2 o'clock yesterday afternoon, blowing a perfect hurricane, the surface of the water being carried up like smoke. The rain came down in torrents, and, wet through, we were obliged to sit up all night. The old craft jumps about so I cannot write no longer.

A postscript records that they managed to get the boat off the rocks the following morning. There is an 'Eagle Point' close to Boa Island on the charts which they prepared and this more than likely was so named by them to mark the scene of their ordeal. Beechey and Wolfe also carried out surveys of loughs Ree, Derg and Corrib for the Admiralty at this time and their charts are still used today as useful aids to navigation; it is suggested that the area in the vicinity of Portlick Castle on Lough Ree was surveyed in greater detail than elsewhere because Beechey was courting the daughter of the house, Miss Smythe, whom he subsequently married; he later became a notable marine painter. In notes accompanying the charts, Wolfe records that he was told that the Lough Erne water was supposed to have affected the health of a regiment quartered in Enniskillen and he also mentions an interesting fact about the level of the lakes:

> In many places within the memory of the present inhabitants, the shores had lost eighteen or twenty feet and islets are now completely underwater in the winter on which once stood private stills for the manufacture of Potyeen or contraband whiskey.

A few years later, in 1841, the Ulster Canal was completed and the lakes were linked with the Ulster waterways network. In the following year William Dargan brought a wooden paddle steamer, *Countess of Erne,* through the canal to Lough Erne. Her first trip to Enniskillen took two days because she ran aground near Lisnaskea. Undismayed, Dargan entertained his distinguished guests aboard until the small hours and she ultimately reached Enniskillen at 1.00 p.m. on the next day, Christmas Eve, to be greeted by a cheering crowd. For the next seventeen years she operated on the lakes, towing boats between the canal and Enniskillen. She carried some passengers, but her principal role was to facilitate the carrying trade on the canal. Dargan operated two other steamers on the lakes, the *Shamrock*, a steam driven boat with twin screws on her bow, and the *Countess of Milan*, a paddle steamer built on the shores of the lower lake in 1855; she was too deep a draft to reach Enniskillen and operated between Belleek and Portora Narrows downstream of the town. A large steamer, the *PS Devenish*, arrived in 1862. She was built in Scotland, dismantled and reassembled at Enniskillen. She was 131ft (39.9m) long and plied around the lower lake carrying passengers, freight and cattle, but her owners went into liquidation and she left the lakes for Bangor, Co. Down; it is not recorded how they got her there.

The *SS Knockninny* arrived via the Ballinamore and Ballyconnell Canal from the Shannon in 1868 after her epic journey through that waterway. Porter established a steamship company and tried to operate her in conjunction with the railway from Cavan; passengers travelled by boat from Enniskillen to Belturbet and by road to Cavan. This was part of Porter's private vendetta against the MGWR, whose direct rail fare from Enniskillen to Dublin was undercut by Porter with the offer of a single fare of 8s 6d. Not surprisingly, this was not very successful but she continued to operate on the lakes as an excursion boat and he opened a hotel at Knockninny, bringing guests there by water from Enniskillen. The tourist trade did not develop but he continued to operate the *Knockninny* and a second boat, the *Belturbet*, until his death in 1903; the *Belturbet* was later acquired by the Lough Erne Yacht Club as a temporary clubhouse.

Another steamer on the lake was the *Rossclare*, renamed the *Lady of the Lake*. She operated a service from Enniskillen to the northern end of the lake in conjunction with the railway from Bundoran up to 1914. A single fare cost 2s saloon and 1s steerage, with family season tickets for £1; these were popular with local families who were put ashore on islands for picnic parties and picked up again in the evening. She was eventually acquired by a local family and renamed the *Pandora*. During the 1921-3 disturbances she was requisitioned by the government, painted battleship grey and used to preserve law and order; nicknamed 'The Ulster Navy' she took part in such affrays as 'The Siege of Pettigo' and 'The Battle of Belleek'.

Some efforts had been made in the 1840s to come to grips with the problem of flooding, without much success. Between 1881 and 1890 a combined drainage and navigation scheme was carried out which aimed to control flooding and guarantee a 6ft (1.8m) depth from Belleek to Belturbet. However, an inquiry into arterial drainage in 1907 heard evidence that the lakes were not being kept at the statutory levels. By this time traffic had fallen to a low ebb and there were no services at all on the lakes from 1915 to 1930. In that year, a large motor launch, the *Enniskillen*, was brought by rail to Enniskillen and launched into the river, but there was no demand for a regular service

and she was used instead for occasional excursions. She in turn became the 'Ulster Navy' during the 1939-45 war and it is recorded that she sank one day during gunnery practice. The *ML Endeavour,* built locally, was used to service flying boats during the war and afterwards became a passenger launch operating excursion trips.

In 1957 a cross-border hydro-electric scheme was introduced and a barrage and lock were constructed downstream of Enniskillen so that the level of the upper lake could be controlled for the power station at Ballyshannon. Today the tourist potential of the lakes has

Erne Navigation: the PS Lady of the Lake at Portora near Enniskillen about 1905

Erne Navigation: a quiet anchorage at White Island on Lower Lough Erne

been realised, facilities around the lake have been improved, a hire fleet, carefully tailored to these facilities, has been developed and considerable use is made of the lakes for water-based leisure activities.

Upper and Lower Bann and Lough Neagh Navigation

Lough Neagh is the largest freshwater lake in the British Isles, but it is very shallow and its capacity to absorb sudden floodwaters is therefore limited. There are six major rivers feeding into it but only one outlet, the Lower Bann, which enters the sea at Coleraine. It was inevitable that flooding should have always been a problem, and even in the mid-1700s people were looking for ways to improve the run-off to the sea. One of the principal obstructions was a great shoal of rock at Portna on the Lower Bann, about halfway between the lake and the sea. The Bishop of Down and Connor, Francis Hutchinson, suggested to the Irish parliament in 1738 that something should be done about removing the shoals and he referred to the annual flooding:

> Ballyscullen Church was not only encompassed by the floods but a great part of the parish had been drowned, those great tracts of rich land, once adorned with trees, were covered and a fisherman, having twice removed his habitation, was about to do so again, complaining that he knew not where to place it, for the Bann followed him.

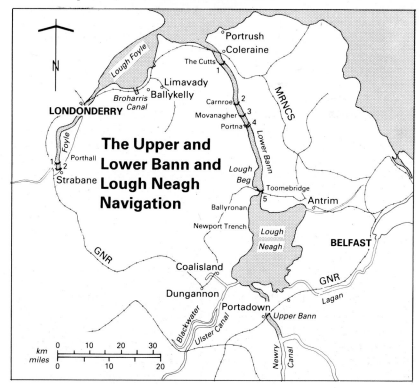

Parliament made an encouraging response but nothing was actually done apart from some works in the river up to Antrim in the 1760s. In 1822 Alexander Nimmo came up with an ingenious idea to solve the problem. He suggested lowering the summit level of the Newry Canal to below the level of Lough Neagh, doing away with all the locks and using the canal as a second outfall to the sea. Not only would this reduce the flooding problem but it would overcome the shortage of water supplies of that canal, eliminate all lock maintenance and produce an estimated 3,000 horsepower flow of water at Newry to generate power from the 45 ft (13.7m) fall. However, it was too ambitious and uncertain a scheme to win support, and it is interesting to surmise whether it would have succeeded.

In 1842 a special Act was passed enabling the Board of Works to carry out schemes to improve navigation, drainage and mill-power in the Lough Neagh basin. At the same time public meetings were held and James McCleery, engineer and secretary to the Lagan Navigation Company, who operated his own steamer company on the lake, assisted an English engineer, Francis Giles, to carry out a survey. Eventually, in 1846, the Board of Works instructed its own engineer, John McMahon, to carry out a detailed survey and estimate the costs. He produced a plan which would make the Lower Bann navigable from Lough Neagh to the sea and at the same time would remove the obstructions in that river, thereby reducing the level of Lough Neagh to about 6ft (1.8m) below its normal level. He estimated that the scheme would cost £183,775, less than half of which would be attributable to the navigation works and the rest to the drainage works. The plan was approved and work began in 1847.

Drainage and Navigation Works

Reducing the level of Lough Neagh meant that works had to be carried out where the Lagan, Coalisland and Ulster canals entered the system. The last lock on each of the navigations had to have the cill lowered and new deep gates made; the Maghery Cut, at the entrance to the River Blackwater, where both the Coalisland and Ulster canals entered the lake, had to be deepened and widened and the channel up the river dredged. The first difficulty that the engineer in charge of the works, Charles Ottley, encountered was a shortage of labour; famine and emigration had reduced the numbers seeking employment and railway construction works were now competing for the available workforce. The works continued for the next eleven years: on the Lower Bann a lock was made at Toomebridge, the extensive rocky shoal was removed at Portna and a double-chambered lock made here for the navigation, three more locks were needed to complete access to the tidal waters at Coleraine, and swing bridges had to be installed and quays built at a number of places. Quays were also built at Antrim and other places around Lough Neagh to suit the new level of the lake, which it was now hoped would remain constant. The final cost of the works was nearly £50,000 more than the original estimate and once again the government was asked to make up this shortfall because the counties claimed that they were responsible for only half the original estimate.

When the works were completed they were transferred to three separate bodies, the Upper Bann Navigation Trust, the Lower Bann Navigation Trust and the Lough Neagh Drainage Trust, appointed and financed by the adjoining counties. This altered completely the original concept that the works would be administered as a single entity with the income from tolls and water power on the Lower Bann subsidising the Upper Bann maintenance works. Instead, the counties to the south of the lake found themselves having to finance not only the original levy for the drainage and navigation works just completed but a steep annual expenditure of about £800 per annum, with no income to meet this. Despite the expansion of Coleraine as a port at the expense of Portrush, the Lower Bann revenue failed to come up to expectations and even here the counties had to face an annual deficit of about £400 instead of the profit which was supposed to offset the original outlay. The cost effectiveness of the whole scheme was therefore very dubious and, although there was some reduction in flooding, the fact that it was a combined drainage and navigation scheme made it fall between two stools, with neither interest satisfied. For example,

Upper Bann: the quays at Portadown about 1910

the greatly increased flow in the Lower Bann made navigation difficult and the *Kitty of Coleraine*, which operated a passenger and goods service between Coleraine and Toomebridge from 1863, eventually gave up the unequal struggle against the current. Even when a more powerful boat was tried she was found to draw too much and was equally unsuccessful.

Lough Neagh Steamers

The usual flatbottomed sailing cotts had been used on the lake from early times and Turgesius had hauled his boats over the shallows in the Lower Bann to reach the lake in the mid-ninth century, but it was not until the Newry and then the Tyrone and Lagan navigation were completed that larger boats found their way on to its waters. At first these were sailed or poled, as on the Shannon lakes, but in 1821 the enterprising James McCleery of the Lagan Navigation Company built a wooden paddle steamer, the *Marchioness of Donegall,* for service on the lake. For the next twenty years she was to tow lighters to and from the Lagan Navigation to various places on the lake. It was suggested that a passenger service should be introduced, but it would have been expensive to operate, and the idea was not pursued. It was left to William Dargan, then completing the Ulster Canal, to commission an iron paddle-steamer, the *Countess of Caledon,* to establish a passenger service. When the railway reached Portadown from Belfast in 1842, he operated a feeder service for passengers. In the same year David Gaussen, a local businessman, commissioned another steamer, *Lady of the Lake,* to operate a service from Ballyronan on the west shore to Portadown; a through ticket by boat and rail to Belfast was only 3*s* saloon and 2*s* steerage and third class on the train. Within a few months Dargan had bought him out and he replaced this boat with the *PS Grand Junction.* It is said that the captain used to signal the number of passengers on board who would be requiring conveyances to go to fairs in Co. Armagh to a look-out man on the roof of Lurgan church. When Dargan retired in 1857 the passenger services ceased and the only steamers operating on the lake in the second half of the century were three steam tugs, the *Shamrock, Primrose* and *Sunbeam.* These tugs sometimes took out excursion parties, and in the 1850s a lady passenger was killed when she went below to the *Shamrock*'s engine room to dry out and her clothes became entangled in the machinery.

Drainage versus Navigation

The Monck commission in the early 1880s and the commission set up in 1887 to inquire into the Board of Works both recommended that the Lower Bann navigation works should be abandoned so that the flow of water from the catchment could be increased to alleviate flooding; they were also very critical of the division of responsibility into three authorities. These recommendations were ignored, as was the advice of Sir Alexander Binnie, President of the Institute of Civil Engineers, who was asked by the government for his views in 1906. He repeated the advice that the navigation would have to be abandoned if drainage was to improve and he drew attention to the very limited amount of traffic using the Lower Bann:

> Putting all other matters on one side and regarding it as a canal for economical traffic, it violates the first principles of canal engineering, for the whole economy of inland navigation is the maintenance of still water ponds between the different locks along which the navigation can be handled at a low cost. In the case of the Bann Navigation, however, we have a canalised river down which passes, against any upward traffic in the winter months, floods at the rate of 400,000 to 800,000 cubic feet per minute. It is therefore not surprising to me that the navigation has not proved a commercial success.

Despite a strong lobby from local landowners who were greatly troubled by flooding, the Shuttleworth commission was reluctant to recommend the abandonment of navigation works so recently completed. It was suggested that alleviating flooding was a high priority but no suggestions were made as to how this was to be accomplished. No action was taken and the counties continued to meet the annual deficits amid increasing complaints from the traders using the navigation of long delays caused by shallows in the river.

In 1925 a proposal to generate electricity from the Lower Bann threatened the navigation, but the plan did not materialise. The Lower Bann Navigation Trust and the Lough Neagh Drainage Trust were abolished in 1929 and responsibility was transferred to the Ministry of Finance but, despite appeals from the Upper Bann counties, this trust was continued and they were forced to meet the annual bill. Limited works were carried out under the Ministry to try to improve drainage, and sluices were installed on some of the Lower Bann weirs so that greater control could be exercised over levels. There was still a limited amount of traffic, which was mostly in sand dredged from the lake for brickworks; this was carried in some of the former Guinness barges which had operated on the Liffey in Dublin between the brewery and the docks. Finally, the Upper Bann Trust was abolished, the navigation was transferred to the Ministry of Commerce and, together with the Tyrone and upper Lagan navigations, it was officially abandoned in 1954.

Several attempts to re-introduce passenger services on Lough Neagh in the early 1900s and again in the 1920s were not successful. A similar attempt in 1965-6 with three motor launches was equally unsuccessful. Today there is considerable activity on the lake with pleasure boating, and the Lower Bann is enjoying much greater use, justifying the decision to retain this navigation when traffic was at a low ebb.

The Corrib Navigation and Cong Canal

Like the Erne, Lough Corrib was used from early times as an important trading route. Here in 1178 a very early piece of canal engineering took place. The friars of Claregalway Abbey became tired of the long detour they had to make to the entrance to the river and they sought permission from the Blakes of Menlo to make an artificial cut through an island to shorten the journey. In time, the Friar's Cut became the main navigation channel and was later widened. Although the cut had made access from the lake to the city of Galway easier, it had not solved the problem of linking the lake with the sea. An unsuccessful attempt was made to achieve this through Lough Athalia to the east of the city in the fifteenth century. Again, in 1715, the Act authorising navigation schemes throughout the country specified an ambitious plan to open a waterway from the sea at Galway through loughs Corrib, Mask and Moy to Killala, but nothing more was heard of this scheme.

In the 1820s Alexander Nimmo drew up plans for a floating basin and a canal to the east of the city. The basin was made in 1830 to an amended design by John Killaly but the canal linking it to the lake was not implemented. Further plans were put forward in the 1830s, but it was not until after the 1842 Act, which authorised the Board of Works to carry out drainage and navigation works, that local land-

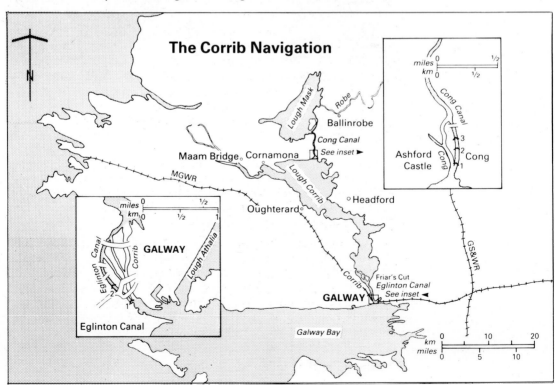

owners began to press strongly for a scheme to be put in hand. At that time there were said to be some 110 boats operating on the lake of from five to eight tons. The Commissioners of Public Works agreed to carry out the works because of the benefits it would bring to a very depressed part of the country, and plans were drawn up. At this stage a company called the Corrib Improvement Company claimed that use had been made of plans which it had drawn up some years earlier but, eventually, this company agreed to accept a sum in compensation and by 1848 the way was clear for work to begin.

Access to the Sea at Last

This time the line of the canal was laid to the west of the city and the work was carried out under the engineer John McMahon. A canal about three quarters of a mile long was made with two locks, and on

Corrib Navigation: the opening of the Eglinton Canal by the Lord Lieutenant in 1852 portrayed in the Illustrated London News

28 August 1852 it was officially opened by the Earl of Eglinton and named the Eglinton Canal in his honour. The event was recorded by the *Illustrated London News* with a fine drawing of the scene as the Lord Lieutenant and his lady were borne aboard the paddle-steamer *O'Connell* through the large sea lock:

> A portion of the route from the landing pier to the basin wherein this tiny craft lay, chanced to be the fish market; and through this not very oderifer-ous locale their Excellencies had to be driven – nay, even to walk a portion. . . . Having gone on board the *O'Connell,* amidst the sounds of music and cheers of the people, deputations and addresses were presented from the Claddagh, as also from the other societies connected with that side of the town. . . the steamer entered the dock for the first time amidst the cheers of thousands.

In the years that followed a number of steamers operated on the lake carrying freight and passengers. In the 1850s and 1860s the *O'Connell* was joined by the *PS Enterprise*, the *PS Father Daly*, named after her originator, the *PS Lioness*, which could accommodate 100 passengers, and the *PS Lady Eglinton*, which was 116ft (35.3m) long with a 16ft (4.9m) beam. The *Lady Eglinton* operated a daily service between Cong, at the northern end of the lake, and Galway, calling at Kilbeg en route; the fare was 3s saloon and 1s 6d for deck passengers. A visitor, Mr J. Gray, described a trip he made in her in the 1880s from Cong to Galway:

> The journey takes about three hours; the little steamer *Eglinton* having to twist and twine her way warily through between those many shoals and shallows that intercept a long part of her course, and which render the navigation of this lake one of extreme difficulty.

An obelisk on the north shore of the lake records that Arthur Guinness, Lord Ardilaun, subsidised the service for twenty-four years 'at great expense. . . for the benefit of the district until the opening of the railway between Claremorris and Ballinrobe in 1892'. She moved to the Shannon Estuary in 1896 but, despite railway competition, a new steamer service was started with the screw steamer *St Patrick* which was built in Galway. There were others, the *Widgeon* and the Shannon Development Company's *Fairy Queen* and *Countess of Cadogan*, which were brought around the coast from the Shannon in 1906 and 1913 respectively. The *Fairy Queen* was a popular excursion boat; meals were served aboard and music was laid on. One passenger told of one such excursion: 'Mr Williams rendered some capital songs during the trip and as the boat neared home, about 10.00 p.m. lusty cheers were sent up for the promoters of the splendid day's outing'. The demand for a service declined, however, and it did not recommence after the 1914-18 war.

The Cong Canal

Work had begun in 1848 on a canal to link Lough Corrib and Lough Mask at the same time as the Eglinton Canal was under construction. Known as the Cong Canal, it is generally described as a great engineering fiasco but, in fact, it would be more accurate to say that its failure was due to a number of reasons. Annual reports were presented by the Board of Works detailing the progress. In the first report the engineer, Samuel Roberts, explained that the workmen were paid 'by task' instead of a daily wage, and he remarked on how little they seemed to be able to earn – some as little as 3d per day: 'I have never witnessed more want of power of exertion among the labouring classes in this part of the country when the work began'. Gradually they did learn to increase their earnings:

> Generally speaking, however, the men are greatly improved in habits of industry, and, of course, in the amounts of their earnings; but the greater portion of them are so perfectly destitute and so wretchedly fed, that it would be impossible to enable them to realise a rate of wages calculated

to support them in a proper manner without paying prices which the economical execution of the work would not permit.

Work went on through the summer months over the next five years on the excavation of the canal and, in the time of the winter floods, the stone work for the locks and bridges was prepared. In 1851 Roberts reported optimistically:

> The lower beds of rock throughout the greater portion of the cutting have turned out of a less cavernous nature than was anticipated and will considerably lessen the difficulty and risk of staunching the canal.

He had completed all three miles of excavation work and two of the three locks when he received instructions from Dublin which must have been very disheartening:

> The masonry in the Cong lock was commenced in March (1854), and was progressing rapidly when I received instructions from the Board, in April, to suspend the execution of all navigation works in this division of the district, and complete only such as were necessary for the regulation of the waters of Lough Mask, for drainage purposes.

It would seem that this decision to abandon the navigation works was made following the findings of a Special Inquiry. This inquiry put forward three main reasons for the recommendation: firstly, the rapid expansion of railways into the west made it unlikely that a navigable link between Lough Corrib and Mask would be profitable; secondly, the strata encountered, which it was anticipated would make it difficult to staunch the canal; thirdly, works which had been started to create employment were now finding it difficult to attract workers, and this had led to demands for increased wages. It was obvious that it was going to be much more expensive to complete the navigation than originally estimated, and public disquiet about overspending by the Board of Works in the early 1850s must have been a factor in the decision to abandon the works. In fact, the amount expended on the navigation up to the time work was suspended was about £40,000. McMahon's original estimate had been £48,178 but this was later reduced to £30,000. In the circumstances, railway competition alone was a sound reason for halting the expenditure of public money on a venture which had limited economic usefulness. We can only conjecture whether there would have been insuperable problems in staunching the canal, but it was these engineering difficulties which were to receive much greater emphasis in public comment in the 1860s. Sir William Wilde in his book about the Corrib, published in 1868, branded it as 'the great canal at Cong (which) would not hold water'. In the same year the report of the Select Committee on the Connaught Lakes said:

> The Cong Canal was one of the follies of the Board of Works and was afterwards abandoned and sold to Lord Ardilaun. The nature of the rock being cavernous limestone it was found impossible to staunch it.

There is no doubt that swallow holes in the limestone were encountered along the line of the canal and that a route further to the west would have been preferable, but it is equally clear that the works were abandoned before it was put to the test. It seems unjust that it should have been condemned as an engineering disaster based on the supposition that it could not have been made to hold water.

The Corrib Today

Maurice Semple, local historian and lover of Lough Corrib, has set out in his three books (*see* Bibliography) the full story of the lake and its two canals. In 1954 he fought a lone battle to try to prevent the opening bridges over the Eglinton Canal being replaced by fixed structures. His appeal to the recently formed IWAI for support in his campaign went unanswered, and low bridges were installed, severing the link between the lake and the sea. Today, with pleasure craft on the lake increasing rapidly, the people of Galway can see the folly of this action. The Corrib Navigation Trustees have at last been galvanised into action to maintain the navigation but it would be far from easy to restore the Eglinton Canal and it is sad that boating enthusiasts cannot pass freely between Galway Bay and the lake.

Lough Gill

The fast flowing Garavogue river through Sligo seems to have deterred any attempt to make Lough Gill accessible from the sea. Surveys were carried out, however, in the early 1800s to establish a link between Lough Gill and Lough Allen. Nothing came of this but the scheme was revived in 1825, following the completion of the Lough Allen Canal, and found to require such heavy lockage that it was not proceeded with. In 1846 legislation was passed authorising a private company, the Sligo and Shannon Railway Company, to construct a ship canal through Sligo to Lough Gill which would enable coasters to reach Dromahaire on the Bonet river. From there it was planned to make a railway connection with the Shannon Navigation at Lough Allen. None of this was achieved, and the company was wound up in 1849.

Despite the lack of access from the sea, steamer services started operating on the lake in 1843. The *PS Lady of the Lake* was built in Scotland and came around the coast to Sligo. This twenty-ton boat was then brought upstream somehow, possibly by being partly dismantled to lighten her. She operated a service between Sligo and Dromahaire which took one hour; from there a horse car took passengers to and from Carrick-on-Shannon. Traffic declined in the 1860s and the service was reduced. In 1873 a much larger boat, the *PS Maid of Breffni*, was built for service on the lake. She could accommodate 300 passengers and was mostly used for excursions; she was also used for carrying corn to the mill at Dromahaire. It is said that it was originally intended to call her *Lady of the Lake* after her predecessor but that one of the people involved in the commissioning was warned by the spirit 'Lady of the Lake' not to use her name. The warning was heeded, but she was not to be a lucky ship and she was wrecked in 1885. A motor boat service was operated in the 1920s and today the *MV Queen Maeve* takes passengers for trips on the lake around W. B. Yeats's 'Lake Isle of Innisfree'.

The Tralee Ship Canal

This canal, one and a half miles long with a spacious basin, was constructed to enable shipping to reach the town of Tralee. In 1828 local commissioners had been authorised to obtain a loan of £24,000 from the Exchequer Loan Commissioners to build the canal with the repayments guaranteed by charges on imports and exports to the town. The scheme envisaged a canal supplied by water from local springs with a lock at the entrance but after work had begun it was decided that the water supply was insufficient and it would be better to make it a tidal canal with a single pair of gates to retain the water between tides. Henry Inglis, an English traveller, viewed the works which had begun in 1832 and remarked:

> The canal, indeed, employs many: but the wages are extremely low; and in this rainy climate, it often happens that the labourers, after working in the canal from five in the morning until eleven in the forenoon, are discharged for the day with the pittance of 2*d.*

About four hundred men were employed but the money ran out before the canal could be completed. When an application for a further loan was made, the Treasury commissioners recommended that the work should be taken over by the Board of Works. This was done, work recommenced and in 1844 a memorial was sent to the government by local interests seeking additional funds to revert to the original plan to make a lock at the entrance. It was pointed out that local springs had exceeded expectations and that an impounded canal would be much more beneficial, retaining a fixed water level in the basin for shipping while boats were locked in and out. The additional loan was authorised, the lock was built and the canal was opened in April 1846.

The *Kerry Examiner* described the scene as the schooner *Defiance of Milford* became the first vessel to enter the canal, followed by a number of other boats:

> The vessels were decorated with flags, boats plying up and down where they had never plied before, the enlivening strains of excellent bands of the Square and Castle Street Temperance Rooms, the unusual bustle and wandering crowds all contributed to produce an effect pleasing and gratifying, perfectly harmonizing with the novelty of the scene and the importance of the occasion.

For the next forty years considerable use was made of the canal. In the 1840s emigrant ships sailed from Tralee to return with meal from America. The Limerick Steam Ship Company called regularly to Tralee Bay en route from Limerick to Liverpool and London; the vessels

Tralee Canal: the basin at Tralee in about 1910

anchored off Fenit on the north shore of the bay and passengers and goods were brought by lighter from Tralee. In time the canal began to silt up, reducing the draft of the boats that could be accommodated, and it became the pattern more and more for lighters to be used between Tralee and waiting ships at Fenit. In 1880 the Tralee and Fenit Harbour commissioners were amalgamated and a deep water quay was constructed at Fenit with a railhead. The canal was used less and less and was finally closed in the early 1930s. In 1945 the local council commissioned an environmental plan for the town including the canal area. In it it was suggested that the lockgates should be replaced and the canal restored as a water amenity area. No action was taken and the present owners, Murphy and O'Shea, building contractors, filled in the basin and some of the canal. Fresh moves are now being made to have the lock restored to create a marina but the fixed bridge at Blenerville would confine boats to the seaward end of the canal.

Belmullet Canal

This canal, about a quarter of a mile long, was opened in the 1880s at Belmullet across the neck of the Mullet peninsula to enable vessels to pass from Blacksod Bay to Broad Haven, avoiding the stormy Atlantic seas. The floor and sides of the canal are lined with granite and it is spanned by a single bridge which last opened about twenty years ago. Despite protests from fishermen and local interests, the new replacement bridge is to be a fixed structure bridge because of the high costs of installing an opening span. Half-deckers, up to 35ft (10.6m), still use the canal, which provides a safe inside route from Clifden to Donegal Bay via the Achill passage. The clearance at the new bridge will be about 16ft (4.8m) at high water neaps when there is a depth of about 7-8ft (2.1–2.4m) in the canal.

10
Conclusion: The Waterways Today and in the Future

The late Harry Rice (top) and Vincent Delany, co-founders of the IWAI, and Ian Bath (bottom) who refused to let the Royal Canal die

THE first half of the twentieth century were not good years for the waterways in Ireland, particularly for those in the north of the country. The tide began to turn slowly but for some the change was to come too late and for the rest it has been a close call.

The strangulation of the Shannon was averted in 1955 by the arrival of the CIE passenger launches, and in the following year Colonel Harry Rice, who together with Vincent Delany had spearheaded the setting up of the IWAI, led a group of boats up the Shannon from Athlone to Lough Key to demonstrate the river's leisure potential. The number of private boats increased in the years that followed, and some small hire firms started operations, but when CIE withdrew their trade boats in 1960 almost all commercial traffic on the river ceased. In 1961 seventy boats assembled for the first official Shannon Boat Rally, which has been an annual event since then. Bord Fáilte, the tourist board, commissioned a study of the river to investigate its potential as a tourist amenity and in 1963 £140,000 was allocated to improve facilities and encourage the setting up of hire fleets. The decision of Messrs Arthur Guinness to enter the hire boat business was a considerable boost, setting very high standards. Within a remarkably short time the Shannon became a major tourist attraction, confounding the earlier critics. In recent years mooring facilities have been greatly improved and the Lough Allen Canal was reopened to Acres lake in 1978. The IWAI finds itself adopting a new role as a watchdog, trying to ensure that the unique quality of the river is preserved.

In the meantime, the Circular Line of the Grand Canal had come under severe threat of closure. In 1963 Dublin Corporation revealed plans to use the bed of the canal for a surface water sewer, with the intention of concreting it in and making it into a high speed roadway. Traffic had reached its lowest ever ebb on the canal and the severing of the link with the sea was considered of little significance by the corporation. Legislation was required to carry out the scheme, and over the next few years the IWAI carried out an intensive campaign to 'Save the City Line', taking to the steets to picket the City Hall at a time when this form of protest was relatively unknown in Ireland. The citizens of Dublin rallied to protect their canal and in 1969 the corporation bowed to pressure and agreed to place the sewer in a tunnel. Today, the city end of the canal is still not used very much because of the absence of safe moorings but there is considerable

Shannon Navigation: boats passing through Clarendon lock, Knockvicar on an early Shannon Rally

activity on the rest of the canal and there is one firm, Celtic Canal Cruisers, offering boats for hire near Tullamore.

The new wave of activity had come too late to save the Ballinasloe Line, which was officially closed to navigation in 1961; part of the canal has now disappeared in bog workings, and a light railway carrying turf to the nearby power station runs along part of its route; in any event a more practical way to make a navigation to Ballinasloe today would be to use the River Suck. The Mountmellick Line was closed in 1960 after ten years of little or no use, and parts of it around Portarlington are now a roadway. The Kilbeggan Line was closed in 1961, a dam was placed across the entrance and it was allowed to dry out, but there are no major obstacles in the way of restoring this canal. The Naas Line, closed to navigation in 1961, is currently being restored to the harbour in Naas and the prospects of opening up the rest of this canal to Corbally have been greatly improved since the new by-pass has taken much of the traffic from the former trunk road, which crosses the canal by a culverted bridge.

In 1978 the government announced that the Grand Canal, Royal Canal and Barrow Navigation were to be transferred from CIE to the Office of Public Works, the body already administering the Shannon Navigation. Six years on, this has still not been achieved but the legislation is currently before the Senate and Dáil. In recent years the canal section of CIE has done a fine job with limited funds and manpower to maintain the Grand Canal and Barrow Navigation, although the latter continues to be bedevilled by the same defects of silting and lack of water in summer. The tidal stretches of the Barrow, Nore and Suir are also increasingly used by pleasure craft today, as indeed are all the tidal waters around the coast.

Grand Canal, Naas Line: a group of IWAI members prepare the upper cill of the 3rd lock for the new gates to restore this canal to Naas

The future of the Royal Canal had seemed very bleak indeed when it was closed to navigation in 1961. Following this closure, seven low level bridges were constructed over the canal from Mullingar west and two on the Longford Line without a single voice of protest being raised. The IWAI, busy trying to save the Circular Line of the Grand Canal, seemed to accept that the Royal Canal was a lost cause. In 1974 Dr Ian Bath challenged this attitude and began his campaign to save the canal, setting up the Royal Canal Amenity Group with the slightly sceptical support of the IWAI. His move came just in time: Dublin Corporation was planning to use the city end of the canal as part of the Eastern By-Pass, and further west yet another low bridge, at McNead's Bridge near Mullingar, was about to begin construction. In response to patient lobbying of government ministers, an *ad hoc* committee was set up to advise the government about the long term

Royal Canal: the harbour at Ballynacargy after the closure of the canal and as it is today rewatered by the local RCAG

future of the canal. Pending the report of this committee, the Minister for Local Government, J. Tully, made the necessary funds available to allow for full navigation clearance at McNead's Bridge and CIE adopted the policy of refusing permission for any further low bridges over the canal. By this time the amenity potential of the canal was being developed by voluntary local community groups in a number of places along the route. It was known that the government was contemplating transferring the Grand Canal system from CIE to the Office of Public Works and it was a real fear that the Royal Canal would be left in CIE's control, as the close proximity of rail and canal made them difficult to separate. However, when the announcement of the transfer did come in 1978, the Royal Canal was included on the recommendation of the *ad hoc* committee. It was stated:

> The Royal Canal is to be developed as resources permit by the carrying out of improvement works on selected stretches. The nature and financing of the works involved will be a matter of discussion between the Office of Public Works and Bord Fáilte and, where appropriate, local authorities and voluntary organisations.

This government commitment to the future development of the canal brought about a change in official attitudes; the local authorities began to show an interest in the amenity potential of the canal. In 1980 the RCAG initiated a lockgate building scheme in premises made available by Messrs Guinness with the co-operation of AnCO, the industrial training authority. Between 1980-4 fifteen pairs of gates were made by AnCO apprentices for the Royal Canal and eight for the Naas Canal with some financial assistance from the local authorities. The Royal Canal gates have now been installed by CIE and over seventy miles, or 75 per cent, of the canal is in-water again. The shelving of the Eastern By-pass road scheme has removed the motorway threat and, in any event, Dublin Corporation had made such significant contributions to the lockgate building scheme that it would have been unlikely to have implemented the plan to fill in the city end of the canal. Today, as I write, over one hundred young people are engaged in various youth employment schemes on the canal and the Minister of Labour, Ruairi Quinn, is supporting the use by the local authorities of a greater labour force under the government's Social Employment Scheme: a success story which is a fitting reward for all the dedication and effort that has gone into the campaign.

The Future of the Waterways

The future of the Irish waterways now seems secure in their new role as recreational and tourist amenities. The last section of canal to be abandoned was in 1974 when the short spur, just under one mile long, leading down to the old commercial terminus of the Grand Canal at James's Street harbour in Dublin was filled in. Such is the change in attitudes that it is doubtful if even this would have happened today. The placing of almost all the waterways under one government department should create a wonderful opportunity for their full potential to be realised. The expertise exists within the Office of Public Works to ensure their development not just as navigations but as water amenity areas and linear parks. A recent study in the UK showed that each mile of restored waterway generated £27,500 of additional trade annually and created seven new jobs in addition to providing recreation and leisure space. In Northern Ireland, where the fate of many of the waterways had been permanently sealed, there is a new emphasis on developing the potential of what remains, and proposals to develop

Royal Canal: the first gate made by the RCAG/AnCO lockgate building scheme is lowered into position by CIE at 3rd lock in Dublin in 1981

the historic Newry Canal, Ireland's first canal, as a linear park have been considered with its possible restoration as a navigation in the longer term. Both administrations, north and south, have shown considerable interest in restoring the Shannon-Erne link and in extending the Erne Navigation to Lough Oughter.

The future is bright, but let us not forget how close we came to losing this important national heritage, so rich in history and lore; let us not forget the men who built them, the canal communities of the past and the people of vision, Harry Rice, Vincent Delany, Ian Bath and those who rallied to their call to save this heritage for future generations.

Grand Canal, Barrow Line: boats assembled for an Easter Rally at Vicarstown during the Year of the Barrow in 1983

Appendix: Summary of Facts

Lake & River Navigations
Canals

Lake & River Navigations

River	Years of construction	Approximate cost in £ stg.	Terminal points	Length in miles
Bann, Lower and Lough Neagh	1847-59	£101,081	Toomebridge, Lough Neagh – Coleraine	32.4
Bann, Upper and Lough Neagh			Lough Neagh – Whitecoat Point, entrance to Newry Canal	9.5
Blackwater (Ulster)			Maghery Cut, Lough Neagh – Coalisland Canal (3.5 miles) and Charlemont, Ulster Canal	9
Barrow	1759-90 (improvement work to 1812)	£220,615	Athy, Grand Canal Barrow Line – St Mullins	41.4
Blackwater (Munster)	1755-c.1765	£12,923	Canal: Mallow – Lombardstown	5
Lismore Canal	c.1814	Financed by Duke of Devonshire	At Lismore, by-passing part of River Blackwater	1.4
Blackwater	No works		Youghal – Lismore Canal	18
Bride	No works		River Blackwater – Tallow Bridge	7.5
Boyne	1748-1800	£181,554	Tidal lock, Oldbridge Lower – Navan	19
Corrib, Lough	1848-52	£61,707	Galway – Maam Bridge	34
Eglinton Canal	1848-52	Included in above	Galway, by-passing part of River Corrib	0.7
Cong Canal	1848-54	£40,240	Lough Corrib, near Cong – Lough Mask	3
Erne, Lough	1881-90	c.£30,000	Belleek – Belturbet	52
Gill, Lough	No works		Sligo – Dromahaire, River Bonet	10
Lagan	1753-94	£97,204	Belfast – Ellis' Gut, Lough Neagh	26.2
Nore	1755-75	£20,044	Kilkenny – junction with River Barrow	17 (Kilkenny Canal 4)
Shannon & Boyle Water	1755-c.1769 (early works)	£277,650	Killaloe – Carrick-on-Shannon	177
	1839-50 (Shannon Commissioners works)	£584,805	Battlebridge and Lough Key – Killaloe	202
Limerick-Killaloe	1755-99 (improvement works to 1814)	£110,336	Limerick – Killaloe	8.75
	1925-29 (hydro-electric works)		Limerick – Killaloe	8

Locks	Minimum size of lock	Peak tonnage: year/tonnage	Ownership and present condition
5 (1 double)	100ft by 18ft (30.4m by 5.4m)	1940s/35,000	Dept of Agriculture, Northern Ireland. Open to traffic
None			Dept of Agriculture, Northern Ireland. Abandoned 1954
None			Dept of Agriculture, Northern Ireland. Abandoned 1954
23 (1 double)	80ft 2in by 13ft 8 in (24.4m by 4.1m)	1840s/75,000	Dept of Finance, Rep. of Ireland (Board of Works). Open to traffic. Purchased by Grand Canal Co. 1894
2			Works never completed
1	71ft 6in by 19ft 6in (21.8m by 4m)		Lismore Estate. Last used in 1920s. Derelict.
None. Tidal			Headroom restricted by Youghal Bridge 22ft (6.7m) at high water.
None. Tidal			As above
20	78ft by 14ft 6in (23.8m by 4.4m)	1830s/10,000	An Taisce and private owners. Became derelict in 1920s
None			Corrib Navigation Trustees. Open to navigation
2	130ft by 20ft 6in (39.6m by 6.2m)		Corrib Navigation Trustees. Obstructed by fixed bridges 1955
3			Works never completed. Board of Works drainage works 1980s
1 (in barrage used occasionally)	112ft by 30ft (34.1m by 18.3m)		Dept of Agriculture, Northern Ireland. No authority in Rep. of Ireland. Open to navigation
			No authority. No works ever carried out
27 (tidal double)	62ft by 14ft 6in (18.8m by 4.4m)	1910s/170,000	Dept of Agriculture, Northern Ireland. Abandoned Lough Neagh to Sprucefield 1954, Sprucefield to Belfast 1958
7 (1 double, 2 flash)	200ft by 21ft (61m by 6.4m)		No authority. Works never completed. Derelict Inistioge – Kilkenny. Navigable on the tide to Inistioge
8 (3 flash)	80ft by 16ft (24.3m by 4.8m)		Dept of Finance, Rep. of Ireland (Board of Works). Early works reconstructed and enlarged by Shannon Commissioners, *see* below.
6	102ft by 30ft (31.1m by 9.1m)	1847/121,702	Dept of Finance, Rep. of Ireland (Board of Works). Open to navigation.
11 (3 double)	74ft 9in by 15ft 2in (22.8m by 4.6m)		Abandoned because of hydro-electric works, *see* below.
1 (double)	105ft by 19ft 6in (32m by 6m)		Dept of F , Rep. of Ireland (Board of Works) and Electricity Supply Board. Lock at Ardnacrusha power station

Lake & River Navigations (*continued*)

River	Years of construction	Approximate cost in £ stg.	Terminal points	Length in miles
Lough Allen Canal	1818-20	£18,805	Battlebridge, River Shannon – Lough Allen	4.25
Maigue	*c.*1720		Adare – Shannon Estuary	8.75
Fergus	1839-50	Included in Shannon Commissioners works above	Clarecastle – Shannon Estuary	20
Slaney	no works		Wexford – Enniscorthy	19
Suir	1756-7 1816-18	£3,000 £16,490	Junction with River Barrow – Clonmel	34.75

Canals

Canal	Years of construction	Approximate cost in £ stg.	Terminal points	Length in miles
Ballinamore and Ballyconnell Canal	1842-59	£228,652	Leitrim, River Shannon – Upper Lough Erne	38
Belmullet Canal	1880s		Passage from Blacksod Bay – Broad Haven at Belmullet	0.75
Broharris Canal	1820s		South shore of Lough Foyle, near Ballykelly, towards Limavady	2
Tyrone Navigation/Coalisland Canal	1732-*c.*1755	£29,000	Charlemont, River Blackwater – Coalisland	4.4
Dukart's Colliery Canal	1767-77	£17,308	Coalisland – Drumglass	3.5
Grand Canal Main and Shannon Line	1756-1804	£746,252	James's Street Harbour, Dublin – Shannon Harbour	79.3
Barrow Line	1783-91	Included in above	Lowtown, Main Line – Athy, River Barrow	28.5
Milltown Feeder	1780s	Included in above	Lowtown, Main Line – Pollardstown Fen	8
Blackwood Feeder	1780s	Included in above	Summit level – Blackwood Reservoir	4
Naas Line	1786-9 (to Naas) 1808-10 (to Corbally)	£28,401	Main Line, near Sallins – Naas harbour (2.5 miles) – Corbally	7.8
Circular Line	1790-96	£52,578 (£112,753 Ringsend Docks)	1st lock, Main Line – Ringsend, River Liffey	3.75 (24.5 acres in docks)

Locks	Minimum size of lock	Peak tonnage: year/tonnage	Ownership and present condition
2	67ft 4in by 12ft (20.5m by 3.7m)		Abandoned because of hydro-electric works in 1920s. Re-opened to navigation to Acres lake 1978
None. Tidal			Limerick Harbour Commissioners. Open on the tide to Askeaton Road Bridge
None. Tidal			Limerick Harbour Commissioners. Open on the tide
None. Tidal			No authority. Tidal
None. Tidal			Waterford Harbour Commissioners. Open on the tide to Carrick-on-Suir

Locks	Minimum size of lock	Peak tonnage: year/tonnage	Ownership and present condition
16	82ft by 16ft 6in (24m by 5m)		Navigation Trustees (lapsed). Derelict but cross-border surveys carried out to assess restoration
None. Tidal			Open to small craft – headroom on new bridge 16ft (4.9m) with 7ft (2.1m) draft at high water neaps
None. Tidal			
7 (one double)	62ft 6in by 14ft 6in (19m by 4.4m)	1930s/57,000	Dept of Agriculture, Northern Ireland. Commerical traffic ceased 1946, abandoned 1954
None. Three inclined planes	10ft by 4ft 6in (3m by 1.3m)		Disused by 1787
36 (5 double)	70ft by 13ft 7in (21.3m by 4.1m)	1845/111,225 (passengers) (1875/379,047)	Dept of Finance, Rep. of Ireland (Board of Works). Open to traffic. Grand Canal Company merged with CIE 1950
9 (2 double)	70ft 10in by 13ft 6in (21.5m by 4.1m)		Commercial traffic ceased 1960. Transferred from CIE to OPW 1985
None			Open to navigation to Milltown Bridge, headroom restricted to 6ft (1.8m) and draft 2ft 6in (0.5m)
None			Closed in 1952 and filled in
5	73ft 6in by 14ft (22.4m by 4.2m)		Closed in 1961. Section to Naas harbour under restoration, continuation to Corbally obstructed by culvert bridge
7	69ft 8in by 14ft 9in (21.2m by 4.4m)		Open to traffic (*see* Main Line above)

Canals (*continued*)

Canal	Years of construction	Approximate cost in £ stg.	Terminal points	Length in miles
Edenderry Line	1797-1802	Partly financed by Duke of Devonshire	Main Line – Edenderry	1
Ballinasloe Line	1824-28	£43,485	River Shannon at Shannon Harbour– Ballinasloe	14.5
Mountmellick Line	1827-31	£33,416	Barrow Line, Monasterevin– Mountmellick	11.5
Kilbeggan Line	1830-5	£14,000	Main Line, Ballycommon – Kilbeggan	8
Newry Canal	1731-42	£48,000	Whitecoat Point, Upper Bann – Newry	18.5
Newry Ship Canal	1759-69	£21,230	Newry – Upper Fathom	1.7
	1830-50 (extension)	c.£110,000	Canal: Newry – Lower Fathom Channel: Lower Fathom – Warrenpoint	Canal 3 Channel 4
Royal Canal Main Line	1789-1817	£1,312,573	Spencer Dock, River Liffey, Dublin– Richmond Harbour, River Shannon	90.5
Broadstone Line	1796	Included in above	Main Line, Phibsborough– Broadstone harbour	0.75
Longford Line	1827-30	£12,497	Main line, near Killashee – Longford	5.2
Strabane Canal	1791-6	£10,945	River Foyle – Strabane	4
Tralee Ship Canal	1832-46	£28,450	Tralee Bay – Tralee	1.5
Ulster Canal	c.1830-41	£231,000	Charlemont, River Blackwater– Wattle Bridge, Upper Erne	45.7

Locks	Minimum size of lock	Peak tonnage: year/tonnage	Ownership and present condition
None			Re-opened to traffic in 1960s
2	70ft 9in by 14ft 7in (21.6m by 4.4m)		Closed 1961. Derelict and partly filled in
3	70ft 4in by 14ft 1in (21.4m by 4.2m)		Closed 1960. Derelict and partly filled in from Portarlington to Mountmellick
None			Closed 1961 and drained
13	69ft by 15ft (21m by 4.5m)	1840s/120,000	Newry Port and Harbour Trust (in liquidation). Last commercial boat 1936, abandoned 1949
1	130ft by 22ft (39.6m by 22m)		Extended and enlarged (*see* below)
1	220ft by 50ft (67m by 15.2m)		Newry Port and Harbour Trust (in liquidation). Closed 1966
47 (10 double)	75ft by 13ft 3in (22.8m by 4m)	1837/46,450 (passengers) 1847/112,181	Dept of Finance, Rep. of Ireland (Board of Works). Purchased by MGWR Co. 1845, transferred to GSR 1938, transferred to CIE 1944, transferred to OPW 1985: closed 1961, restoration work in progress.
None			Harbour filled in 1877, middle section filled in 1927, final section filled in 1956.
None			*See* Main Line above. Harbour and 300 yards (274m) filled in.
2	108ft by 20ft (32.9m by 6m)	1900s/20,000	Strabane and Foyle Navigation Co. Disused from 1932
1			Murphy and O'Shea, Tralee. Closed in early 1930s, harbour and part of canal filled in
26	62ft by 11ft (18.8m by 3.3m)	1890s/16,000	Dept of Finance, Northern Ireland and Dept of Finance, Rep. of Ireland. Parts sold to private landowners. Last commercial boat 1929, abandoned 1931

Bibliography

Historical and Travels

Blair May, *Once upon the Lagan*, Belfast, Blackstaff Press, 1981.

Canaliana, Robertstown Muintir na Tire, 1965-80.

D'Arcy, Gerard, *Portrait of the Grand Canal*, Transport Research Associates, 1969.

Delany, Ruth, *The Grand Canal of Ireland*, David & Charles, 1973.

Delany, V. T. H. and D. R., *The Canals of the South of Ireland*, David & Charles, 1966.

Ellison, Cyril, *The Waters of the Boyne and Blackwater*, Blackwater Press, 1983.

Feehan, John M., *The Magic of the Shannon*, Mercier, 1980.

Flanagan, Patrick, *The Ballinamore and Ballyconnell Canal*, David & Charles, 1972.

Gardner, R., *Land of Time Enough*, Hodder & Stoughton, 1977.

Harvey, R., *The Shannon and its Lakes*, Hodges Figgis, 1896.

Hayward, R., *Where the River Shannon Flows*, Dundalgan Press, 1940.

McCutcheon, W. A., *The Canals of the North of Ireland*, David & Charles, 1965.

McNeill, D. B. *Irish Passenger Steamship Services. North of Ireland*, David & Charles, 1969.

McNeill, D. B. *Irish Passenger Steamship Services. South of Ireland*, David & Charles, 1971.

Malet, H., *Voyage in a Bowler Hat*, Hutchinson, 1960.

Malet, H., *In the Wake of the Gods*, Chatto & Windus, 1960.

Martin, Michael, ed., *Inland Waterways Association of Ireland Silver Jubilee, 1954-79*, IWAI, Athlone, 1979.

Nowlan, David, ed., *Silver River: A Celebration of 25 Years of the Shannon Boat Rally*, IWAI, 1985.

O'Farrell, Padraic, *Shannon through her Literature*, Mercier, 1983.

O'Sullivan, T. F., *Goodly Barrow*, Ward River, 1983.

Praeger, R. L. *The Way that I Went*, Methuen & Hodges Figgis, 1947.

Ransome, P. J. G., *The Archaeology of Canals*, World's Work, 1979.

Raven-Hart, R., *Canoeing in Ireland*, London, Canoe and Small Boat, 1938.

Rice, H. J., *Thanks for the Memory*, Athlone Printing Works, 1952.

Rodgers, Mary, *Prospect of Erne*, Fermanagh Field Club, 1967.

Rolt, L. T. C., *Green and Silver*, Allen & Unwin, 1949.

Scott-James, R. A., *An Englishman in Ireland*, London, J. M. Dent, 1910.

Semple, Maurice, *Some Galway Memories*, Semple, 1969.

Semple, Maurice, *Reflections of Lough Corrib*, Semple, 1973.

Semple, Maurice, *By the Corribside*, Semple, 1981.

Stokes, William, *A Pictorial Survey and Tourist's Guide to Lough Derg*, London, Schulze & Co., 1842.

Wakeman, W. F., *Three Days on the Shannon*, Dublin, Hodges and Smith, 1852.

Wibberley, Leonard, *The Shannon Sailors*, New York, William Morrow, 1972.

Wilde, Sir William, *Lough Corrib*, M'Glashan, 1867.

Wilde, Sir William, *The Beauties of the Boyne and its Tributary The Blackwater*, M'Glashan & Gill, 1850.

Guides

Balfe, T. and Weaving, J., *Shell Guide to the Shannon*, Irish Shell, 1977, 2nd ed. 1981.

Barrett, E. C., *Irish Inland Waterway Holidays*, Fodhla Printing Co.

Delany, R. and Addis, J., *Guide to the Grand Canal and Barrow Line*, IWAI, 1983.

Delany, R. and Addis, J., *Guide to the Barrow*, IWAI, 1977.

Delany, R. and Addis, J., *Shannon Guide*, IWAI, 1978.

Delany, R. and Bath, I., *Guide to the Royal Canal*, IWAI, 1984.

McKnight, H., *The Shell Book of Inland Waterways*, David & Charles, 1975.

Ransome, P. J. G., *Holiday Cruising in Ireland*, David & Charles, 1971.

Children's Books

Delany, R. and Addis, J., *Irish Inland Waterways*, Folens, 1978.

Hartford, D. M., *Arrow II Explores – An Irish Adventure*, Volturna Press, 1977.

Nowlan, Nora, *The Shannon*, Frederick Muller, 1965.

Ransome, P. J. G., *Your Book of Canals*, Faber and Faber, 1977.

Index

Lever, Charles, author, 91
Levitstown, 69
Lewis's Topographical Dictionary, 32, 38
Liffey, River, 11-2, 19, 32, 48, 74-9, 82-3, 98-9, 101, 148, 169
Lighters, 24, 32, 36, 114, 117-8, 152, 154
Limavady, 38
Limerick, 45-6, 48, 50, 53, 55-7, 59-61, 105, 107, 112, 124, 129-31, 140, 142-3
Limerick-Killaloe Navigation, 49-51, 54-8, 65, 123
Limerick Navigation Company, 50-2, 54-5, 59, 65, 71, 124
Limerick Steamship Company, 175
linen trade, 23, 34, 36
Lioness PS, 172
Lisburn, 33-5, 116, 119
Lismore Canal, 63
Lisnaskea, 162
loans *see* debentures
locks, 9, 21, 22, 24, 27, 29, 30, 31, 48-9, 51, 65-6, 79, 100, 128, 149, 152, 158
lockhouses, 49, 54, 96, 105
lockkeepers, 16, 45, 52, 57, 96, 97, 102, 118, 143
Lombardstown, 62-3
Londonderry *see* Derry
Londonderry Journal, 38
Longford (Line), 93, 107-8, 147, 179
Lord Hertford, lighter, 33
Lough Erne Yacht Club, 161, 163
Lough Neagh Drainage Trust, 167, 169
Lowe, John, engineer, 40
Lower Bann Navigation Trust, 167, 169
Lowtown, 96-7, 143
Lucan, 11, 79

Maam Bridge, 170
Macartney, Sir George, chief secretary, 13
Macartney, Sir John, canal company director, 82, 98
McCann, James, canal company director, 122, 140
McCleery, James, boat operator, 37, 166, 168
McCormick, Thomas, contractor, 56
McGreevy, James, bank ranger, 143
McLaughlin, T.A., hydroelectric engineer, 133
McMahon, John, contractor, 83, 93, 107-8
McMahon, John, engineer, 157, 166, 171, 173
McNead's Bridge, 179, 182
Macneill, John, railway engineer, 154

Maelshechlainn, 10, 11
Maghery, 30, 37, 167
Maguire, John, inventor, 91
Maid of Breffni PS, 174
Maigue, River, 11, 57
Mallet, William and Robert, boat builders, 145
Mallow, 62-3
manure trade, 16, 80, 103
Marchioness of Donegall PS, 168
Markham, William, contractor, 72
Marquis Wellesley PS, 57-8
Marshall, John, boat builder, 145
Martello towers, 46
Martin, Thomas, contractor, 43
Mask, Lough, 111, 172
Matthews, Benjamin, debt collector, 79
Maynooth, 101, 108
M-boats, 141
Meath River Navigation Company, 122
Meelick, 46, 48-9, 51-4, 124, 125, 132-3
Midland Great Western Railway (MGWR), 130, 139-40, 148, 160, 163
military protection, 57, 93, 97, 103, 105, 139, 141, 147
Millar, Archibald, engineer, 81-2
Milne Transport Inquiry, 112
Mitchell, Humphrey, engineer, 134
Moira, 36, 119
Monaghan, 153-4
Monasterevin, 68-9, 81, 94-5
Monck Commission, 111-2, 155, 159, 168
Monks, Daniel, engineer, 30, 42, 44
Monks, John, contractor, 43
Monks, William, canal manager, 31
Morgan, Andrew, hotelkeeper, 90
Morrell, River, 76-7
Morres, Redmond, canal company director, 78
Morres, Sir William, 67
Mountaineer PS, 57-8
Mountmellick (Line), 94-6, 178
Moy, Lough, 170
Moyvalley hotel, 106
Mudge, Captain, surveyor, 123
Mullingar, 83, 99, 101-2, 105, 108, 146, 148-9, 179
Mullins, Bernard, contractor, 80, 83
Mulvany, Christopher, engineer, 134
Mulvany, William Thomas, engineer, 111, 157-8
Murphy, Father P., 138
Murphy and O'Shea, 176
Murphy, Thomas, lockkeeper, 143
Myers, Christopher, engineer, 29

Naas (Line), 51, 83, 95, 103, 178, 183

Napier, David, engine builders, 37
Navan, 41-5, 122
Neagh, Lough, 10, 12, 19, 22, 27, 30, 32, 34-8, 57, 111, 114, 116, 118-9, 150, 156, 165, 167
Nevil, Francis, collector of HM revenue, 19
Nevill, Arthur, surveyor general, 12
Newgrange, 122
Newry, 19, 23, 25, 29, 32, 36, 114, 115, 153, 156, 166, 184
Newry Navigation, 12-3, 19, 20, 21-8, 30, 32, 40, 48, 114-5, 150, 153, 166, 184
Newry Navigation Company, 26, 114
Newry Port and Harbour Trust, 115
Newry Ship Canal, 20, 22-3, 26, 29, 44, 112, 114, 184
Nimmo, Alexander, engineer, 26, 60, 166, 170
Nonsuch, canal boat, 58
Nore Navigation, 50, 62-3, 64, 65, 66, 67-8, 136, 179
Norton, William, Tanaiste, 134

Oates, James, engineer, 81
O'Briens Bridge, 51, 57, 59
Ockenden, William, engineer, 23, 50, 62, 65, 67-8
O'Connell PS, 172
O'Ferrall, More, landowner, 105, 107
Oldbridge, 40-1, 43, 122
Olga SS, 131
Oliver, C.D., engineer, 122, 136
Omagh, 39
Omer, Thomas, engineer, 22-3, 29, 33-4, 41-3, 48-9, 54, 65, 68, 74-9, 84, 86
O'Neill, Thomas, dockmaster, 146
Ormonde, Duke of, 10
Ottley, Charles, 167
Owel, Lough, 10
Owen, Richard, engineer, 35-8

Page, Thomas Hyde, engineer, 100
Pandora PS, 163
Parliament (Imperial), 15, 117
Parliament (Irish), 12-3, 15, 19, 29, 30, 32, 35, 43, 48, 50, 52, 62, 65-6, 71, 76, 98, 99, 101, 165
Parliamentary Committees (Irish), 11, 15, 17, 22, 28-9, 40-1, 49-52, 62, 65, 67-8, 71, 76-7, 100
Parliamentary Commissions and Inquiries (Imperial), 62, 88, 103, 111-2, 117, 122-3, 154-5, 159, 163
Parliamentary Petitions (Irish), 11, 19, 32, 42-3, 48, 50, 65, 68
Parnell, William , author, 15
Parteen, 55, 59, 133
passenger services, 25, 58, 71, 80, 88-92, 105, 107-8, 122, 129-31, 134,